A
HEDGE
FUND TALE

of Reach and Grasp

Barton

BIGGS

A HEDGE FUND TALE

of Reach and Grasp

... or what's a Heaven for?

WILEY
John Wiley & Sons, Inc.

Published by John Wiley & Sons, Inc., Hoboken, New Jersey.
Published simultaneously in Canada.

For general information on our other products and services or for technical support, please
contact our Customer Care Department within the United States at (800) 762-2974,
outside the United States at (317) 572-3993 or fax (317) 572-4002.

Wiley also publishes its books in a variety of electronic formats. Some content that appears
in print may not be available in electronic books. For more information about Wiley
products, visit our web site at www.wiley.com.

Library of Congress Cataloging-in-Publication Data:
Biggs, Barton.
  A hedge fund tale of reach and grasp / Barton M. Biggs.
    p. cm.
    Includes index.
  ISBN 978-0-470-60454-0 (hardback); ISBN 978-0-470-89239-8 (ebk);
  ISBN 978-0-470-89240-4 (ebk); ISBN 978-0-470-89241-1 (ebk)
    1. Hedge funds. 2. Securities industry—United States. I. Title.
  HG4530.B5154 2010
  332.64'524—dc22

                                                          2010015496

Printed in the United States of America
10 9 8 7 6 5 4 3 2 1

. . . With melting wax and loosened strings
Sunk hapless Icarus on unfaithful wings;
Headlong he rushed through the affrighted air,
With limbs distorted and dishevelled hair;
His scattered plumage danced upon the wave,
And sorrowing Nereids decked his watery grave;
O'er his pale corse their pearly sea-flowers shed,
And strewed with crimson moss his marble bed . . .

—Erasmus Darwin, "Icarus"

Contents

A HEDGE FUND TALE

of Reach and Grasp

Introduction

Ah, but a man's reach should exceed his grasp, or what's a heaven for?
—Robert Browning

A Hedge Fund Tale is a business and investing book masquerading as a fable. I have come to believe that professional investors, especially hedge fund types, must not only have superb analytical and judgmental skills, tremendous intensity, and a dollop of luck, but, to survive and be successful, they must also profoundly comprehend that they are going to be vulnerable to and enslaved by extreme mood swings and terribly susceptible to hubris. Both can be mortally dangerous not just to their investment health but also to the well-being of their most intimate life relationships. Too dramatic? I don't think so!

This book is about the investment management business, the rise and fall of hedge funds, and the various forms that the plagues of the

1

great financial panic assumed. It is in the form of a fable because I use disguises to mask identities, just as I did in my previous book, *Hedge Hogging*. However, at its core, it is a book about people—investment people—and my faint hope is that their stories will help future investors deal with the ecstasy of financial victory, the black dog of despair, and the mortal sin of hubris.

Hedge funds were the gold rush of the past 20 years and, like all bubbles and manias, ended with a bust that destroyed many of the egomaniacs and most of the latecomers, and even took out some solid citizens. The immense wealth accumulated in a few years by mostly young hedge fund managers—who haven't hesitated for a moment to spend it ostentatiously and often rudely—has generated great animosity and envy from everyone else. It's a tale worth exploring, as it is littered with compelling stories of triumph and tragedy.

Almost by definition, those who are willing to live by raw performance alone are mostly people who believe their investment life reach should exceed their grasp. Beating the stock market inflames even a normal ego. Becoming very rich very fast has swiveled many a head to the point of madness. As the ancients warned us, "Those whom the gods would destroy they first make mad," and "Pride goeth before destruction and a haughty spirit before a fall." Remember, Icarus, whose reach exceeded his grasp, sank headlong "through the affrighted air" when he went too close to the sun on "unfaithful wings."

Over the course of my 40 years in the professional investment arena, I have known many a charming, ambitious Icarus who has flown too high. The business breeds them in profusion. The protagonist of this book, Joe Hill, is an imaginary character, but his path from rags to riches to perdition personifies the arc of the lives of so many hedge fund people I have known. I have noticed no correlation between hedge fund success and being born on the right side of the proverbial social tracks or having gone to the fancy colleges and the best business schools. A glittering resume helps a lot in getting a job, but a majority of the winners I have known have undistinguished pedigrees; brains, guts, drive, and intuition put the points on the board. Performance investing is a numbers game.

That's why I spend space on Joe Hill's background. The early chapters of this book try to develop his character in terms of his will to win, his intensity, and his toughness, and then his loneliness and love. I try to make him an appealing figure, a hero, because I want to show how even someone who is fundamentally a sound and admirable character can get sucked into the vortex and destroyed.

The business of investing is also about the interaction of social relationships within the office. As I try to describe in Chapters 3, 4, and 5, the normal stresses inherent in people working together day after day in an investment management company is intensified by the stresses of performance investing and both internal and external competition. You have got to be tough and develop a thick skin or you'll be overwhelmed.

Within a large hedge fund firm the intensity is far higher, as demonstrated in Chapters 7 and 8 and then in later chapters of the book. When the market environment gets really difficult and there are life-or-death decisions, the most intimate relationships and lives—both in and outside the office—often fracture. The environment and stress become comparable to an infantry unit in combat or life on a destroyer in the North Atlantic in World War II. The fledgling investor should know what he or she is getting into, as the only defense mechanism is a prepared mind.

This hedge fund tale of Joe Hill is not an American tragedy in the sense of Theodore Dreiser's hero. This is a modern hedge fund tragedy: the story of what happens when a good man's reach exceeds his grasp. As F. Scott Fitzgerald so succinctly put it, "Show me a hero and I will write you a tragedy."

Chapter 1

Big Neck, Virginia

J oe Hill grew up in Big Neck, an old textile town of 20,000 people in the rolling flat lands and gentle blue hills of rural Piedmont Virginia. Once, maybe a century ago, the mills had offered jobs and a measure of prosperity, but Big Neck was too far from Washington, Charlottesville, and Richmond to have benefited from their fancy suburban sprawl, and the mills now struggled along with light manufacturing and electronics. The railroad still ran through the center of town, but the heavy freight trains just thundered through on their way to somewhere else. American prosperity had more or less casually, thoughtlessly passed Big Neck by, and the population was down from 35,000 a quarter of a century ago.

Big Neck was integrated, hardworking, stalled, middle America. There was nothing upwardly mobile about it, but the town functioned. The climate was mild, the schools were decent, and, all things considered, it wasn't a bad place to grow up in. Although it wasn't a small town, everybody knew a lot about you by the time you had lived there for

10 years or were 13 years old. You had a public history, which maybe was Dolores's problem.

Dolores was Joe's mother. She was white. Joe's dad, Big Joe, as he was called, was black. Their son was the result of a high school romance, conceived by accident just after graduation. The pair lived together after Joe's birth in a rented dingy row house on Elm Street, separately but amicably enough when whatever magic there once was, wore off. In the years that followed, Big Joe and Dolores were distantly friendly, held within a tenuous orbit by their mutual love for their son.

Little Joe was a big strong baby who would stand in his playpen and violently shake the railing, laughing and yelling at the same time. Big Joe's friends were impressed. "Joe, that boy is going to be a banger," they would say. "That kid is going to be all muscle and fight."

Big Joe was a foreman in the mill. He was a large, contemplative, handsome mahogany-colored man whom people looked up to and who didn't waste a lot of words on idle chatter. "The first screw to get loose in your head," Big Joe liked to say, "is the one that holds your tongue in place." A couple of years after his split with Dolores, he married a black woman and they had three girls. Joe's half sisters idolized him and frantically competed for his attention.

Despite his second family, Big Joe was involved in his son's upbringing. On his way home from work, he would drop by before dinner most evenings. Since Big Joe was a good natural athlete, he encouraged his son to play sports and, as the boy grew up, they ran pass patterns on a field down the street and played one-on-one basketball in the driveway. When the mild southern Virginia weather cooperated, they played golf. About once a week, you could find the two of them out on the scruffy municipal golf course lugging their old bags over the bedraggled, wandering links. There were pullcarts available for three dollars, but they always carried their bags.

"Makes no sense for us to pay six dollars between us when we got strong backs and like the exercise," Big Joe would tell his son. "Besides, we ain't long on money."

By the time he was 12, Joe could outdrive his father and hit a golf ball nearly 300 yards. But his favorite sport was football. Football was— and is—the big sport in the mill towns of rural Virginia, and Joe played his way up through the Midget and Peewee leagues. His father was one of the youth league coaches, and he never missed a game or practice. Never! Yet, during these games, Big Joe discovered that within Joe's seemingly happy-go-lucky, well-adjusted personality burned a fierce competitive fire. Sometimes Big Joe worried about this intensity. The boy concealed it from others, but one day after his team lost a Peewee game, the 12-year-old boy kicked the stuffing out of the backseat of his father's aging car. Big Joe made him pay for the repairs, once again saying: "We ain't long on money, son. Best you learn now that temper tantrums are expensive."

Joe was also an obsessive perfectionist; he could not bear to lose in a one-on-one basketball game or on the golf course. A muffed golf shot would cause Joe to pound the offending club against a tree, and a lost father-son basketball game would send him sulking, silently furious, back into the house. Although Joe got mad, he worked hard at practicing so that he could do better the next time.

As for Dolores, life seemed to have passed her by. She worked long hours as a waitress. Though in the early years she dated other men, she never married. As she aged, she became thick around the waist and lost her looks. Her face became pale and pinched, her eyes dark and anxious, and her hair stringy. She didn't appear to be a happy person. There was a certain unspoken, lugubrious bitterness in her attitude as though she sensed she had been ostracized.

Subconsciously, Dolores worried that her son's biracial background was a disadvantage and her worry made her feel guilty. She focused on Joe, but he grew secretly ashamed of her as he grew older and she became less predictable. Once as a young boy, on a soft, golden October afternoon, Joe was gang tackled during a Peewee football game. The play ended with Joe at the bottom of a pile of aggressive boys. Suddenly, Dolores detached herself from the cluster of other parents standing on the far sideline and bolted across the field screaming, "Leave him alone," and then began pulling the other boys away.

Years later, Joe would recount that suspended moment—when he was imprisoned at the bottom of the pile under the brilliant, windless sky of early autumn—as perhaps the most mortifying moment of his life.

Yet, Dolores made some important contributions to Joe's childhood. Forced to listen to three televisions blaring endlessly in the tavern where she worked, she insisted on minimal television at home.

In fact, the only time TV was permitted was when a sporting event was on or Big Joe came to visit. Father and son would watch sports in Dolores's congested, high-ceilinged living room, which was dominated by a sagging couch on a gray carpet stained with 20 years of footprints and spilled soft drinks. Dust motes reeled in the shafts of sunlight as they watched games there, sunken into two stuffed armchairs, while Big Joe explained the complexities and nuances of football, basketball, and baseball. At these moments, Joe felt like he was part of a real family. It was as close as they ever came to a communion.

But, as soon as the game was over, Big Joe would leave and Dolores would insist that Joe turn off the television and read a book. She loved to read and she was determined that her son would be an educated man. "You gotta be somebody," she would tell him. "You gotta be smart; you gotta make money; you gotta get out of here." Listening to her, he didn't discard her exhortations. Joe understood, albeit dimly, her dissatisfaction with the monotony of her life, and early on he knew he wanted something better—a lot better. But it seemed as though the fastest, easiest way out of Big Neck and into money was through sports.

In an effort to combine Joe's love of sports with his education, Dolores gave him a card football game called *Running Back* on Christmas day. The game and its statistics became his obsession. He created a league with two divisions of four teams and stocked them with players from the actual National Football League. Then he played endless games and kept detailed statistics for each quarterback, running back, and receiver. The mathematics of quarterback ratings and yards gained after the catch were complex, and he became engrossed with the analysis of the statistics and the ebb and flow of his players' careers. *Running Back* was the beginning of his interest in numbers and the message within them.

As Joe played his way up through the age groups in the youth sport leagues in town, it became apparent that he was by far the best athlete of his age in town. Big and strong, he was superbly coordinated and almost prenaturally fast.

By the time he entered junior high, Joe was a lean, handsome, dark-complexioned boy whose biracial background was apparent. He had learned at age nine from an older boy's snide comment that he was a mulatto, a half-breed from an unwanted pregnancy, but after he gave the boy a bloody nose, no one ever mentioned it again—at least not to his face. Nevertheless, it was always with him although he never spoke of it. Was he white, he wondered, or was he black? Which crowd should he naturally hang out with or did he have *entree* to both?

He eventually came to realize, however, that outside of Big Neck, the rest of the world viewed him as black because of his dark complexion. When he came into contact with the outside world, he couldn't go around with a sign on his back affirming that he was half-white. Nor did he want to. In fact, as time went on, if anything, he became prouder of his blackness than his whiteness. Partially, he recognized, this was because he was more comfortable with his father than with his mother.

Nevertheless, Joe was a socially, athletically, and intellectually confident boy. Schoolwork came easily to Joe, so easily that Dolores considered taking him out of the Big Neck public school system and sending him to St. David's, the Jesuit Catholic school in town, which was considerably more rigorous academically. Big Joe objected, not because of the religious conversion that a scholarship would entail, but because the athletic program at St. David's was weak.

In junior high school, Josh Gibson noticed Joe. Gibson's family had lived in Big Neck forever, and he and his older brother owned the mill where Big Joe worked. Gibson lived five miles from town on a 200-acre spread of rolling land with several hundred beef cows, and by Big Neck standards he was immensely rich. The mill was very profitable, and everyone knew he was the biggest customer of the Merrill Lynch office on Third Street. He was perhaps 40; a bald, heavyset man. His belly bulged over his belt, his neck bulged over his collar, and his eyes bulged out of an open, friendly face. He was as affable as the day was long. He was married but without children, and he genuinely cared about kids, the town, and his employees at the mill, but above all, he loved jocks and sports.

Gibson had always liked Big Joe, and he began to hear chatter on the mill floor that Big Joe had a kid who was some kind of a super athlete. In the fall of 1983, Gibson had gone to one of his Peewee League football games, and as he got to know the boy he came to like him more and more. He recognized Joe's intelligence, and he was particularly intrigued with Joe's statistical bent with numbers and with *Running Back*. As Gibson listened to Joe talk about *Running Back*, the boy's natural reserve evaporated. Gibson and Joe shared a love of numbers.

But Gibson also cared about the land, his land. He was easily moved to quote Robert Frost's lines "the land was ours before we were the land's" which meant, he explained to Joe, that a man had to physically work his land to have the land accept him. There was a tract of 50 acres that had once been part of his farm with an old mill that lay between his place and the river. "My place is lopsided without it," he would tell Joe. He yearned for it. "The corn in that bottom is doing right well. That was always good ground for corn. No better on the river."

Joe was with him the afternoon the owner of the parcel sent word he would sell. He would experience the elation on Gibson's face, and that evening observe how Gibson went into the twilight to gaze down at the fields, the dark green mass by the river, that was now his land. They later would walk through the grove of cedars to the disintegrating structure of the old mill; the stone dam hung with moss. At night, the motionless water above the mill looked like slick, black metal.

Joe fell in love with that piece of land. From the river, it swept away to the hills and the sky. It was thick and green and beautiful. During summers he worked for Gibson one summer clearing brush and another rebuilding the stonework on the dam. It was hard, manual labor and he relished it. At noon he would eat his sandwiches up on the meadow and then roll over on his stomach and inhale the land. He loved the rich, fragrant odor of the black earth and the grass. Years later, when the financial plague came, the feel of the land, the work, and the smell of the soil saved his sanity and maybe his life.

Gibson also harbored a secret fascination with the stock market. Like Joe, he loved to pore over statistics and valuations. As the year passed, and they became almost kindred spirits, Gibson began to jabber at Joe about his stock ideas. His mill was a supplier to Wal-Mart and he was intrigued with the company and its lean modus operandi. He bought the stock in early 1982 and hung on to it.

On a Saturday in May of 1984 Gibson took both Joes out to lunch at McDonald's. When they had settled into a booth, Gibson said, "Look, son, I know you're a good athlete, but even more important, I think you're a smart young guy with a fascination and gift for numbers. The stock market is numbers and brains and intuitions. I want to get you interested in it, so you know what? I'm going to give you 15 shares of Wal-Mart. The stock closed at $31.40 yesterday so that's like $470, but I want you to promise me you won't sell it for two years. After that you can do what you want with it and the money. Is it a deal?"

Big Joe looked puzzled and Little Joe looked stunned.

"That's real generous of you, Mr. G," Big Joe said. "But tell me again why you're doing this."

"Plain and simple. I want to get this man-boy of yours interested in the stock market, and not just football, and I think Wal-Mart is going up and that'll get his attention."

"Mr. G, you know I want to play in the NFL someday," Joe said.

"Yeah, I know that and I'm rootin' for you. But I want you to use those big muscles in your head and not just the ones in your legs and arms. Will you agree to the deal?"

Joe looked at his father, who nodded. Then he replied: "Yeah, of course I will. It's the first money I've ever had, and you're right, I'll watch it real close. You've showed me how to look up stock prices before. Guess I'll have to ask Mom to bring home her restaurant's copy of the *Richmond Post Reporter*."

"Okay," said Gibson. "I'll open an account for you at Merrill Lynch on Monday morning. I'm going to tell them to send you the same research they send me. And I'm going to tell my guy there to keep his mouth shut about this."

"Should be interesting," said Big Joe. "Only stock I ever owned is Virginia Electric & Power and it's been a dog."

"Well, Wal-Mart ain't no dog," said Gibson with a big grin. "It's a hungry tiger."

And that's how it began. Joe followed the stock's progress. As Figure 1.1 shows, Wal-Mart's shares soared and by July of 1987, the

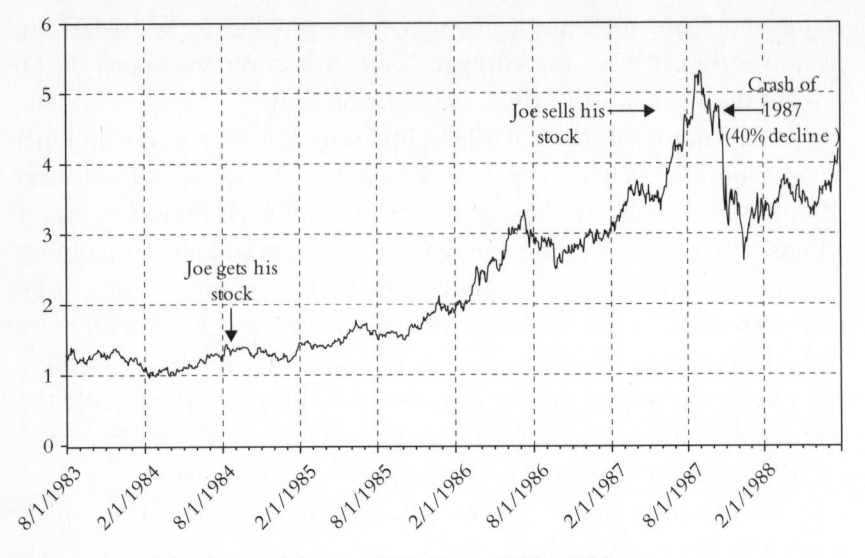

Figure 1.1 Up, Up, and Away—Wal-Mart: 1983–1988

stock was selling in the $90s. (Note, price data have been adjusted for subsequent stock splits.)

Gibson had never had such a winner, and at that price he sold out his position. Joe followed him; after all, he said to himself, "What do I know?" But the money certainly got his attention. When Gibson told him about the capital gains tax, he was appalled at the Internal Revenue Service's share of the profits. Nevertheless, it felt marvelous to have $1,350 in the bank, and he began to think about finding another stock. Maybe, he thought, I have a magic touch.

His elation faded as the stock kept climbing throughout the summer of 1987, touching 106. Then, to his astonishment, came The Crash of 1987, and at one point Wal-Mart hit 56. In the long run, though, the Crash of 1987 was barely a blip on the radar screen (see Figure 1.2).

Over the next 12 years, Joe watched in awe as Wal-Mart soared to an adjusted price of 1,380 on the last day of 1999, a peak it has not yet reached again. Once, much later, he calculated that the $471 worth of stock that Gibson had given him over a cheeseburger on that May afternoon would have been worth $20,700 in 1999. Watching

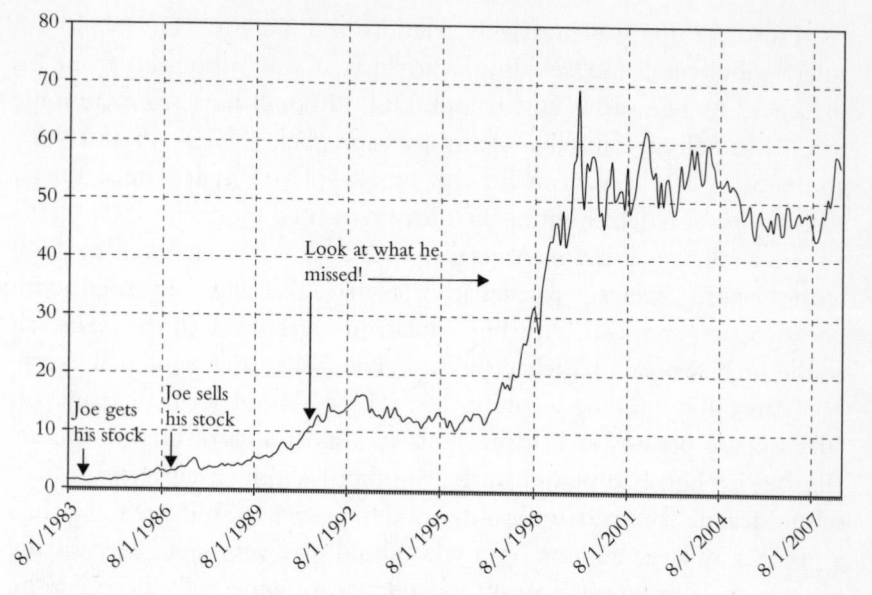

Figure 1.2 Patience Is a Virtue—Wal-Mart Long-Term History

the stock market as a teenager, Joe learned that a great stock is the most fabulous wealth creation vehicle imaginable, but that the markets require a stout heart and patience. He was hooked.

By freshman year, Joe stood several inches over six feet, weighed almost 200 pounds, and had the broad shoulders, thick hands and powerful legs of his father. He could effortlessly flick a football 40 yards on a line, and outsprint any wide receiver or running back on the Big Neck High team by several yards. His energy was boundless.

Joe was supremely confident in his natural athletic skills and his ability to perform under pressure, and he used those assets to make some pocket change. Frequently, he would challenge his friends to foul shooting, golf putting, or football throwing contests so he could win some money. As his prowess (and his winnings) increased, his friends either wouldn't play or would demand substantial advantages. Joe loved the pressure—and the money.

However, Joe was invariably friendly and inclusive. He would not tolerate bullying, and any boy who bullied was ostracized from his presence. As one of his best friends said, "I could be a real nice dude too if I had all his natural assets in my back pocket." The anointed star and captain of every team he was on, he played high school varsity basketball and baseball but his first love remained football.

In rural, small-town America, everyone in town goes to high school sports events—particularly football. Parents, old men with cheap cigars, and kids with big, idolatrous eyes flock to the fields, sit in the high, wooden bleachers, and carefully watch the game that every-one cares about so desperately. Most high school football games in Virginia are played on Friday nights in almost a carnival atmosphere. Big Neck High had played in the Southern Virginia, eight-team high school league for years with only moderate success, but Joe's class had a number of large athletic boys who could play very well. Joe was the big star, scoring almost as many touchdowns running with the ball as he did passing. When at the beginning of each game the starting lineups were announced, and the public address system echoed across the field: "At quarterback for Big Neck High, number twelve, Joe Hill," a huge roar would rise from the crowd. The team lost one game during his junior year and the next year Big Neck was undefeated. Both years Joe was voted first team All-State. Suddenly, everyone in town knew Joe. He was an all-star; a town hero.

With his fame and athletic achievements, the girls came easy. Except for the physical part, no girl really attracted him or was his close friend and confidante. He had no idea of the concept of find-ing intimacy with a girl. But there was plenty of sex available, and Joe lost his virginity at age 16 to the blandishments of an 18-year-old—a fox, with incredible legs and a bulging bosom. He realized afterward that he was just a trophy for her. The realization turned him off; he felt demeaned by what should have been a transforming experience. It instead made him feel cheap and used.

It was only the first of a number of fast, secretive spasms with different and diverse girls. He had decided that sex for him was going to be careful. No romances, no unwanted pregnancies. Perhaps because of this scruple and the covert nature of the act, affection and

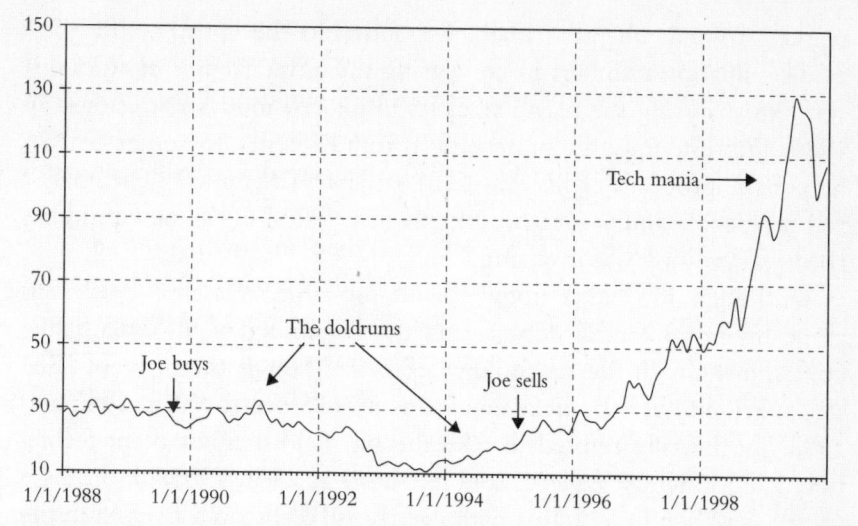

Figure 1.3   Patience Is a Virtue II: IBM 1988–1999

intimacy did not play a part in these relationships. After he had sex, there was always an empty, hollow feeling as though he had somehow missed the essence of the experience, and he invariably wanted to be away and gone from the girl. In fact, he always wanted to take a shower, and wash the dirt off, so to speak. Girls, as far as he was concerned, were boring chatterboxes, hard to talk with, and generally to be avoided.

In general, Joe had difficulty maintaining intimate relationships with his peers. The only person he confided in was Josh Gibson. Gibson never missed an athletic event Joe was involved in, but it was hard for Joe to pay much attention to him in the post-game turmoil. Instead, they would have lunch on Saturdays and talk about sports, the market, and stocks. Gibson traded a lot, and a couple of times he brought along his broker from Merrill Lynch. Joe was not impressed with the man.

Occasionally an analyst from New York would visit the Merrill Lynch office, and Gibson always would urge Joe to attend the presentations with him. Joe liked these sessions, and he scanned the reports he was sent. He felt he was learning more and more about the way the market worked. He particularly responded to the apparent precision of the valuation numbers in comparing the attractiveness of stocks. It was like analyzing the player statistics in his boyhood board games. In 1989, after listening to a presentation from Merrill's computer analyst, he put the proceeds of his Wal-Mart sale into IBM at 27. The analyst was personable and passionate, and his description of the new products IBM was creating was inspiring.

Although Joe didn't know this at the time, this stock pick was to be his first financial debacle and the beginning of his endless discontentment with the technology sector. Although the price of IBM shares drifted over the next few years, it collapsed to 10 in 1992 and 1993. Joe initially refused to take the hit, held on, but then, feeling bored and lonely at college, sold his shares at 24 in 1995, absorbing a small loss. Then he watched with dismay as IBM soared fivefold in the tech mania of the late 1990s (see Figure 1.3). Again, Joe learned that patience is a virtue and that technology analysts are glib and sound good but can be very wrong.

Chapter 2

Arizona Union

I n the fall of his senior year, the college scouts from Virginia Tech
and Penn State came to check Joe out. Although they praised his
athletic ability, they said he lacked the really great arm of a big-
time Division I quarterback. Maybe he could be converted to a wide receiver, they thought, or a defensive back. He was definitely a talent they
wanted to recruit. But, Joe was disappointed that he wasn't getting more
attention from the famous Division I football schools. He dreamed of
going to bowl games and playing for a national championship team.

Joe also wanted to get out of Big Neck and make a lot of money.
He was tired of skimping. The Wal-Mart experience had whetted his
appetite, but nothing like it had happened to him in the stock market
since. He had continued to follow the market and read the material
Josh Gibson gave him but neither of them had found any great stocks
in a difficult market environment. Joe determined that the only way to
make money was to play in the NFL.

One December afternoon Joe got a call from Josh Gibson, who
wanted to talk about Joe's post-graduation plans. They met in Gibson's

simple, workman-like office. When Joe entered the room, Gibson didn't get up and continued to sit at his big wooden desk

"Pardon me for not getting up," Gibson grinned. "I didn't ask you here to shoot the breeze. This is serious; I think you're making a mistake. Your SAT scores are good enough to apply to an Ivy League university or another first-rate college, and those schools give academic, not athletic, scholarships to kids who have excelled in a sport. There are some wonderful colleges where you could be a scholar-athlete and get a fine free education that will be worth something."

"I don't want to play amateur, Division II or III football at those schools," Joe told him. "I think I can make it big in Division I, and then I really want to play in the pros where the big money is. And, let's face it, I'll never make the pros from Division II."

"The Ivy League has twenty players active in the NFL right now. Their alumni care about football, too; they just aren't insane. It's not professional football like the NCAA Division I. Furthermore, the Ivy League alumni are far more influential and better placed to help you with a real job after you graduate," Gibson said.

Joe would have none of it. "I'm going to play Division I football. The scouts that have seen me play say I have NFL potential. Just wait and see."

"Do you realize that only one out of every thousand college football players makes it to the pros? Suppose you get hurt? Suppose you don't make it in Division I. Then your scholarship is gone and you got nothing. Besides, the big money is in business and the stock market, not in smash mouth football."

"Maybe," said Joe. "I appreciate your interest. I really do, but I have to make this decision for myself."

"Okay, go get 'em," said Gibson with a large but flat smile.

Later, Joe would admit that that foolish decision cost him six years and that he blew a huge opportunity. "I was a just a dumb kid," he would say.

That winter, Virginia Tech, a Division I national powerhouse, wooed Joe hard, and he went to a three-day recruiting weekend there with

50 other prospects. The visit was complete with tryouts, tours, lectures on "the tradition of the program," and girls. They offered all the conventional goodies, but made it clear that after the first two years the continuation of the scholarship depended on his making the team. Joe was a little over-awed. The "program" seemed huge. He felt he did well at the quarterback tryout, but there were two other boys who could throw a ball farther and harder than he could. Also, the current starting quarterback for Tech had two years of eligibility left.

"We want you," the quarterback position coach told him. "You're fast and have good ball sense. We'll find a place for you."

"Not exactly a ringing endorsement," Joe told his father when he got home.

Virginia Tech was pressing him for a commitment when a scout from a giant commuter college outside of Phoenix, Arizona Union,[1] came along. The scout was a friendly guy, soft-spoken, and he knew a lot about Joe. He talked with the Big Neck High coach, took Big Joe to dinner, and visited Joe and Dolores at home. He even brought Dolores a bouquet of roses, which was a big hit. She told him no one had ever given her flowers before, and Joe thought he saw tears in her eyes. He made a mental note to bring her flowers when he graduated.

The scout told them AU had been around for 30 years, had an enrollment of 40,000, but had only gotten into big-time football five years ago. The chairman of the board of trustees had made his fortune selling insurance to immigrants and was determined to put AU on the map as a serious university. He was convinced that the way to achieve this status was to become a Division I football power. Therefore, he had given $25 million (all tax exempt, incidentally) to the athletic department, stipulating that it was for football and that the stadium be named after him.

The trustees had hired Pete Johnson, a head coach who had a reputation as a winner but who had been censured by the NCAA for recruiting violations. Johnson's salary, the scout told them, was four times that of the president of the university.

---

[1]Arizona Union is a fictitious university and not representative of any other educational institution in the country.

After this long pitch, the scout invited Joe to a football weekend in February, and said, assuming he did well, they would offer him a full scholarship. He would be assigned an alumni rep who would take care of "spending money and wheels." When he graduated, the alumni rep would arrange a great job for him. "After I play in the NFL, that would be helpful," Joe told him.

Big Joe laconically appraised the scout from AU as "a straight shooter" and really liked him. He strongly encouraged Joe to "check out the AU opportunity." When Joe went to talk it over with Gibson, Gibson told him in no uncertain terms that he thought it would be a mistake.

"Third-rate cow college. A degree from there means nothing. They'll exploit you on the football field and then spit you out." Joe listened and said nothing.

In late February, AU flew Joe out to Phoenix for a three-day week-end. As he came out of the airport gate, there was a good-looking blond-haired girl in a T-shirt holding a sign with his name on it. Joe introduced himself, and she smiled a little wanly as she told him her name was Leah and she was to be his guide for the weekend. As they walked to her car he couldn't help noticing that her blue jeans were so tight they practically clove her in two. She drove him the 20 miles to the campus, and they talked. Her eyes were tired, but she was informative.

"You guys are staying in a motel out by the stadium. Then I'm taking you to the football jocks' dorm. It's really nice. Not like being in a grungy regular dorm. They have their own rooms and lounges, and a kitchen with a chef that makes really good, healthy food with snacks anytime they want them."

"Where do you live?" Joe asked.

"I'm in a regular dorm. You see, I got a cheerleader scholarship but my real job is to do what they tell me as a hostess for you guys."

"Yeah," said Joe. "What does that mean?"

"You know, be available for the athletes. As us girls say, to keep the animals content and satisfied. Doesn't make you feel great about your-self." She was tough, Joe thought, but interesting.

After he had checked into the motel, they went to the large, four-story football dormitory. As she had said, the players lived in relative luxury, each having his own private small room with a TV. The bathrooms on each floor were spacious with showers, hot tubs, and a steam room. On the first floor, there was a movie theater, a small barber shop, and an elaborate weight room with four or five guys lifting. Then she ushered him into an enormous dining hall hung with exhortative banners such as "When the Going Gets Tough, the Tough Get Going," "Angry People Win Football Games," and "Make Something Happen."

At the far end was an elevated platform with a mahogany table and chairs. The backs of the chairs had silver nameplates on them.

"This is where head coach Johnson and his assistants sit," she told him. "They eat lean and watch as the players get bulked up on pasta."

"What's Coach Johnson like?" he asked.

"Good old boy; South mouth charm on the outside and barbarian toxic on the inside," she replied with a smile. "But don't quote me!" She was beginning to warm up.

As they chatted, Joe was surprised to learn that AU played football all year. Coaches insisted that the players come to practice and do two hours of daily weight training but cared little about whether they attended classes. Many maintained their eligibility by enrolling in softball courses and majoring in weight training.

Then they walked to the nearby practice facility. The locker room was huge, with wood-paneled lockers, thick carpets, and blaring rock music. Next to it were several spacious meeting rooms with auditorium chairs, blackboards, and screens. Joe was in awe—the locker room was nicer than his entre house.

That evening, in the brisk Arizona night, a bus took the 40 recruits to a large private room in a fancy suburban restaurant. Joe sat next to a barrel-chested guy with thick wrists and a steely stare. His narrow face was anonymous but for the crooked memory of a broken nose and intense gaze.

"I'm Jack Scott from Omaha. I'm a running back. Call me Scooter. I gave that name to myself and it stuck. I owned Friday nights back home. I was All-State Nebraska the last two years, and I'm sure counting on making it big here."

The other boys looked at him quizzically, not quite sure what to make of his bravado. But Scooter continued to babble, delivering a summary of his triumphant senior year during which he had scored 19 touchdowns in 10 games. Joe began to feel more at ease and barely suppressed a grin.

"I heard they play six-man high school football in Nebraska," said Joe deadpan.

Scooter grinned at him. "So you're a smart-ass quarterback, aren't you?" Scooter drawled. "Well, it ain't six-man, pal, and I can tell you I'll be the best thing that ever happened to you. Not only will my running open up your passing game but I can catch good. Great soft hands."

Then, Thomas Billow, the chairman of the trustees, stood up to address the recruits. A gray-haired man, he wore a Hermes tie and an expensive suit with a matching handkerchief in the breast pocket. His voice was husky and full of money. He told them he wanted to welcome them to AU. Then he spoke briefly about the university's history and the boosters' plans to make AU a national sports power.

Then he introduced head coach Johnson, describing in detail his record of turning around programs at Michigan State and Georgia Tech but omitting the suspensions for recruiting violations.

The coach stood up, looked around the room, and shouted, "Like Vince Lombardi said, winning isn't the most important thing. It's the only thing!" The boys cheered, but Joe thought it was corny. He'd been hearing that Lombardi comment since he was 10 years old.

The coach continued, "We got running backs with four point two speed to get around the corner at the next level and three-hundred-pound linemen with thirty-six-inch waists and fifty-two-inch chests who can bench press the Field House to knock people over. We're planning to kick some serious ass! But just remember one thing, guys. Pretty coeds don't have sex with losers!" The boys cheered again.

The next morning, he said, would feature a written multiple choice psychological test, a brief physical exam, and tests for strength, agility, and speed on the practice field. In the afternoon, they would break up into position groups.

The next day was a blur of activity. Joe felt he did well in the field drills, and his time in the 40-yard sprint attracted attention. Following the afternoon session, they jogged over to the stadium and watched the varsity offense run plays against the defense. Back in Virginia at a little over six feet two inches and 210 pounds he had felt big. Here, he realized he was on the small side. The starting varsity quarterback looked like he weighed at least 30 pounds more than Joe.

At the end of the varsity scrimmage, the quarterback position coach introduced him to his alumni rep, Bill Harrison, a tall, lean man with tanned, hollow checks, olive skin, a pencil moustache, and hair parted in the middle and frozen into place. Harrison was smooth as a snake and oozed charm. He owned three Honda dealerships around Phoenix, and he told Joe that he wanted to be his best friend. He said his "clothes allowance" would be $300 a week, and the car would come when he had "settled into the routine of things in the fall." And after graduation, a job as a car salesman awaited him. Joe didn't tell him that being a car salesman was not what he had in mind.

Harrison then shook hands with him and gave Joe a blue blazer with the AU crest on it, which Joe wondered if he would ever wear. Later back in his room, Joe found five $100 bills in the breast pocket. That got his attention.

That evening Leah escorted him to a party at a large house owned by the AU Athletic Association. Sweating kegs were set up and a vast barbecue was arrayed on the terrace. Twenty girls, many with pineapple colored hair and fireproof smiles, circulated among the recruits. Joe saw Scooter sitting and talking animatedly to a tall, dark-haired girl in a halter. Scooter later winked at him as the girl led him inside and upstairs.

As he ate dinner with Leah, he asked her what it was like to go to school at AU. "About half the students here are part-time and commuters, and the students are into football big-time. Believe it or not, making it in Division I would really help admissions."

"There are some good courses here," she added. "It's pretty casual, and honestly, its reputation is lousy, so being a graduate isn't worth much. Still, it's a college degree, and that means something when you apply for a job. I haven't seen my father in almost ten years and my mother was a maid at a fancy hotel outside of town until her back got so bad she couldn't work. I need the money and I need the degree."

They talked some more. He told her some about Big Neck and his background. For the very first time, he was actually confiding in a woman. She lit a cigarette, exhaled, and said, "Yeah, I know smoking is disgusting." She smiled at him with a real smile and asked, "You want to go upstairs? That's part of the program."

For a moment Joe was tempted. But somehow casual sex seemed shabby, and suddenly he thought of what it had done to his mother.

"You know, Leah," he said, "I don't think so." he paused and, to take the sting out of it, and added, "But I'd like to see you when I come back for summer practice. I've got an early plane tomorrow. Can you run me back to the motel?"

"Perfect," Leah said. "They'll think we've snuck off and I won't get dinged for being inhospitable."

He laughed but then he was sorry he had. She was surprisingly articulate and sensitive.

"Don't laugh," she said with a sly, sad smile. "If we're both lucky we won't be totally damaged, beat-up, second-hand goods by the time we get out of here."

His decision made, Joe reported to AU for football in late June. AU was a year-round football factory. Joe spent mornings in the weight room, listening to audio books to drown out the pounding rock music and stifling monotony. But there was no escape from the endlessly boring team meetings.

Practices often involved a lot of standing around in the hot, dry Arizona sun, which baked even the artificial turf. Repetition makes perfection, coaches believed, so players endlessly ran and reran plays. Sometimes, Joe felt as though his brain had congealed into an inert lump of gristle.

Coach Johnson watched the practices and scrimmages from a tower under a beach umbrella. He used a loudspeaker system to broadcast his lacerating sarcasm, which he apparently thought was both funny and motivational. A guy who ran a play wrong heard, "Number 26, you're depriving a village somewhere of an idiot." A senior who was trying to come back from an injury was warned "Spagnola, you're really not so much a has-been, but more of a definite won't be." A lineman who missed an assignment was told, "Smith, if you were any more stupid you'd have to be watered twice a week." A defensive back who got beat was informed, "Young lady, you have delusions of adequacy." Burps often punctuated these gems.

During that first hot summer, Joe felt he was doing well, but there was a lot of fresh meat on those practice fields. As time went on, it became clear AU had too many talented quarterbacks, and that Joe really didn't have an exceptional arm. He wasn't big by Division I standards. He read defenses well and could scramble, but he realized that playing QB for AU was going to be a long struggle and would involve being "redshirted" for a year, maybe even two.

Redshirting is a common way to extend a player's eligibility to five or more years. NCAA rules say a player has only four years of eligibility. However, if a player isn't officially part of the squad and doesn't play in any games, that year doesn't count. Most players foolishly like this idea as they still have all the benefits of being fed, paid, and playing college football, and the extra development time may improve their chances of eventually playing.

Joe also began to realize that he wasn't going to make it to the NFL and that he had better start taking life after football seriously. He still desperately wanted to play college football and began to wonder whether he should transfer to a Division II or III school, where he was sure to be part of the starting lineup.

By September, the coaches had decided to convert Joe into a defensive back. When Barnett, the coach of the defensive backs, called Joe into his office and told him the news, he was disappointed but not surprised. He knew he had no chance of playing quarterback until his senior year. He actually liked playing defensive back, knew he was good, and was reasonably sure he could be a starter.

During this meeting Barnett, also told him that he was to be redshirted for one year to gain experience. "You'll still get your regular walking around money every month. Is that okay?" asked the coach, fully expecting the usual answer that it was fine.

"No, it's not okay," said Joe. "I want to get on with my life. I don't want to spend five years here."

Barnett glared at him. "What a lousy attitude. This is Division I football. It's the Big Twelve. Maybe you should go play intramurals, bro'."

Joe looked him in the eye. "Maybe I should transfer—bro'."

Barnett's demeanor abruptly changed. If a body could help them, they had to humor the body. Joe became a defensive back, but he was marked down as a malcontent.

It was not a dramatic transition for Joe, who had occasionally played safety in high school. By his second year, Joe was a starting cornerback. He was fast, had good hands, and hit hard. As the season progressed, his confidence grew. He knew he physically could play well at this level.

He enjoyed transcendent moments when he made big plays. In a game against Penn State he was in deep coverage and the ball was batted up in the air. He leaped, tipped it, and then caught the ball with one hand, bounced off a tackler, and sidestepped another. Suddenly, he saw the whole field and instinctively cut back against the flow of tacklers, felt an arm grab him but in a flash had broken away, and then he was by them all, the green, empty field stretching in front of him. When he reached the end zone after an 80-yard run into daylight with the roar of the crowd engulfing him, he turned and looked back up the field. For a few seconds, the world stood still—his pursuers stopping, his teammates running toward him, the AU players on the sideline screaming his name. It was a moment of pure, exquisite exultation. AU didn't get invited to any bowl games, but the team finished 9–4 his sophomore year.

By Joe's third season he fully understood that big-time college football was a business. Nobody at AU cared whether Joe went to class, but he signed up for a full academic load anyway. The coaches did care whether he went to the weight room every morning for two hours. In fact, they took attendance. The defensive backs' coach asked him why he was wasting his time in class. He told Joe, only half joking, that if he cared so much about getting a degree, AU would give him an honorary one in weight lifting or phys-ed.

By this time, Joe had learned that the coaches saw the players as just glorified cannon fodder. Guys got hurt and were forced to play anyway resulting in more serious, permanent injuries. He had a series of minor nagging injuries, and he worried about concussions. He didn't really savor tackling the big running backs anymore. Still, there was nothing like the rush of winning on Saturday afternoons.

Outside of football and class, Joe spent his free time in his room reading with the door closed. The anti-intellectual culture of the coaches was such that he felt it was sensible to bury his textbooks and growing library deep in his closet. He consumed newsmagazines and the novels his mother sent him, and he studied the assignments from his business and economics classes. He was frustrated because there was nothing in his coursework that related directly to the stock market. He carefully pored over the Merrill Lynch research reports he received every week, analyzing the numbers to determine which stock was the best buy. It was like studying his *Running Back* players as a kid.

In his room, at practice, sitting in the meetings, he sometimes felt an overwhelming loneliness—a loneliness that was to plague him as he grew older. Somehow, the loneliness was connected to fragments of his past, to the sunsets, the stadiums, and particularly to those times when he and Gibson walked that land down by the river and he had fallen in love with it. But there was no understanding why or what the ineffable meant.

But he understood one thing: He was different from the other players. He was not part of the raucous life of the team. He liked them well enough, and they liked him, but he abhorred the monotonous brutality of practice.

Moreover, the boisterous, companionable football dormitory life was not for Joe. Twice in the first year he had gone to parties and drank way too much. Reeling with the liquor heavy in him, he had random, meaningless sex. Afterward, he was left with a hollow, drained depression.

Joe watched as many of the AU players—after they had used up their eligibility or were too busted up to play—left college without a degree, broke, a little punchy, and with bum knees and shoulders. He noticed there weren't any job offers from alumni reps unless you had been a big star and had made it to the NFL. Then maybe you could sell insurance in Phoenix for the chairman or cars for the big auto dealer.

Joe knew he was better, smarter than that, and he was dismayed by the insouciance of most of the other people he was around. He began to take his classes almost more seriously than football, and his particular concentration centered on working for his business degree. In the back of his mind he knew he wanted a stock market job.

Joe majored in business administration and found the subject interesting, but the classroom environment was often sloppy. The most compelling instructor was in accounting, of all things, and Joe took five courses over two years. To his surprise, he found himself engrossed with the subject. Its logical consistency appealed to him. But then again, he had always liked numbers.

His other focus was American literature, and he was surprised and pleased when his writing instructor offered to help him get a job in journalism. It was the first time that someone whose intellect he respected had responded to him because of his thinking, rather than his athletic skills. However, he was shocked at how little journalism paid. His determination to build his business knowledge and skills soared.

At AU, football players didn't have much opportunity to mingle with the rest of the student body. Joe saw other students at class, but most of the classes were in big lecture halls, although he sometimes was recognized and approached by guys who wanted to talk football. He dated Leah a couple of times but nothing sparked.

AU brought Big Joe and Dolores to a few games during Joe's years as a starter. AU treated them like minor royalty with complimentary accommodations and excellent tickets. He liked seeing them, felt obligated to have them, but was glad when the weekend was over. Having a big black father and a white mother with dyed blond hair just emphasized to his teammates what they already knew—that he was a half-breed, a mulatto.

Josh Gibson came to a couple of games each year and was at the Penn State game when he ran the interception back for a touchdown.

They usually had dinner together after a game, and they talked a lot about stocks. Joe began to realize that Gibson was an amateur playing a game against professionals. He didn't do the research work on the stocks he owned himself. Even though he incurred a small loss when he sold IBM too soon in 1995, Joe's total portfolio by now was worth almost $4,000 and he recognized that wasn't going to get himself any attention from a broker until he had many times that much. He read and reread an interview with Warren Buffett about how you should invest only in companies whose products you understood, and he increasingly tried to combine that principle with stocks that sold at low price-to-earnings ratios.

As it turned out, Scooter, the cocky running back he had met at the recruitment dinner, became his best friend. Scooter was a charming, happy-go-lucky, confident guy who had blossomed into a major attraction and was rumored to be a draft prospect.

At the beginning of their senior year, Scooter asked Joe for the loan of two hundred dollars. Joe agreed, but asked why he needed the money. In truth, Joe already knew. Scooter was a human sieve, running though money like it was water. He sported diamond stud earrings, and on this particular day he was dressed in a three-piece, double-breasted light-brown suit with a pale-blue shirt, all from a major Phoenix clothing store.

"My pops told me lend money, lose a friend," replied Joe, deadpan.

"Come on, pal, I'll pay you back."

"With all the yards you're gaining and the touchdowns you're scoring, I would have thought they'd be getting you big walking around money."

No, said Scooter. He was getting the same $300 a week he had always received.

"That's ridiculous," Joe told him. "Tell your alumni rep you want more."

"I don't want to piss him off," said Scooter. "It's only money."

"Yeah," said Joe. "There are more important things in life than money but the trouble is they all cost money. Get tough, asshole!"

Scooter did, and the alumni rep grudgingly agreed to make it $400. Scooter complained, but the guy told him to take it or leave it. Joe felt demeaned by the exploitation. "You're a wimp! They should have at least doubled it," Joe almost shouted. "Go back and tell that guy you want $600 and if you don't get it that sore ankle of yours is going to get a lot sorer."

Scooter did just that, and then sulked and limped the next day at practice. The following morning Joe was summoned to Head Coach Johnson's spacious office in the Athletic Center. The air conditioning was on full blast, but the heavyset coach had dark splotches under the armpits of his blue shirt. The office smelled of cigar smoke and sweat. Johnson was all smiles and charm when he talked to the press and always referred to the players as "his kids," but today he wasn't kidding.

"You know what, Hill," Coach Johnson told him. "You're a smart guy. Maybe too smart for your own good. I hear you been fussin' around studying the stock market instead of next Saturday's game plan. Why don't you apply those brains to better understand what UCLA is going to throw at you this Saturday rather than fucking up my star running back's curly blond head."

He leaned back in his chair and fiddled with a cigar. Joe was no longer intimidated by the coach, and, in fact, as he stared back at him he thought, *What a brutal, phony asshole you are.* Johnson continued, "Just so you understand what you're messing around with, let me make it simple. We're playing UCLA in the L.A. Coliseum this Saturday. The place seats like eighty-five thousand, and we get half of the gate over the two-million dollars UCLA takes off the top. If Scooter don't play and the big crowd don't come to see the great white hope running back, we'll be lucky to gross $100,000. This program and my salary live on gate receipts. This building and that fancy stadium of ours are financed with tax-exempt bonds. Sure, the alumni boosters help some, but they're a bunch of hillbillies with no real money. This cow-town university is not Harvard or Yale with thirty-billion-dollar endowments. We live hand to mouth."

Joe hadn't thought about the economics of the operation before. "I understand," Joe replied. "But, with great respect, sir, we're a hot team. We've been drawing big crowds. The guys, particularly Scooter, ought to get more walking around money."

"Son, you're supposed to be into football, not labor relations. We win football games with crazed maniacs, not accountants. I don't like troublemakers even if they are good cornerbacks. Do it again and you're out of here with a very big, very bad black mark."

"I've already got a black mark," Joe mumbled as he stood up to leave.

"Wise guy. Rabble-rouser. Troublemaker" Johnson said to his back.

Joe was still angry when he talked to Scooter. "This precious program of theirs is exploiting us. We could get a bunch of the starters to say either more money or no play. This UCLA game is a potentially big payday and an ego trip for a bunch of old men but it doesn't do anything for us."

Scooter didn't laugh. "That's treason, you're talking, dude. I don't want to be blacklisted as a troublemaker for a lousy three hundred dollars. I want to play in the NFL. They pay even rookies thirty thousand dollars a game." (Scooter got the opportunity to play in the NFL and was drafted by the Chargers after college . . . but his career didn't last long.)

That was the end of their great rebellion. They played UCLA that Saturday in the Coliseum, which was almost full, giving AU a big payday. Scooter had a good game, but they lost 28–21. Joe didn't care. The whole thing pissed him off. He was sick of the phoniness, the violence of the game. He didn't want to play in the NFL anymore. He was thinking more and more about life after football.

By the spring of his senior year, Joe found he did not have enough credits to graduate. Frequent travel and team meetings had kept him from completing the minimum attendance requirements on all of his courses. Since walking around money for seniors was discontinued at the end of the football season, about half of the seniors quit school in January and didn't graduate. Not Joe. He decided to take a summer course to complete his degree.

At last, Joe had an undergraduate degree in business administration. He headed for New York City with high hopes and $500 in his wallet. He wanted to work as an analyst on Wall Street . . . where the streets were supposedly paved in gold and where he'd make lots of money.

Chapter 3

New York and the Firm

After arriving in New York, Joe checked into a YMCA. Having seen an ad in the *Wall Street Journal*, he went to an employment agency that specialized in staffing financial firms.

"An undergraduate business degree from a university like Arizona Union doesn't cut it. Without an MBA, you aren't qualified for placement with a big name commercial or investment bank," the recruiter told Joe. "They do have training programs for the best and the brightest, almost like two-year financial boot camps, and afterwards you're looking good for a big money career in investment banking. Guys who have been through the programs do the interviewing and almost all of them attended fancy universities. They tend to hire people like themselves." Joe thought the agency guys seemed a little sour.

"I know a fair amount about the stock market and investing," he told him. "Since I was a teenager, I've followed the market. I'm really just looking for an opportunity."

"Yeah, sure. It won't matter, though. Ordinary guys like you and me that went to hick colleges aren't really eligible. A firm like Goldman or Grant & Company gets five hundred resumes and interviews a couple of hundred. They only look at the fancy Ivy League colleges and places like Stanford and Amherst. Arizona Union ain't going to do it for you. But maybe I can place you in a back-office job."

He continued, "Back office means you are in the bookkeeping department. Front office is where the people who interact with clients are. At a firm like Grant & Company, the portfolio managers and their analysts are the elite. Back-office jobs don't pay anything like front office."

"Does that mean I'm stuck in the back office forever?"

"It all depends. Maybe you can work your way out."

"What do they pay?"

"Maybe $50,000." Joe thought the guy didn't seem very interested or helpful. He obviously figured placing Joe wasn't going to get him a big commission.

A few days later, the agency sent Joe to Grant & Company, a major investment bank, to interview for a job in operations. Several years earlier, Grant's extensive back-testing had found high SAT scores and playing a team sport at the college level were the two best predictors of success at the firm. The human resources man who interviewed Joe observed that he was a handsome, dark-complexioned guy who was slim but had strong, broad shoulders, a thick neck, and long, sinewy hands. His SAT scores were better than decent, and he had played big-time college football. He offered Joe a job in operations at Grant Investment Management.

Sue Girardi, the operations manager at Grant, was a plain, square-bodied woman with an angular face and a nasal voice. She was in her mid-forties, and had a direct way about her that Joe responded to instinctively. He frankly told her about his ambitions.

"So, you want to be an analyst," she said. "Next, you'll be thinking of being a portfolio manager. Well, we are the ones who keep those smart guys from the Harvard Business School from selling what they don't own." She looked at Joe skeptically, thinking that he looked like a stud. She wondered how he would fit in with her people and how long he was going to stick around. "My staff is my family," she told him. "We get along and help each other out. So mind your manners."

Joe worked in the "engine room," an open space with no windows on the twenty-first floor of 1300 Avenue of the Americas. He shared the space with 20 other men and women, all of whom worked at terminals. All day he reconciled accounts—settling trades, making sure all the entries hit, checking the account statements. It was tedious work, surrounded by nice, but boring, people. Most of them were middle-aged women who had worked their way up from being secretaries, save for the few men who had mostly gone to some junior college. As for Sue, he found she was tough but fair, and determined that the work be done correctly and on time.

Portfolio managers at Grant were a distant aristocracy, and the ana-lysts were their dashing young lieutenants. These Brahmins didn't mingle with the peons in operations. But when Joe did their performance runs, he noticed that about half of the portfolio managers had results that were below the relevant benchmarks they were competing against. Buy high, sell low, follow the momentum seemed to be their investment style. Nevertheless, they had the interesting jobs and made the big money.

After a few months of a steady paycheck, Joe got a room on the fifth floor of a walk-up boarding house in the East Village that loomed up from the gloomy groin of the street. He made sure he got to work early and left late. With his facility for numbers, the job was not diffi-cult, and he caught some errors, earning an "Atta boy" from Sue. Grant's gym was reserved during the day for managing directors and principals, but the peons could use it after six. Joe began going three times a week, and it was there that he met Doug Scott.

Doug was a small, lean Californian with an easy smile and con-siderable charm. They found they both lived in the East Village, and would often ride the subway home together after the gym. Doug had majored in business at UCLA and was clearly smart and knowledge-able about stocks and markets. He originally had applied for a job as a research assistant at Grant & Company, but despite a strong academic record had been sent to equity sales. He was a natural—had a friendly, likeable personality, and was very capable. He had been in equity sales for five years, and he told Joe he was earning around $700,000, which he implied was slim pickings in his world.

"You've got to keep plugging, dude," he told Joe. "After going to a university that nobody has heard of, you're going to need some credentials in order to get out of the back office. Why don't you go to business school part-time and get your MBA at night? It's a drag, and although the NYU Stern School of Business is not Harvard, it has a good reputation. The firm will pay for it."

Joe knew he was right. If he was ever going to be an investor, he had to get some credentials. The portfolio managers and analysts might be well-dressed, overbred mediocrities, but they had the education and the investment tools he lacked. He knew he couldn't stand up to them in a conversation about the stock market. His accumulated self-confidence of Big Neck and the AU years was slipping away. He had to remedy the situation.

Joe applied to and was accepted by Stern at least in part because of Sue's letter of recommendation and the Grant & Company imprimatur.

"So you're going fancy on me, Joe. I'm all for people bettering themselves, but don't let me catch you doing your homework during working hours. And no leaving early for school. We've got our work to get through."

Joe signed up for a full course load and went to class at night. Going to school after working all day was a hard grind. Sometimes he had to struggle to keep awake in class, and it was tough to get all the assignments done. The level of teaching and time demands were far different from the undergraduate curriculum at AU. He found himself studying on the subway and even during the 40 minutes when he went to the company cafeteria for lunch.

The men in operations were nice enough and they liked to chatter about sports with Joe. However, they were not guys he felt any inclination to hang out with. Most of them were older and had families. He knew no one in the city, and so on the weekends, he had vast expanses of time. He jogged in Central Park, studied at the small table under the reading lamp in his bare boarding house room, and read stock market books in the cavernous New York Public Library. It was a lonely, frugal, ascetic life. Joe almost missed AU—almost, but not quite.

Once again, his loneliness came back. Studying alone in his room or at the library, he would suddenly be overwhelmed by the futility of it all. His whole life seemed like nothing but fragments of vanity; his past valueless, his future meaningless unless he might by some single stroke of luck discover the unifying fulfillment.

In late November, Joe asked Sue for a Friday off so he could go back to Big Neck for the weekend. Friday night, he had an early dinner with Big Joe. They talked about sports and Big Joe told him that the high school team was struggling. As they walked toward the field, his father was as laconic as ever.

"I'm proud of you working for a famous firm like Grant & Company," Big Joe told him. "But then I've always been proud of you, son."

"I've got a crappy job there, Dad, but I'm trying to work my way up."

"I know you will, son. I know you will!" It was about as intimate an exchange as father and son had ever had.

At the field, with all the familiar sights and smells, the memories of what had been flooded over Joe. It had been more than five years since he graduated, and the players seemed so much smaller and more fragile than those he remembered. At halftime he shook hands and embraced old friends and teammates, and after the game a group of them went to The Big Easy, one of the town's taverns.

All of Joe's old friends were married and had jobs in town selling cars, pumping gas, or at the mill. They regarded Joe with awe because he lived in New York and worked for a famous firm, and looked skeptical when he told them how menial it actually was. Joe began to feel bored. His initial gladness at seeing them wore off, and he found he didn't really have much to say. At the end of the evening, as he walked home down the same old dark streets he knew so well, he felt strangely depressed.

The next day Joe had lunch with Gibson, who was looking old and shriveled.

"The proverbial one returns to the scene of his triumphs!" Gibson said as they sat down.

"Hardly," said Joe with a wry grin. "I'm not feeling very proverbial these days." He then proceeded to confide in Gibson. "You were so right way when you told me to go to a good college instead of a football factory. Big mistake, and now I'm stuck in the back office."

"Joe," said Gibson. "You're a very smart, gifted guy. Grant is supposed to be a great firm. You'll get a break. Getting an MBA is dead right. Keep paying attention to the stock market. Work hard and keep your nose clean."

"That won't be hard. There's nothing to get it dirty with," Joe told him.

During lunch, they talked about stocks. Josh seemed to like to dwell almost masochistically on his mistakes even though Joe knew he had made some good money in the ongoing bull market. He was still flagellating himself for selling Wal-Mart way back in 1987.

At this lunch Josh described in detail his adventures and errors in Digital Equipment. Since the early 1980s he had used Digital Equipment computers in his plant, and he told Joe how much he admired the company, its products, and its sales organization. The salesman on his account was "such a fine person and was so optimistic about the future of DEC." Josh had watched the stock soar in the mid 1980s, and, after the Crash in 1987, he and Joe had gone to a meeting with the Merrill Lynch computer analyst. Did Joe remember the meeting? Of course, Joe told him, he remembered. With the proceeds of his Wal-Mart sale he had bought IBM after the same meeting.

The analyst had gone on and on about how state-of-the-art Digital's word processor was. Impressed, Josh had bought the stock at 108 in early 1989 when the equity market was still depressed after the Crash. Unfortunately, the supposedly great management was a one-trick pony and had failed to develop new products. The best sales organization in computerdom was worth very little with obsolete equipment. In the next few years as the broad market gradually rallied, Digital Equipment traded down with the declines interspersed with sharp rallies. Discouraged and frightened by the sharp fall, in the summer of 1990 he sold half of his position at 70 and then sold the other half in February of 1992 at 57. The company eventually was acquired at no premium for 56 on June 12, 1998.

"I should have kicked it out back in 1988 right after I bought it when the stock acted so badly. Sell your losers; ride your winners. Instead I did the opposite. Don't listen to salesmen or analysts."

Lying in his old bed that night, he was restless in the familiar room. In the quiet of the night, he heard the distant hoot of a freight train and the low rumble as it rounded the bend and made the uphill run toward town. Suddenly an ineffable sadness swept over him. He couldn't wait to get back to New York, and yet he didn't know why.

Back at work, Joe noticed a dark-haired woman with a round, wholesome face and big green eyes whose name was Pat. She was maybe five years older than he and was nice looking but with no cheerleader body after having sat at a desk for 10 years. She smiled at him a lot, and one day when he was eating lunch by himself and studying in the cafeteria, she came and sat by him. They chatted about the firm and the work. She had been a secretary for five years, then took some advanced computer courses, and eventually had been promoted to professional staff. But now she had gone about as far as she could go.

After that first lunch, she would collect him for lunch a couple of times a week, and several times on a Friday night they went out for drinks with Pat's friend Marlene and a few other co-workers from the engine room. Against his better judgment, Joe tagged along because he had nothing else to do, and he guessed he was a little bored and lonely with his existence as a hermit.

The women in the engine room were a close-knit group but there were petty jealousies. Most were either single or divorced. About once a year Marlene organized a trip for all of them to some exotic party town. Joe gathered that sometimes things got pretty wild on these trips as they partied and picked up men. Pat told him she had gone a couple of times.

Marlene was 40, divorced, big and brassy with dyed blond hair, and liked to flirt. She did not flirt with Joe. Somehow, the women in the office had come to consider him Pat's property, which was okay with him as long as no one took it seriously. Marlene worked for David Dawes, the head of U.S. equities for Grant. Dawes's position gave her some power, and she enjoyed using it. She was much more outspoken and assertive than Pat. He found them both amusing.

Joe knew nothing about the culture of a big Wall Street investment company so he listened carefully when the women gossiped about the firm and the men who ran it. The women thought many of the top brass were smart and hardworking, but that some were mediocre dilettantes at best. They were the privileged elite, the investors, because they had the good fortune to grow up in fashionable suburbs or on Fifth Avenue and had gone to the right prep schools and universities. Marlene liked her boss—David Dawes. He was a good guy, no genius, she said, but he didn't need to be since his wife supposedly was rich. He was fair and competent.

Joe and Pat's easy, if sporadic, relationship continued in the months that followed. They talked freely about work and the firm. Pat occasionally asked him about his business school courses, but when he talked about his excitement and enthusiasm, she was not responsive. It was almost as if she didn't want him to get an MBA. Joe enjoyed Pat's company, but he wasn't physically attracted to her and didn't want to get intimately involved with her. He never asked her to spend time alone with him and simply thought of her as his office confidante. Yet, after having lived for years in a world of men, he was intrigued by this completely different casual relationship.

All this changed that summer, when Pat asked Joe to join her, Marlene, and a few other friends at a rented beach house on the Jersey shore for the weekend.

The beach house was shingled and weather-beaten and more of a shack than a house but the view out over the long stretch of beach and the dark blue ocean was startling. Pat showed him to the small room he was to share with Jack, another guy from the engine room. He put on swimming trunks and went to the beach.

It was a beautiful sunny day with the big, heavy Atlantic surf pounding in. Pat, Marlene, and two other women from work were sitting in beach chairs and they eged him appreciatively. Although he had seen these women day after day in their business attire, it was strange to see them lying in the sun in their skimpy bathing suits. Pat didn't exactly have a bikini body and Marlene looked dumpy. He began to feel a little uneasy.

He stretched, and then told Pat he was going for a run. He set a pace that discouraged company. He ran a long way down the broad beach in the hot afternoon sun past children playing in the shallows of the surf. The salt spray in his nostrils was like the ocean's perfume. After a couple of miles he broke off into the sea and swam hard for 10 minutes. The water was cold, but it felt wonderful. It was as though layers of New York grime and boring reconciliations were washing off him.

When he got back to the house, the beach party was already under way with loud music and a cooler full of beer, wine, and rum. Someone was grilling steaks and hamburgers. He could hear Marlene's loud, raucous laugh. He changed into a polo shirt and shorts and found Pat. They ate and drank amid snatches of conversation with Marlene, her date, and the other guests.

Much later, when it was dark Pat grabbed his hand and pulled him over to a dune where they could see the white surf pounding in and a long path of moonlight over the dark blue ocean. He lay back on the dune, enjoying the dull ache from his earlier exercise and the liquor in him.

"You know," she said, "I was thinking about leaving Grant until they began hiring hunks like you." He sensed the comment was rehearsed and that the slightest advance on his part would quickly and gratefully be received. "You're different," she murmured slurring her words just a little. "You're going to business school. You'll be discovered. I know you're going to be a hotshot investor, make tons of money, and forget about little old me." He was determined to shift the conversation away from him.

"Tell me your life story," he said casually. "Then I'm going to bed."

Her story was predictable. As she rambled on about a series of failed relationships, including a long affair with an older, married man from Grant who eventually left her and returned to his wife and family, Joe half-listened and thought about his options. Clearly, Pat was trying to seduce him and wanted to consummate their "relationship" but Joe knew it was not smart to have a one-night stand with a girl he had to see at work every day. Then, again, he thought, what was the harm in having some casual fun? He gazed up into the endless vault of stars in the night sky. There were no answers there.

They walked back across the now-deserted beach up to the house. He thanked her for inviting him and gave her a quick kiss good-night and went up to his room. He thought she looked at him wistfully. He had barely undressed and got into bed when the door opened.

Pat stood there in a thin nightgown through which he could clearly see her body. "Jack is in my room with Marlene," she whispered. "You're not going to make me sleep on that bed all alone, are you?"

She seductively walked over to the bed, slipped under the covers, and put her hand on his upper thigh. It had been awhile since a woman had pursued him so aggressively, so insistently. He decided he was not going to ask her to leave his room.

When he got up Sunday morning, Pat was gone. Jack was in the other bed with his mouth open, snoring. Joe dressed quickly and went downstairs. It was another beautiful, hot summer day with the sun shimmering off the sea and the big waves rolling in. Pat was in the kitchen making coffee. She kissed him and squeezed his hand.

Joe began to feel trapped. He got up and abruptly said he was going for another run. Pat started to protest, but then seemed to change her mind.

He took a long jog far up the beach, and as he ran, he began to feel more and more uncomfortable with the Pat situation. He was disconcerted by the intensity of Pat's behavior. He did not want anyone to think that she was his girlfriend. Had he inadvertently misled her? It would be unseemly to be rude, so he would finish the weekend, and then, back in New York, gently distance himself from her.

When he finally returned to the cottage, he sat down in a remote corner of the porch with his accounting textbook. Twenty minutes later, she found him.

"You're about as sociable as a computer terminal," she chided him.

"Sorry, but as usual, I'm loaded with homework," he told her.

"I've missed you!" she said.

"My accounting book has missed me even more." She looked hurt.

That evening there was another noisy beach party with a drifting crowd of people, most of whom he didn't know. All of them seemed to have had too much sun and too much to drink. He wondered again what he was doing here, but then a sleek, deeply tanned, attractive woman about his age in a tube top with a lithe body began talking to him. She was an analyst at J.P. Morgan, she told him, and he suddenly found himself interested in her. Then, just as suddenly, Pat interrupted the conversation, put her arm around his waist in a proprietary way, and told him they had to eat. Joe later looked for the woman, but she was gone.

That evening seemed endless to Joe. He was bored and uncomfortable, so he told Pat he was going back to the cottage to pee, and instead he snuck off to his room. He lay on his bed with a book and had just drifted off to sleep when Pat opened his door and climbed onto his sagging, narrow bed. She whispered, "Can I get an encore?" and turned off the lights.

They had sex and quickly fell asleep, but Joe slept fitfully and dreamed that he was being pursued by some voracious animal. When he awoke and saw the softly snoring figure with messy hair next to him, he felt a desperate, overwhelming need to escape. He looked out the window and saw the sun pouring in through the ratty venetian blinds and he could smell the fresh, salt ocean air. Suddenly, he had a sense of clarity. He needed to leave . . . now. He dressed quietly, scrawled a note of thanks saying he had a paper to write, and hitchhiked to the train station.

The first morning back in the office after the long weekend, Pat stopped in front of his work station. "I can't wait for lunch," she softly said. Joe steeled himself.

"Pat, I've got some studying to catch up with."

"I won't bother you," she said. "We'll catch up this weekend."

"Pat, I want to keep being your friend, but there isn't going to be a next weekend. I had a wonderful time but there's no encore."

She gasped. "So it was sex and run," she said, her tone changing abruptly.

"Pat, it was great fun, but for me it was just fun. Like between two good friends. Let's have lunch next week when I get caught up," and he turned back to his computer. She walked away but her eyes were damp.

Later in the day when he passed Marlene in the hall, she glared at him. "What's the matter with you? Pat says you won't come down next weekend. I thought we all had a great time."

"I enjoyed it very much. It was wonderful to be at the ocean and with you all, but I don't want to make a habit of it, and frankly, Marlene, I don't want Pat to get the wrong idea."

Marlene flared her nostrils. "You might have thought of that *before* . . ."

In the weeks that followed, Joe would occasionally have lunch with Pat, but their conversation had lost its spontaneity. He went out a couple of times with a group from the room for drinks, but it was uncomfortable because Marlene mostly seemed to glare at him and the other women gave him no more than a cursory nod. He chastised himself for getting involved physically with Pat and he resolved never to be so stupid again, but he was too preoccupied with work and school to be deeply concerned.

Besides, he was beginning to see some career daylight. A few months before the ill-fated weekend, David Dawes—the managing director who ran the U.S. equity group—had come in to check a performance figure on one of his accounts. Dawes was a tall, lanky, fit-looking man in his mid-forties with an aristocratic face He was charming, well-liked, and respected. That morning, he noticed *Manias, Panics, and Crashes* on Joe's desk.

"Hey Joe," he said. "Great book. Kindleberger is the best. You reading investment stuff?"

"Yeah," said Joe, surprised that Dawes even knew his name. "I'm trying to, but I've got a lot of business school stuff to get through."

"I've got a whole bookcase in my office full of good investment reading. The classics. Help yourself. You going to business school?"

"Yes sir," said Joe. "I want to be an investor."

"That's great!" said Dawes, "They tell me you played college football. What position did you play?"

"I played quarterback in high school but ended up as a cornerback in college at Arizona Union."

"Great," said Dawes. "I was a tight end at Princeton. Half the time I sat on the bench. I didn't play much until my senior year. But it was *great*. I loved it!"

Joe consumed Dawes's books, one by one. He read old classics like Mackay's *Extraordinary Popular Delusions and the Madness of Crowds* and Graham's *Security Analysis*. Then he read modern stuff: Sobel's *Panic on Wall Street*, Soros's *The Alchemy of Finance*, Dreman's *Contrarian Investment Strategy*, and even Galbraith's *The Great Crash*.

He bought Charles Ellis's *Classics I* and *Classics II*. He didn't just read them but underlined and consumed them. He found investment numbers and concepts endlessly fascinating. Unraveling a company's accounting was like solving a puzzle. It reminded him of his boyhood days tracking his football board game statistics.

The more he read, the more he thought that value investing was his thing. He liked dealing with hard numbers about what a company was worth, and then comparing them to the price of its stock. Over the years, value had beaten growth by almost three percentage points annually—a huge difference.

When it was time for Joe to return a book to Dawes, he made a point of trying to do it when Dawes was in his office by himself. When that fortuitous circumstance occurred, Dawes often talked with him about the book. Over time, Dawes became impressed with Joe's urge to better himself and his quick comprehension of investment concepts.

"Read this new one," he said one day, handing Joe Menschel's *Markets, Mobs, and Mayhem. This guy has a great attitude*, Dawes thought. He asked HR for Joe's resume and became even more interested when he found out that Joe had been second team All Big 12 his senior year. Too bad he had gone to such a hick college.

Joe also continued to keep in touch with Doug. At the end of the year, Doug was moved to proprietary trading, where he would be trading the firm's own capital, an activity that Grant was emphasizing.

"They want to be like Goldman Sachs," Doug explained. "Prop trading can be a really big, high-margin profit center, and the investment banks—because they're brokers—have an edge since they see the order flow from their customers and, let's face it, have big research departments who can move a stock when they change their mind. I work at staying close to the star analysts. Of course, everyone has to be careful about inside information but still there's an edge."

"Why do you want to do it?" asked Joe. "You're making good money in institutional sales and there's less risk."

"Yeah," replied Doug, "but that was yesterday. Commission rates keep going down and the role of the salesman is becoming far less important than it was twenty years ago. Back then a great relationship institutional salesman would become a portfolio manager's best friend,

and because he could manipulate the PM, he was of incredible value to the firm in getting tough deals done."

"So what's the deal?"

"I sit on the equity floor with six or seven other guys. We are allowed to buy or sell short anything that moves. Stocks, indexes, commodities, currencies, fixed income."

"What do you know about commodities and bonds?" Joe asked.

"Not much, but they're all trading animals subject to fear and greed and momentum. And I can learn. You know there are *eating* sardines which is what you guys in investment management do, and *trading* sardines which is what prop traders buy."

"Who will you report to?" Joe inquired.

"The group I'm in works under what we call our warlord. The firm probably has thirty prop traders overall who work for like six warlords. The warlords compete with each other to become the trading Taipan who runs the whole business. The firm gives me like fifty million of capital. I can leverage it up, and at the end of the year I get a payout of twelve percent of the profits. The firm will pay for an assistant and for my travel. The tough part is I can't have a drawdown—in other words, a loss—of more than ten percent. If I do, they close me down."

"Suppose you're up twenty percent and your equity is sixty million. Does that drawdown rule mean they'll close you?"

"Exactly. No ten percent drawdowns. They'll punch you out and sit you down until the end of the year or until the warlord thinks your head is on straight again.

"Isn't it the exact opposite of what the great long-term value investors like Warren Buffett preach?" asked Joe.

"Definitely. It's momentum trading. *Fast money* like that program on CNBC. Sell on weakness, buy on strength. But if you score, they'll give you more money the next year and probably a bigger payout."

"Doug, that's great, but why did they pick you? You've never been a trader."

"They want to have fifty prop trading lines working next year. They've heard I've had some good calls with clients, I know the analysts, can maybe slyly front run them, and I guess they think I'm a smart, savvy guy. If I succeed they've got a winner that can make them some serious money. If I flop and lose ten percent, it costs them max six million and I'm either out on the street or back in sales."

"Sounds good to me," said Joe. "Maybe I should be trying to be a prop trader."

"You gotta get out of that dead-end operation first."

"Yeah, I know," said Joe.

In August, Dawes asked Joe to have lunch in the cafeteria. At that lunch, and in two more lunches over the next six weeks, they talked easily about sports, the markets, and the books Joe was reading. Dawes wanted to know what playing Division I football was like, and Joe was very candid with him about the rigors and phoniness of AU. Dawes was fascinated, and he respected what Joe had experienced. He also was surprised, maybe even astounded, at how perceptive Joe was becoming about investing. He began to send Joe research reports, which Joe studied intensely. Joe made it a point not to be too obsequious but he knew Dawes could rescue him from operations.

Three months later, when Dawes needed another analyst to work with his group, he asked Joe if he was interested. He warned him that no one was going to give him a tutorial on being an analyst. He was going to have to learn on the job. Joe, of course, was absolutely thrilled and jumped at the opportunity. He was moved to a desk in the analysts' bullpen the following Friday.

About six weeks into his new job, Pat called Joe and demanded that he have lunch with her.

"I must talk to you. We have to go somewhere out of the office." As they walked up Sixth Avenue, he had a sense of foreboding. They bought sandwiches and sat in the open-air plaza at Rockefeller Center.

"I'm pregnant," she said. "I can get an abortion for three thousand dollars but I want to have the baby."

Joe stared at her. "You didn't take any precautions?"

"No! Do you think I do that kind of thing all the time? Why didn't you?"

Joe grimaced. She was right. He should have had a rubber with him, but he hadn't expected sex to be on the weekend's agenda. On the other hand, he now had come to suspect it had been on Pat's agenda all along.

He squeezed her hand "I'm so sorry," he murmured. "Pat, I'll help pay for the abortion. I'll go to the doctor with you. I'll do anything you want, but I definitely do not want a baby." Tears welled up in her eyes, and abruptly she stood up and stormed off back toward the office.

Sue called him the next afternoon and asked him to come to her office. Marlene was waiting there, too. Although Joe had thought of Sue as smart and fair, he was uneasy and wasn't quite sure why Marlene was in the room.

"Joe, I'm talking to you unofficially, but we're all family here. Pat is a nice, wonderful girl," Sue said, speaking deliberately in her nasal voice. "She wants to have the baby and will make a fine mother. We think that at the very least you two should move in together."

Joe felt his guts recoil. He looked Sue in the eye. "I feel terrible about the pregnancy, but there is no way I am moving in with Pat or anybody else. I will pay half the cost of an abortion, do everything I can, but there is no long-term relationship coming."

"Suppose she has the baby," asked Sue. "Will you help support the child and be involved?"

Joe squirmed uneasily. Before answering the question, he thought for a moment. He wondered how much Sue knew about his background.

"The answer is no. I'm twenty-four years old. Pat is twenty-nine. I don't want a child at this point, and I can't afford to help support one. I would like Pat to have an abortion—soon."

Marlene almost screamed at him: "You should have thought about all that before you seduced a nice girl like her!"

Is that her version of what happened? Joe thought to himself. He could feel the anger and resentment welling within him, but he was determined to control himself, and he measured his words.

"I didn't seduce Pat. She seduced me. Let's not distort the truth here," Joe said.

Marlene ignored him. "You took advantage of our hospitality."

"Come on, Marlene, give me a break. I wasn't the only one sleeping with someone in that cottage. I didn't go to Pat's room; she came to mine. Yeah, I wasn't prepared for it, and I'm willing to pay my share of the cost of the abortion, but don't try to unload a major guilt trip on me."

"You think you're a big, fancy swinging d**k, don't you?" Marlene snarled.

"All right, you two," Sue interrupted, "this squabbling doesn't solve anything. It's complicated and I haven't decided what to do or even if there is anything to do. I want to think about it. Now let's get back to work."

A couple of days later, Pat called him at his desk and they walked out together. When they were outside, she grimly told him that Sue had talked with her and that she was taking a week off to have the abortion. He wrote her a check for $2,000, which cleaned out his bank account. She took the check, glared at him, and as she turned toward Penn Station, he tried to kiss her cheek but she angrily pushed him away.

The following Tuesday, when he called Marlene at the office and asked how Pat was, he got a frosty "Just fine, no thanks to you." However, he felt a lot better when Sue called him later that day and said, "You know, Joe, it was unfortunate but I think it worked out for the best in the end. Good luck."

Chapter 4

Onward and Upward

I n 1998, Grant & Company Asset Management was a major, worldwide investment management firm with assets of $250 billion. The investment management division was based in New York. David Dawes ran U.S. equities, one of seven major product groups, assisted by a deputy portfolio manager. Three other portfolio managers ran smaller specialist categories—technology, emerging growth, and small- and medium-cap value. There were five analysts, one of whom was Joe. In total, the group managed around $30 billion.

Somewhat to his surprise, Joe found he could hold his own and perhaps more than his own against the other four analysts and even the portfolio managers, who theoretically had more experience and a better education. All the portfolio managers and three of the analysts had graduated from Ivy League colleges and had gone to full-time business schools such as Harvard, Stanford, and Columbia. Two of the portfolio managers were also CFAs (Chartered Financial Analysts), which was a well-regarded accomplishment and the equivalent of an MBA.

The analysts were assigned industries, and they were expected to follow developments in the companies in their industries. They did this by keeping in touch with brokerage specialist analysts who were supposedly experts in these companies, by going to meetings put on by the managements, by attending conferences, and occasionally by visiting the companies. The firm's analysts from time to time were also asked to research companies that a portfolio manager found interesting. A written report and recommendation were expected.

The analysts all wanted to become portfolio managers, and thus intensely competed to appear bright and alert, and above all to show good investment judgment. Several of them sucked up to Dawes (shamelessly in Joe's view)—one of them, whose father was an executive vice president at General Electric, even organized a golf game for Dawes with his father, while another regularly played squash with two of the portfolio managers at the Racquet Club on 51st Street.

This ass kissing, nepotism, and squash games pissed off Joe. He hadn't gone to the right schools, didn't know the right people, and had never even seen a squash court. However, as he had always been able to do, he masked his insecurity with an intense demeanor.

Occasionally, an analyst would come up with an idea on his or her own, but it was relatively rare. The analysts were reactive instead of proactive. Joe noticed this and decided he would take the initiative to try to find some winners on his own in his assigned industries—aerospace and defense. He studied his companies intensely, but hesitated to make a recommendation so soon and he worried that if his first selection flopped, his credibility would be severely damaged.

Ironically, his first investment recommendation came from an unlikely source. Football.

Upon being released from the Chargers, Scooter had been recruited by a Los Angeles–based insurance company, Sun America, as a sales trainee for wholesalers in their variable annuity business. Joe and Scooter had kept in touch, and Scooter asked him to check out Sun America's variable annuity equity products that he was being trained to sell.

Joe had studied the firm's annual report, read the brokers' research, and talked with two of the analysts who covered the company. Sun America was a financial services company that specialized in a broad range of retirement savings and investment products and services. At the time, the shares were selling at around 15 times earnings, which seemed low considering the company's earnings apparently were compounding at 20 to 25 percent a year. Joe told Scooter equity variable annuities should be an easy sale in the bull market. "It won't matter that you majored in pool," he told Scooter. "Just don't get that smile of yours damaged."

"Hey," said Scooter. "I'm ready for some easy money. The sales guys tell me they've got a layup setup where you can trade shares in international and emerging markets funds and it's a sure thing."

Joe asked, "How does that work?"

The system, Scooter explained, involved buying or selling shares in an international stock fund. Investors made late-day trades based on U.S. market changes, assuming that fund shares would make corresponding moves when European and Asian exchanges opened the next day. So far it was legal, Scooter said, though it tended to hurt long-term shareholders by sapping fund performance.

"Sleazy," said Joe.

At Scooter's urging, Joe visited Sun America, meeting with the shareholder relations guy, and then with the CFO. Sun America was complex, and the accounting was difficult, but Joe became convinced the business model was for real. The company was well-run and innovative and senior management was reputed to be very smart. The chief executive, Eli Broad, had a reputation as an innovator and a winner. At 15 times earnings, the stock was cheap as long as the bull market lasted.

When he got back to New York, Joe wrote up Sun America and presented the idea to Dawes and the committee. When he had finished, the senior analyst, Bill Hansen, whom Joe had sensed was jealous of his relationship with Dawes, challenged him on the company's accounting. Hansen, never shy of voicing his overly aggressive opinions, loudly bellowed, "The stock is already up twenty-five percent on the year and is really just a bucket shop sales organization."

Joe stared at him. It was like looking at a large empty house at night in which all of the lights were out. Hansen was just being a jerk, but Joe remained unperturbed. At AU he had learned that you could get away with challenging coaches and self-appointed superiors if you disarmed the sting of your disagreements by saying, "With respect" or even "With great respect." Now he employed that ruse.

"With great respect," Joe said, "it's a bull market play but both the business and the stock price have momentum going for them. It's a very well-managed company. Yeah, they're an aggressive sales organization, but a lot worse stuff is going on in the IPO market. I think Sun America is a winner."

Dawes and two of the other portfolio managers accumulated a big position in the high 40s and 50s. (See Figure 4.1.) Over the next few months the Sun America stock price rose 15 percent. Then, out of a clear blue summer sky, on August 20, 1998, American International Group (AIG), the global reinsurance conglomerate, made an offer for Sun America at a premium of almost 40 percent to the then existing price. It was a *friendly* deal in the sense that it had been negotiated by the two managements prior to the announcement.

The morning the deal was announced, Dawes virtually came running into the analysts' bull pen. He grabbed Joe, and embraced him.

"AIG is buying Sun America for stock!" he shouted. "Forty percent premium! It's a great fit. AIG is a superb company. Congratulations! Hey dude, your stocks are on fire. I want more!"

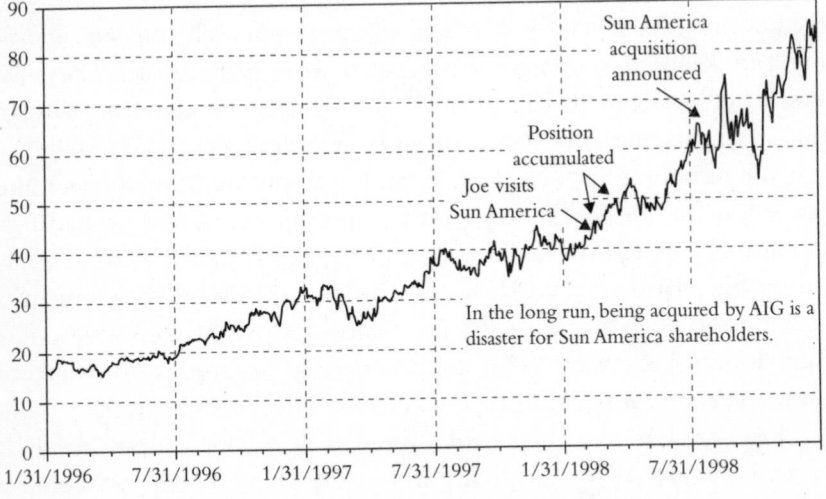

Figure 4.1　Great Buy, but Lucky—Sun America 1995–1998

When Dawes had left, the squash player analyst murmured a trifle grimly, "I thought football players were supposed to be dumb."

"They are," said Joe, "but sometimes they get lucky."

The guy grinned sourly at Joe. "I don't know about that, but like they say, never confuse genius with a bull market."

One mid-September afternoon, after Joe briefed Dawes on a company visit, Dawes asked him to play for his football team in Greenwich that Saturday.

"It's two-hand touch. Our team, which we call the Footballers, has some good athletes, guys my age that played college sports—but we want to win. We're playing one of the best teams in the league."

Joe jumped at the opportunity.

"Nothing I'd rather do than play football," he replied.

"Great!" said Dawes and slapped him on the back.

Dawes picked Joe up at the train station and brought him to the field. The feel of running on green grass on that crisp fall day and the fiber of a football in his hands elated him. As for the Footballers, it took them about five minutes to realize they had struck gold. Joe might not have had a Division I quarterback's arm, but he could still throw a ball on the line 40 yards and he was faster than anyone on the field.

The Footballers won by three touchdowns that day. Joe passed for two touchdowns (one of which was a 30-yard strike to Dawes), ran for one more, intercepted three passes, and had a wonderful time. The Footballers were so impressed with his razzle-dazzle game that they asked him to join the team.

He played every game through mid-December and the team made its league playoffs.

Meanwhile back at the firm, Joe was working long hours and loving it. He was feeling increasingly confident about his ability to compete with the other analysts. They had been to the Harvard Business School and he hadn't, but they were not fanatical and he could outwork them. Nevertheless, he minded his manners and was defferential and friendly to everyone.

Joe's second recommendation was the conglomerate United Technologies. In the late summer and early fall of 1998, the stock sold at $20. He read everything he could find on the company, and went to their principal facility near Hartford to call on the CFO. He became convinced that not only was the stock cheap, but earnings were going to surge over the next three quarters. In early September, he put the stock on the agenda for the weekly research meeting with the portfolio managers and analysts, which alerted everyone that it would be discussed.

Joe had a 10-page presentation that he labored over—two pages of what he hoped was concise text and numerous charts and tables. He was compelling as he made the case that United Technologies (UTX) was an extremely well-managed, rational company, and that its different businesses were dominant in their respective industries. He argued the shares were now very attractively priced, and business was clearly improving. The stock was not widely owned.

The investment story was not understood or appreciated.

When he had finished, Hansen challenged him. "It's just a disconnected conglomerate with a lot of lousy businesses pasted together masquerading, you know, as a real company. Otis Elevator and Sikorsky are cyclical, low-quality operations. The stock is going to sell at eight times earnings forever. No *sophisticated* investor would buy it."

Joe maintained his composure. "With great respect," Joe said, "I think UTX is transforming itself and its image into a well-run industrial growth company. Its basic businesses are solid, well-managed, and quite dominant in their industries. I tried to model earnings over the next five years based on their existing order backlogs, and when I showed my numbers to the CFO, he agreed with them. You could have a double play here with earnings rising faster than the consensus expects and an expanding multiple."

The next week Dawes bought the stock in size on a dip in late September at 19; three months later it was 29 and by the next spring it had almost doubled. Joe later wished that he had recommended selling the stock at that point because its glory days were over except for one final spasm in the last gasp of the tech mania several years later (see Figure 4.2).

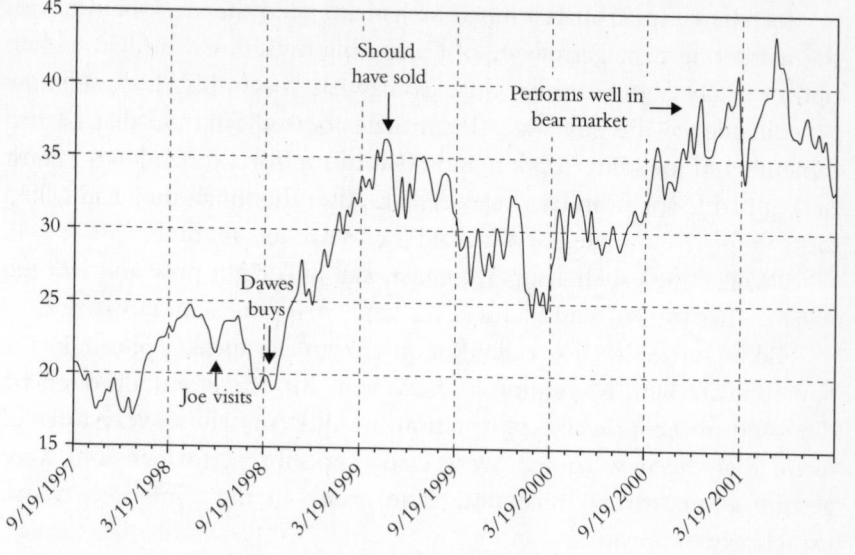

Figure 4.2 A Timely Buy—United Technologies

A month after recommending to buy United Technologies, Joe had another stroke of fortune. He also covered technology, and at their weekly meeting he argued that Cisco, which had just experienced a sharp sell-off and was now selling at just over 13, was very attractive. The conventional wisdom on Wall Street was that Cisco's business was slowing dramatically, but Joe believed the analysts were wrong and that the new Cisco routers were state of the art. He maintained that Cisco's order backlogs were exploding and earnings would turn out to be better than expected. He argued they should buy the shares.

Again Hansen disagreed. "Cisco was last year's stock," he stated categorically and somewhat sourly. "Technology is the wrong place to be in the current environment. Earnings will be disappointing and the company's backlog was shrinking. There was always misinformation and disinformation floating around about Cisco that sucked in naïve investors," he said, looking at Joe.

When he finished, Dawes asked Joe, "What do you say to that? Aren't you being naïve? How do you know those new routers are taking off?"

Joe cited a small analyst lunch he had attended the week before with the marketing manager of one of Cisco's big divisions, who had spoken optimistically about the backlog. Somewhat sheepishly, Joe told how by coincidence the guy was a Penn State football fan, and that he had remembered Joe's interception and 80-yard run for a touchdown against his big bad Lions from two years earlier. After the lunch they had talked football for five minutes, and he told Joe to call me anytime.

"Well, if he's such a super contact, call him right now and let's see what he has to say," said Hansen, his voice dripping with sarcasm.

Taking a chance, Joe called the guy from the speaker phone in the conference room. Miraculously, he was in his office and although he disclosed no proprietary information, he did confirm in very forceful terms that the new routers were vastly superior performers and were getting a very strong reception. The group in the conference room was clearly impressed.

"See what happens when you get off your ass and go out and meet companies," said Dawes, looking at the other analysts.

"We get it, boss," said Matthew, the squash player analyst. "The problem is none of *us* ran back an interception against Penn State for six big ones."

Everyone laughed. Dawes and the portfolio managers bought Cisco over the next few days between 13.50 and 14.50 (see Figure 4.3).

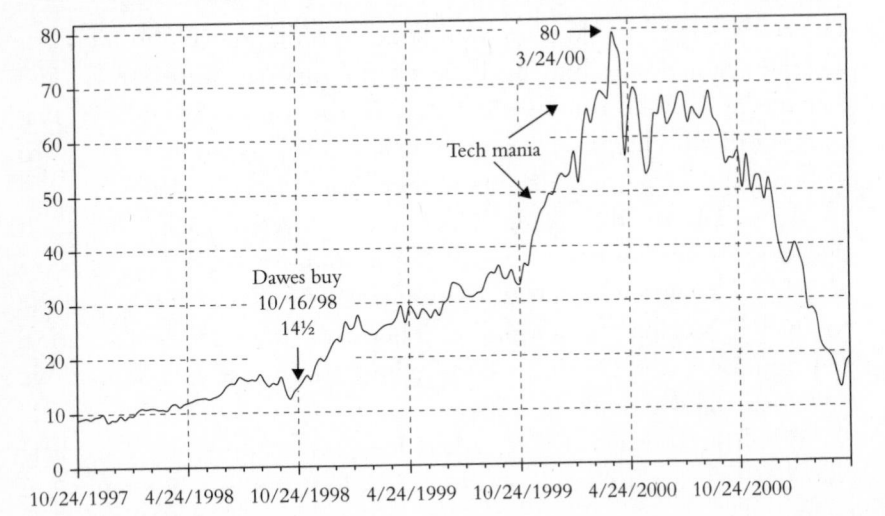

Figure 4.3 Jesus Christ, Superstar—CISCO

By year-end it was 28 and was about to soar even higher. At the time Joe knew his three winners were beginner's luck but it still felt wonderful. His confidence was growing and he felt that just maybe he had good investment intuitions.

In large part thanks to Joe, Dawes's football team was now winning their games, so teammates' wives and older children began to appear at the games. In early November, Dawes brought his daughter, Emily, a senior at Princeton, to a game and introduced her to Joe. Emily majored in history and played lacrosse on a team that the year before had reached the Final Four of the National Championship. She was good-looking in an athletic way with long shapely legs, a big smile, and a firm handshake. During the game, Joe was acutely aware of her presence. It was a rough game as two-handed touch can be—and their opponents were tough. The Footballers won it when Joe made a diving catch in the end zone. After the play, he looked up and realized to his dismay that she had left.

When the game was over, he felt strangely let down. "Forget it," he told himself. "This girl majors in history at an elite university and probably has 1600 SAT scores. She probably has an intellectual boyfriend whose family owns a bank and is going to be a Rhodes Scholar."

In December, the Footballers held their traditional dinner. Following the last game of the regular season, a player would host a dinner for the players and their wives and girlfriends. It was David Dawes's turn, and he mentioned to his wife that he wanted to invite Joe. She was hesitant, wondering if he would feel out of place.

"He's considerably younger than the rest of you and from a completely different background. After all, he is black."

"Half-black. His mother is white." He looked her in the eye. "All things considered, he's a poised young guy and a lot more hard-working than those sons of the Johnsons and Brownings. Besides, he's been a huge addition to the football group. It would be incredibly rude of us not to invite him."

Joe readily accepted Dawes's invitation. He liked the guys on the team and also knew they were good connections for him. However, he had no idea what he could talk to their wives about. With some trepidation he put on slacks, his AU blue blazer, and his newest tie, and took the train to Greenwich, Connecticut.

It was the first time he had been in a Greenwich home, and its scale and furnishings astounded him. The Daweses greeted him warmly at the door, and escorted him to the living room. There he stood like a fish out of water, with a beer in his hand, admiring the stone fireplaces and antique Wilton weave carpet. He guessed that this one room and all its furnishings cost more than his mother's house in Big Neck. The Footballers, who were all elegantly dressed in sports jackets, finally broke the ice. They slapped him on the back. "Dude, you made our season!" they told him as the chardonnay and beer flowed. "How are things going at Grant?"

Their wives were another matter. They seemed to come in two varieties, slim, almost skinny women who had starved themselves to low body fat perfection, and plump rosy-faced mother figures. They did have two things in common; almost every woman in the room was blonde and they all had that tight, neat, and proper WASPy look.

Joe was feeling distinctly out of place when suddenly Emily came in. She was dressed simply and demurely in a plaid skirt and a blue cashmere sweater that tried—but failed—to hide her voluptuous curves.

Joe felt as though an all-powerful gravitational force pulled them toward each other. From the beginning their conversation flowed easily. Nothing seemed forced or contrived. After 20 minutes, Emily said, "Let's get some dinner and then go sit in the library. I'm not up for mingling with the old folks and being asked endless, idiotic questions."

"Sounds wonderful to me," Joe told her, "but you don't think it's being rude?"

"Who cares? Daddy has told me a lot about you, and the only reason I'm here is because I knew you were coming." *Could she possibly mean that?* thought Joe.

They took their food from the silver chafing dishes arranged in the dining room. There were softly lit ancestor portraits above the sideboard and much fine porcelain. Emily led him to a quiet corner of the big library near the fireplace, where they settled into English Chippendale wing chairs and put their plates on Irish Sheraton side tables. His chair was obviously antique and it felt beautiful, old, and fragile. The library was full of books that looked as though they had been read, and there were antique wooden ladders on rollers to access the high shelves.

Most of the party was in the living room, and the buzz of conversation gave Joe and Emily privacy. As the evening progressed, a few other groups drifted into the library but left the pair undisturbed. Emily asked Joe where he grew up, and he told her about Big Neck and gave her a sanitized version of AU. Emily laughingly compared it to her teen years in Greenwich and at Andover. She told him how much she loved lacrosse and being part of the team. The Princeton coach was demanding but understood the academic load the girls were carrying. Nevertheless, there was lots of competition to get playing time, and she said her position on this year's team was by no means assured.

Around 10 o'clock, the party broke up. Emily offered to drive him to the station to catch the train back to New York. They sat talking in her car with the engine running. In fact, they talked right through the first train and were still at it an hour later when they heard the last train hoot as it neared the station. Joe jumped out of the car.

"When am I going to see you again?" he asked, grabbing his jacket.

"Next Friday I have to be in New York. Will you have dinner with me?"

"Absolutely!" he shouted. "Of course! How do I call you?"

"You can't. I'll call you at your office," she yelled as he ran up the steps to the platform.

My God! he thought as the trained pulled out of the station. *She just asked me to have dinner with her!*

If it was not love at first sight, it was pretty close to it. Joe had never met a woman with the background, intellectual depth, and education of Emily, and never before could he remember having experienced so compelling a physical attraction. But it was more than that. He felt an overwhelming urge to enter her life. They had so little, yet so much, in common. On the train, in the grip of his excitement, he could not stop grinning.

For Emily, Joe was the real thing and different from the usual guys she dated. His having a black father and having gone to college on a football scholarship excited her. She was liberal, a little rebellious, and fed up with preppy, Ivy League guys who wanted to compare SAT scores. Besides, she found him and his toughness physically very attractive.

The next weekend they had dinner in a dingy booth in a small restaurant on 45th Street and again talked nonstop, and then she took the train from Penn Station back to Princeton Junction. The following two Saturday nights he went to Princeton and they went out to dinner. The second Saturday he also went to her lacrosse game, and she introduced him to her best friend, who stared at him intently.

"So you're the hoss that has got Emily off her feet. It's quite a feat. This creature hasn't been the same since."

"I hope so," Joe replied. "I hope so."

"Both of you shut up," said Emily, blushing.

The fourth weekend, as he was walking her to Penn Station to catch her train back to Princeton Junction, they stopped at the deserted corner of Fifth Avenue and 37th Street. Impulsively he swung her around to face him and took her in his arms and kissed her on the mouth.

"I love you," he said, the words spontaneously but definitively welling up from within him. "I've never said that to anyone before," he whispered. "I didn't even know I was going to say it. It just came out. But it's the pure, utter truth."

"I love you, too," she whispered. He looked at her in the ashy, blue light and thought how beautiful she was.

He reached for her hand and smiled lovingly at her, stunned by what had happened to them in just a short month.

At that moment, the emotional barrier was broken. He felt free . . . well, almost. At work, he had been feeling guilty around Dawes who apparently did not know that Joe was seeing his daughter. Dawes had rescued him from obscurity, invited him to his home, and now he was having a clandestine affair with his daughter. It was one thing to hire a poorly educated analyst; it was quite another to have him courting your daughter.

Over the next few months, they saw each other almost every weekend. Joe would go to Princeton, and she often came to New York.

They never went out with anyone else, and although they kissed and held hands, they never made love.

Instead, they either went out to dinner in large, impersonal, noisy restaurants or cheap little hole-in-the wall bistros with tables covered by red-checked tablecloths and drank cheap red wine, looked at each other, and talked. They talked endlessly about everything. They found each other infinitely fascinating. Backgrounds, families, his work, her life at Princeton, the lacrosse team, hopes and fears were poured back and forth across tables or as they walked the cold and windy streets of New York. They imagined their souls discovering each other. They felt as though they had known each other forever. They became best, intimate friends . . . but not lovers.

Although their physical life was restricted, their intellectual intercourse flourished. He knew that she was majoring in history at Princeton, but he was astounded at her grasp of history and appalled at his own ignorance.

"Let's do it together," she told him. "History and literature. We're going to complete your blighted formal education and enrich mine."

For Joe's birthday, Emily bought two copies of Paul Johnson's *Modern Times*, and chapter by chapter, they worked their way through the historian's masterpiece. It was hard to find the time each week to do the reading, what with his investment work and business school assignments and her full course load and lacrosse, but somehow they did. She was the most important thing in his life and Joe would happily make any sacrifice to enrich their relationship.

They did other things as well. They walked in Central Park, and once they went to the Rainbow Room and danced. Joe almost trembled at the touch of her body. *What is happening to me?* he wondered. He kissed her that night in the street.

By now Joe had his own room in a fourth-floor, walk-up apartment in the Village that he shared with two other guys. He couldn't imagine asking her to go there. It was just too messy. When he came to Princeton, she thought of bringing him to her dorm, but again, intimacy was impossible.

"We could go to a hotel," she said to him one night, after he kissed her furtively in dark corners of the street.

"You wouldn't be comfortable. I know you wouldn't be happy there. Besides, this is a love affair, not a sex affair."

She looked at him lovingly and wistfully. "I'm not sure one can exist without the other," she told him.

"We don't need to have sex. You're younger. You're still in college. I don't want to betray your father."

As soon as the words were out of his mouth he knew they sounded ridiculous, pompous, phony, but he wanted to be respectful of her.

As it turned out, they didn't have to wait that long. In late March, Emily's parents went to Palm Beach for 10 days. The first weekend they were gone Princeton was scheduled to play Brown in women's lacrosse at Providence, Rhode Island, on Saturday afternoon. This was the opportunity they had been waiting for. Joe rented a car and drove up I-95 to the game and sat in the bleachers. When the game was over she ran up to him and kissed him lightly on the cheek and whispered very softly.

"I hope you brought your toothbrush!"

"Of course I did, and my pajamas too."

"You're not going to need them, but the toothbrush is another matter."

He looked at her standing there in her shorts and game jersey, sweaty, with skinned knees, holding her helmet and lacrosse stick like a warrior maiden, and knew she was the most desirable woman in the world. His face, seemingly of its own accord, broke out into a huge grin.

"Wipe that look off your face. Why don't you just announce to all my teammates that you're in love with me," she said half-jokingly.

They drove back to Greenwich and stopped in a restaurant for dinner and drank a bottle of good chardonnay, extending and savoring the anticipation but also feeling just a little awkward and shy.

When they got to the Daweses' house, Emily said, "Come on, we're going to my room. I've got a queen-sized bed that even you will fit into. However, sharing a bathroom isn't on my intimacy agenda. Use my brother's bathroom down the hall."

He undressed except for his shorts and a T-shirt, cleared the pillows off the bed and lay down. She suddenly emerged from the bathroom and stood in the doorway. He had seen her so many times fully clothed, modestly dressed, and now to see her standing there naked—so exposed, so vulnerable, so beautiful—stunned him. She walked over to him on the bed and lay with her back to him. Her skin was the color of pale moonlight. He gently pulled her to him, experiencing the firmness of her back and tracing the perfect curve of her hip. He lay against her, their bodies touching, and he kissed her gently and tenderly.

Afterward, they wondered how anything so beautiful and simple could be permitted. How could they be allowed to get away with it? How could the world still be the same? Had anyone else ever experienced anything like this? Wasn't it wasteful to be doing anything other than this, ever?

As the spring progressed, Joe and Emily became even more intimate. They found so many things that they wanted to do together, and they seemed to be able to continually find new subjects to talk about. In April, they went away for long weekends and never, even for a moment, were bored. They talked for hours about their backgrounds, *Modern Times*, the agnosticism of the founding fathers, and their own religious beliefs. The Daweses were committed Episcopalians, and twice Emily and Joe went to church at Princeton and twice in New York.

They began to assume that their relationship was permanent although neither confided in anyone. Joe had no one to confide in, and Emily was not a girl who talked about romantic relationships with her friends. They had no need for other company. Joe sometimes wondered if it was healthy to be so totally self-sufficient or if it meant they were unsociably isolationist. Was there perhaps an unspoken fear on both their parts that their love would wither under outside scrutiny? He didn't think so but he couldn't help wondering about it.

Sometimes in the middle of the night he would wake up racked by even more frightening thoughts. Was his background or race an issue with her? How would her parents react? Without her a long life of loneliness loomed. He was sure he could never find or love another woman.

The fear that this most precious of all relationships, this incredible thing they had created, this emotion he had experienced, never even known he was capable of, could be snatched away was agonizing.

Emily had left a pair of her sneakers with Joe and he would stare at them as they rested next to his. They were so much smaller, so feminine, and yet so sturdy and strong, just as she was. "Man, you've got it bad when you're worshipping her Adidases!" he said to himself. He knew what an old friend would have told him. "Savor it, cherish it, and don't screw it up."

Chapter 5

Crisis and Confrontation

After Emily graduated from Princeton, she moved to New York. With the help of the head of the history department at Princeton, she got a research job at the prestigious Council on Foreign Relations.

It was early July and Emily and Joe were enjoying Sunday brunch when Emily said to him, "I've always been really close to Daddy, and I want to tell him I've been seeing you and that it's serious—whatever that means."

"I hope it means everything," Joe said.

"Of course it does, but did you hear me? I want to tell Daddy."

As that thought sunk in, Joe was truly frightened for a moment. "It could be the end of us," he said.

"Don't be dramatic," she told him. "Nothing could be the end of us, and, anyway, Daddy is truly open-minded. Mom is another matter.

She can be a little stuffy. Besides, I'm just telling him—not her. And I'm not asking for his permission."

"Are we dodging the issue of my race?" Joe asked. "Emily, there are going to be serious, big-time issues."

"There are issues in almost every relationship. Mom's parents were filthy rich and had lived in Greenwich for a hundred years. Daddy was from New Jersey and didn't have any money. They thought he was a gold digger."

"Yeah, but he went to Princeton and wasn't half black," Joe told her.

A week later, Emily confided in her father and held nothing back. "This could go all the way," she told him. He was surprised, but his immediate reaction was supportive. He told her how much he liked Joe and how capable he thought he was. That evening with considerable trepidation he informed his wife, adding that he was happy for both Joe and Emily.

"I'm very high on him. I'm happy both for him and for Emily!"

Andrea Dawes was appalled. An attractive 52-year-old woman with a wide, somewhat clenched face, a long nose, and lightly tinted brownish blond hair she kept herself in good shape by playing golf and working out with a personal trainer at the Green Acres Country Club gym. From an old Greenwich family, she had graduated from the Kent School and Vassar. She had the confident demeanor of a wealthy woman who was utterly sure of her place in society and had inherited a considerable amount of money.

Basically, she was a snob, although she would have been astounded and angered if confronted with this characterization. Her mother, Emily's grandmother, had deeply instilled in her a sense of class consciousness, that you consorted only with what she called *the right people*. The right people were mostly affluent WASPs. Even as Emily was growing up *en famille*, the old lady would dismiss someone they had met with a cold smile and a curt "N.O.C.D.—Not Our Class, Dear." Of course, the old lady had conveniently forgotten that she herself born in a small town in Ohio, had married wealth, and had acquired position from Emily's grandfather.

"You have to be joking!" she hissed, angrily. "David, sometimes you're hopelessly naïve. He certainly is *not* what I have in mind for Emily. You told me before that his mother was a waitress and his father was a mill worker. What does he know of our way of life?"

Mrs. Dawes envisioned Emily marrying some handsome hunk, someone she'd be proud to call her son-in-law. He would be from a well-known family, have gone to Yale (preferably Skull and Bones), and then to the Harvard Business School. The wedding would be in June with the reception on the great porch of the Green Acres Country Club overlooking the rolling, manicured, deep green fairways. It would be on one of those long perfect, early summer evenings with the magnificent setting, a small band playing Cole Porter, and golden light filtering and magical. Everyone would be beautiful, and she would be gracious and proud. Then the enchanted couple would live happily ever after in bigger and bigger houses in Greenwich, and she would ferry her perfectly behaved, adoring tow-headed grandchildren to the club for their tennis lessons.

Joe Hill did not come anywhere near complying with that model. She understood that some women would find him attractive and that he had a *decent* job, but she couldn't think beyond his race and background.

Dawes had always been intimidated by his wife's rages, and as if he was reading her mind, he equivocated, "I'm not sure how serious it really is."

"Well, my intuition is it's plenty serious. Come to think of it, I suspect Emily had him to my home that weekend we were in Florida. There were some warning signs. It's *your* fault. You invited this man, *your* employee, to *my* house for that stupid, juvenile football party, and he seduced *your* own daughter. In our bed for all I know. If he's as smart as you say he is, he's probably figured out I'm rich and is after my money."

Dawes didn't know if he was seeing tears of rage or sorrow in his wife's eyes. Why did she always say *my* home and *my* money? Wasn't it *our* home and didn't he have something to do with the money?

David Dawes was the vernacular "good guy," but Andrea was the dominant personality in their marriage. She was the one, who, so to speak, "wore the pants" and made the big decisions. She had strong opinions, and she was capable of fierce rages. Although Dawes was well paid, much of it was in restricted Grant stock rather than cash. Her inherited wealth was what enabled them to have three children in expensive schools, belong to four clubs, live well above their means, and have a sprawling Tudor mansion in Greenwich, a ski chalet in Aspen, and a beachfront house in Palm Beach. But, that certainly didn't excuse her behavior.

Andrea now paused and looked at him with disgust. "David, you fool. He's what mother would call *an adventurer*. You'd better find out more about him. You got us into this mess, befriending stray football players, and you have to get us out of it before it's too late."

Dawes called Marlene the next morning. He knew Marlene was a gossip and not always a reliable source of information, but he had no choice. By lunchtime every woman in operations would know he was inquiring about Joe Hill, but he had no alternative.

"Marlene, tell me—off the record so to speak—about Joe Hill," he said.

Marlene's anger with Joe was still festering. She recognized, albeit grudgingly, that Pat had pushed herself on Joe, but she was still offended that Joe had not responded to Pat. It was as though Joe's rejection of a more serious relationship with Pat was a slap in the face to the older single or divorced women who had labored so long for the firm and still had romantic aspirations. Pat was the best they had and it was insulting that Joe was not even faintly interested. After all, he was from the wrong side of the proverbial tracks, too. She took a deep breath and vented.

She told Dawes that when Joe came to the firm, friendless and alone, some of the women in operations had befriended him and included him in social events. She said Joe had gone out with them for drinks after work on numerous occasions and had focused his charm on one particular woman. Marlene didn't say who the woman was, but she asserted that this woman was a good, moral person. Unfortunately, this woman had fallen in love with Joe. She had invited him to a beach party weekend last summer at which Marlene was present. She had seen the whole thing. Joe had cruelly taken advantage of this innocent woman's vulnerability and seduced her—not once but *twice*. Joe had then dropped the woman—*cold*. She emphasized "twice" and "cold."

Marlene paused, evaluating his response. Dawes was shocked and speechless. Taking a deep breath, she went on. And then when the woman had become pregnant, Joe had refused to do the honorable thing and adopt the baby. He had insisted instead on an abortion and then chiseled on paying for it. Marlene vehemently insisted Joe was a social climber of the worst kind, an immoral womanizer, and a bad guy.

Dawes sat there stunned and appalled. All this was going on in his division and he had known nothing about it. He was not a prude, but he had never imagined Joe, his prodigy, in this light. He could hardly believe it. This coarse lecher had come from the sweaty pleasures of a beach party couch to charm and seduce his beautiful and intelligent daughter. This was not the man whom he had befriended and sponsored. If it was true, he had totally misjudged him, Emily was in danger, and his wife would be even more furious than she already was.

He thanked Marlene and called Sue. He had known her for years and trusted her judgment. He told her what Marlene had said.

"The matter has been settled as far as I'm concerned," Sue said. "Joe paid for most of the abortion. His work in operations was exemplary, and I hear he is doing well for you as an analyst. The man is bright and works very hard."

Dawes paused, then replied, "We've known each other a long time, Sue. What I'm going to tell you is in complete confidence. I didn't tell Marlene any of this. I'm asking because my daughter Emily is in love with him."

"I see," said Sue slowly. "Of course I understand why you are so concerned. I wasn't at the beach that weekend, but I suspect Marlene's version of Joe's activities is grossly exaggerated. I should tell you that at the time Marlene was having an affair with another man in operations. I don't like that kind of stuff going on within my group because it often leads to trouble."

She continued, "Your family is your problem, and I wouldn't dream of telling you what to do." She paused. "I will say this. The woman he was involved with is a good woman, but I'm not sure who seduced whom. Joe is a tough, confident guy, but my sense is that he's a very decent person. I think you should talk to him directly."

"He's also a very talented stock analyst. I don't want to lose him," Dawes said. "But above all, I don't want Emily to be hurt."

Sue had been at the firm a long time and was a little cynical. *Analysts,* she thought to herself. *Analysts. When the market is going up, who needs analysts? When the market is going down, who needs stocks?*

That evening, still in the grip of panic and dismay, Dawes told his wife what he had learned. In actuality, she was less concerned about his sexual adventures at the firm than his background and its consequences. Her mind began racing. What if this was a serious relationship? She was appalled at the implications.

"My God!" she said to her husband, "Suppose they did get married. I couldn't imagine having his mill-working father and unkempt mother on the receiving line. And then we might end up with black grandchildren. Wouldn't you just love having your black grandchildren running around the Green Acres Country Club? Think of what people will say. Think of what our friends will say. We will be humiliated."

"You're being ridiculous," David snapped, feeling the anger welling up. "It's almost the twenty-first century and you're talking like a racist. You're worried about appearances and being embarrassed." It was as close as he had ever come to directly challenging her.

She glowered at him. "I'm not a racist. I'm just being realistic. Marriage and bringing up children is hard enough as it is without tremendously complicating things with a mixed-race marriage. You know that as well as I do! I'm thinking about Emily's long-term happiness. David, you simply have to put an end to it—immediately!"

"What do you want me to do?"

"Tell that man to stay away from her! If you won't, I will! Fire him for sexual harassment and getting that other woman pregnant. The man must be a serial lecher." She stomped upstairs.

David Dawes slept very poorly that night. The next morning he spent a miserable hour in his office staring out the window. He knew that somehow over the years his wife's personality and money had come to dominate him. He recognized he should talk with Joe, if only to satisfy his wife.

Sitting there, he felt the first, strong stirrings of rebellion against her. She was archaic, out of date, a traditionalist. Sometimes he thought of her as an *asphalt* wife. Most of their friends wouldn't really care if Emily married a black man. When they first heard about it, sure, it would give them something to cluck about for a couple of weeks but then it would pass.

What should I do? he asked himself. Now that the first flush of panic, dismay, and rebellion was fading, he knew he should talk with Joe. The guy had the potential to be the best analyst he had ever hired and his daughter was madly in love with him.

When Joe came to his office, Dawes recounted what Marlene had told him, softening it a little with Sue's caveats.

Joe grimaced and his stomach churned. "It's true. I want you to know, though, that it also all happened before I ever met Emily. I should never have slept with Pat at that beach party. It was a stupid thing to do. But I never led her on before or afterward."

Dawes again was shocked. "I always thought Pat was a *nice* girl," he said.

"She *is* a nice girl," Joe replied.

"My wife and I demand you immediately stop seeing Emily. We intend to tell her the same thing," Dawes blurted. He turned his head from Joe and bit his lip, disgusted with himself.

Joe bowed his head and was quiet for 30 seconds. "I'm sorry, David, but I can't agree to give up Emily. She is the love of my life. I'm going to tell her about Pat. I should have done it before, but honestly, it didn't seem that important. If she still loves me and wants us to continue, I'll resign from the firm."

Dawes didn't know what to say. He was deeply moved by Joe's expression of love for Emily. Besides, he truly liked Joe and didn't want to lose him from the firm, from the team, or for Emily, for that matter. Deep down, he wasn't really that bothered by the Pat affair. Over the years, a lot worse things had happened at the firm. He sighed. He recognized that a mixed-race marriage had its inherent difficulties, but he was a romantic and believed love conquered all. He wouldn't mind having Joe as a son-in-law, if Emily really loved him. Nevertheless, though rebellious, he was still intimidated by his wife. He could sense one of her monumental rages coming on.

"David," Joe said, "I deeply appreciate everything you've done for me. You been so kind and generous, but I'm sorry. There's no way I can give up Emily. I'm going to call her now." He stood up.

Joe left Dawes's office and called Emily.

"We need to talk. Now."

"Sweetheart, but what's going on?"

"Family crisis and true revelations required," he told her, trying to strike a light tone.

"Serious?"

"Your father talked to me. Life or death," he said.

"Death is not possible for us," she replied. "You know that."

As they walked through Washington Square Park—with the late afternoon twilight and abundance of flowers bursting out all around them—he told her—in brief, bleak sentences—about Pat and the abortion. She listened intently, but he couldn't read her face. When he was done, she took his hand and pulled him to her.

"All this happened before you ever met me?"

"Yes. And there has been nothing since, with anyone. You know that."

"Joe, I never thought I was your first." She kissed him lightly. "But I had better be your last!"

He knew then that it was going to be all right. They talked some more as the setting sun touched the light, virginal green of the high branches of the elm trees. Those sun-kissed young leaves were as fresh and pure as their love, Joe thought. Then he told her of his conviction that if they were to continue he must resign from the firm. He liked her father and felt an obligation to him, but now it would be uncomfortable for both of them at the firm. There was too much water under the proverbial bridge and there would be gossip. She immediately understood his thinking.

"You can get another good job, can't you?" Emily asked.

"I'm pretty sure I can. Thanks to your father and the football game, I've met a lot of senior people in the business. A couple of them have already offered me stuff."

Emily went home to Greenwich the following Saturday. After lunch, as the cook cleared the dishes, Mrs. Dawes said severely, "Your father and I want to talk to you, dear." Emily well aware of her mother's upholstered sensibilities, knew what was coming, and had tried to prepare herself. Nevertheless, she sighed. Mrs. Dawes did most of the talking, describing in excruciating detail all the reasons that Emily shouldn't even consider a serious relationship with, much less marry, someone like Joe.

"Sorry, Mom, but I'm going to keep seeing Joe. He's my true love. We have magic that I've never even come close to feeling before. To tell the truth, I hope that six months from now we are married."

The words hung in the warm afternoon air. Emily looked into her mother's eyes but it was as though a curtain had been pulled down that shut her off from what was behind the unblinking surface of those eyes.

"Marry! You must be mad! You barely know the guy. Thirty years ago my mother would have sent you abroad for two months so that you could get over it."

"That was then. This is now. We know what we're doing."

"And as for *magic*, you're being dramatic. Emily, I dislike saying this but it's not magic, it's just sex. I'm sure the man is very experienced. Get over it!"

Emily could feel the anger welling up in her. "You have no idea, Mom. He's the love of my life!"

Mrs. Dawes sighed. It was time to be firm. "Your father and I will not continue to support you if you go on seeing him! Continuing this relationship will irredeemably taint you."

Emily gazed down the gentle incline of the lawn. "Mom, you seem to forget I have a trust fund."

"I'm sure he knows that also." The words hung in the air.

Emily stood up. "That's the end of this conversation. As a matter of fact, he doesn't know and wouldn't care if he did."

On Sunday morning, when the Dawes family got up, Emily was gone. There was a note on the dining room table that read, "*Will keep in touch. Love, Emily.*"

As time went on and the bull market climbed, Joe began to feel out of it.

"What's the matter?" Hansen asked him at their weekly meeting. "You got acrophobia, kid?"

One of the other analysts in his team was coming up with a succession of small and medium-sized technology companies whose shares were soaring. Joe's reading had instilled in him a sense of speculative history and a profound value orientation, and what was happening with the Internet and technology stocks was far beyond his comprehension as a value investor of the way the world should work, and it seemed that everyone was just becoming caught up in the madness of the moment.

One afternoon Dawes called him and asked him about Parton Networks. "Lehman's telecom analyst is big on the name," he said. "They're arranging a trip up there to hear the story. Maybe you should go. You know, Joe, you don't want to get too negative on telecom. The space is working."

Joe signed up for the visit and did some work on Parton. In the mid 1990s the senior management of Parton Networks, a Canadian telephone company, made the decision to transform the company into a telecom-tech enterprise. They determined to shed the old image of a stodgy, slow-growth telephone company, develop and promote a new growth business plan, and change the name to Parton Networks. The middle-aged, somewhat sleepy and slightly dowdy lady was going to be given a face-lift, undergo a full-body contouring dermassage, be outfitted with a new sexy wardrobe, and get reincarnated with a more glamorous name and image. They had succeeded.

In the full flush and incandescent brilliance of the tech boom, the shares of Parton Networks soared from the mid 60s in June 1998, nearly tripling in 1999. The stock was levitating at 50 times earnings. Joe was mystified as to why, since the earnings were almost entirely from its historic, slow-growth, fixed-line telephone business. Maybe he was missing something, and he thought he'd better figure it out.

Five other investors and analysts came along for the visit to Montreal in 1999. One of them, according to the Lehman Brothers program, was a portfolio manager at Bridgestone, a major multistrategy hedge fund. Multistrategy firms were growing rapidly and were appealing to prospective clients because they could easily switch from one investment style to another within the same firm.

The chief financial officer of Parton, Mark King, was a slim middle-aged man with a long, tanned, aristocratic face. That morning he was wearing tight blue jeans made from some expensive fabric Joe couldn't identify and a tailored, dark blue sports jacket with a handkerchief in the breast pocket. When he entered the room, he slipped off the jacket, revealing a snug, short-sleeved, button-down shirt. The resume supplied by Lehman Brothers affirmed that he had graduated from Harvard, Yale Law School, and the Stanford Graduate School of Business. King seized Joe's hand and squeezed hard. Joe had come to wonder about men who seemed determined to project their strength and power with vice-like handshakes.

King launched into his comments with no small talk. "I want to prove to you today that our stock is *undervalued* at the current price. We are convinced we can grow earnings at twenty percent a year so our PEG ratio, in other words our price/earnings valuation to growth ratio, is only a little over two. The famous consumer growth stocks, such as Coke or Procter & Gamble, sell at PEG ratios of three even four times. We are very shareholder oriented so the price of our stock is absolutely crucial to our strategy, but I don't want to lecture you; I want to have a conversation with you." He gazed at them while twiddling a gold pen. He had a patronizing voice, shaped by too many advanced degrees.

The Lehman analyst spoke: "The stock market agrees with you, so you must be right. As you know, Mark, I've had a buy on your stock for the last year."

"We appreciate your help and we won't forget it," Mark replied. Joe suspected what that meant. *No wonder*, he thought, *we don't trust analysts that work for investment banks.* The Lehman analyst smiled modestly.

Joe's natural inclination and his reading had instilled in him a profound distrust of high price/earnings ratios. At Stern his most compelling lecturer had been a confirmed value investor and disciple of Benjamin Graham and Warren Buffett. The current valuation of tech stocks simply made no sense to him, and he couldn't understand how a company whose basic business had at best nominal GDP growth prospects could be expected to grow 20 percent a year except by financial engineering. He hesitated and then spoke up.

"With respect, Mark, it seems to me that technology growth companies, even the great ones, should not sell at the same PEG ratios as consumer growth companies, because they generate very little true cash flow. Even a tech company with a dominant competitive edge has to spend its free cash flow on research and development because perpetual obsolescence is, by definition, inevitable in the tech world."

He paused and took a deep breath. "If development efforts are successful, the technology company's capital spending consumes its cash flow because it has to build plant and equipment to produce new products. As a result, even the great tech companies have a relatively low return on equity. If a tech company stops or fails with its R&D spending and building new products and lives on its fat, in a relatively few years it will be anemic. In a few more, it will have to liquidate the company."

They were all looking at him. This was pure, unadulterated heresy.

"By contrast, a great consumer franchise company, although it needs a continuing advertising investment, generates substantial free cash flow that can pay dividends or buy back stock. Thus, a fifteen percent growth trend for a consumer products company is of better quality and deserves a considerably higher P/E ratio than the same growth rate for a tech company. Also, tech companies, even the great ones, are more cyclically sensitive. In fact you could say they are not *ruler* growth stocks but are really *cyclical* growth stocks."

In the hard lights of the conference room, the CFO gazed at him with surprise and dislike. He began to get angry. Who was this upstart to come to his house and challenge him?

"What you say, young man, may have been true in the past, but it is not true today." King continued, "We do spend to fund our own R&D, but we can't just depend on the productivity of our in-house research. We are a company of entrepreneurs. So we rely far more than previously on venture investing in in-house research cells and outright purchases of smaller companies with promising technologies to mitigate the obsolescence and 'time to market risk.' So in fact a premier tech company like ours does generate free cash flow that we can employ to offset options issuance. Our venture investing has been very rewarding, and we have harvested some big gains as the companies went public. This strategy works.

Intel, for example, reported that at the end of March its venture portfolio was worth around ten billion dollars with a cost of two billion dollars."

When Mark King spoke, he intoned each word precisely as though it had great significance. This guy is a pompous phony, Joe thought.

Now King paused, apparently to give them time to digest what he had just said. "Because we can use our shares to buy potential competitors with disruptive technologies, the danger of being blindsided is much less than it was for tech companies in the past. Ergo, for the professional investor, owning the great technology growth stocks of this era is far less dangerous in terms of obsolescence risk than it used to be. As for tech companies having cyclical sensitivity, this tech cycle driven by the Internet is different."

Cohen, the hedge fund guy who was sitting next to Joe, nudged him and whispered: "This asshole definitely went to some fancy Ivy League school. I should know. Listen to the way he intones this crap." Joe nodded and then asked King: "But aren't all your competitors, both large and small, following a similar strategy and trying to buy the same companies that have breakthrough technologies? Doesn't the bidding drive up prices so that huge sums like five to ten billion dollars are being paid for companies with nothing but one product and no sales? I know it's only paper, but it's your paper, and aren't you diluting your existing shareholders?"

King's face reddened. "You have completely missed the point! We have a virtuous circle going. Our venture investing is generating new technologies and cash flow. We have a major advantage because our market capitalization is so huge, and with our P/E of fifty we can pay billions of dollars in our stock for enterprises with very little earnings and suffer minimal dilution. The paper of the premier tech companies is also the currency of choice for entrepreneurs because it is so liquid, and the share prices of the premier companies are far less volatile than tech stocks in general. Being big is a huge competitive advantage in this new environment."

Cohen interrupted. "Bernstein research has calculated that over the last 25 years there was only one chance in three that the average large-cap tech growth stock would retain its high growth status for the next five years, only one in nine it would retain growth stock status for ten years, and only one in twenty for twenty years. Yet at the valuations the dozen or so premier tech growth like yours are at today, investors are betting that these companies can continue growing twenty to thirty percent for a decade. To accept this, you have to believe it's totally different this time."

King looked at him and shook his head. There were damp splotches of sweat under his armpits. "You're the guy from a hedge fund. You're probably short our stock and you've been dead wrong. Lehman forecasts that with the business model and opportunities we have, we will keep growing twenty percent a year for a decade. And, yeah, I do believe it's different this time. Besides, the Internet and its infrastructure represent the most dynamic invention of all time. No new product has ever achieved so much penetration so fast."

"There have been life-changing, breakthrough inventions before. What about the telephone, the radio, the PC?" asked Joe.

"It took forty-six years for a quarter of American homes to be wired for electricity, thirty-five years for phones, and twenty-two years for radio to reach the same penetration level. The PC took only sixteen years but the Internet got there in seven. Internet years are really like dog years. Thus we would argue the opportunity for growth is greater." King was almost snarling now.

"Sorry, Mr. King, but that's ridiculous," replied Cohen, "If Internet years are like dog years it just means your growth window is shorter. The opportunity for rapid growth early is bigger sooner because the penetration rate is higher sooner, but to the extent that growth is front-end loaded, the high growth cycle will be shorter. You guys could be looking at a growth bust."

Joe interrupted. "Mark, the other part of it is that the way you operate to some extent inflates earnings. You spend relatively very little on R&D and instead use your high share price to buy potential competitors. You hold those companies in an investment account below the line and write off losses as nonrecurring items when they actually are recurring. Thus in effect you're overstating reported earnings."

Mark King glowered at him but Joe went on.

"With respect, sir, although the Internet continues to grow, the dot-com companies are losing money and burning cash. They cannot finance in the junk bond market or by selling more equity and, in fact, are running out of cash fast. Haven't they bought equipment from you, most of which has been financed by your captive finance company? If some of them go bust, won't that equipment be returned and won't that create a glut and cause price weakness? Yet as I understand your accounting, you've booked those transactions as sales and included the full profit in earnings without allowing for the contingent liability."

"You must have been bit by an accountant, fella," snarled King. "It takes imagination and an unfettered mind to be a successful investor in the new industrial revolution that is technology. You're a new analyst at Grant, is that right?"

"Yes sir," said Joe. "But I got bit not by an accountant but by Graham, Dodd, and Buffett."

"Never heard of them," said King. "Never heard of them."

"Antiquities!" the Lehman analyst snapped.

"Have you guys heard of Buffett?" asked Cohen, the hedge fund guy.

"Yeah, and he has completely missed this whole tech and telecom thing."

Now King tuned and looked directly at Joe. "Well, young fellow, the Japanese have a saying 'the protruding nail gets hammered' that you would do well to remember. Investors in our stock believe in us— a company of entrepreneurs and creators. Our share price has been climbing for years."

"Maybe so," said Cohen. "But remember the Hans Christian Andersen fable about the emperor who went on parade naked? It was a child that blew the myth that he was wearing beautiful clothes. The hot air always goes out of the balloon a lot faster than it went in."

King got to his feet. "Now my associates will show you some of our new routing and switching facilities. Like everything else, they are state of the art."

After the tour was over, a van took them to the airport. "You didn't make any friends today," the Lehman analyst said to Joe in a surly tone of voice. "What did you want to piss the guy off for?"

"I didn't mean to give him a hard time," Joe replied. "I was just asking questions."

"Ignore that ass-kissing analyst," the hedge fund guy murmured to him afterwards. "You made one friend. Me! My name is Mickey Cohen. I work at Bridgestone. I like guys that have been bit by accountants. Those were good questions you asked, good points you raised."

They sat together on the flight back to New York. "What do you think of Parton Networks as a stock?" Cohen asked Joe.

"Hey," said Joe, "I'm just a rookie but I think it's a phony. It's a plain, old telephone company dressed up in fake tech clothes. They've had a virtuous circle going for them, but God forbid it turns vicious. The accounting is virtually fraudulent. Their basic fixed-line business is slow growth and is threatened on many fronts. The whole price structure is going to collapse. They've used all kind of tricks to inflate earnings. They hype the stock price so they can use it as currency to buy start-ups instead of spending money on R&D. The stock should sell at ten to twelve times earnings, not at a P/E of fifty."

"I couldn't agree with you more. I'm not running money right at this moment but if I were I'd short it. Even monkeys fall from trees and this is a mighty ugly monkey."

Cohen asked him a lot of questions about Grant and what industries he covered. They talked more about stocks.

At the end of the short flight Cohen said to him, "Look, if you ever get the hedge fund itch, give me a call. We are always looking for smart young guys."

"Thanks," Joe said. "I'll keep that in mind, but Grant has treated me well and I really like the guy I work for."

"Loyalty is in short supply in our business," Cohen replied. "Good luck."

A few weeks later, with Parton's stock price soaring from 255 at the time of the meeting to over 370, Hansen walked into the analysts' bull pen and said loudly, "Hey, mister defensive back, what did you miss at Parton? That guy you roughed up is throwing touchdown passes! Looks like he's completed a bunch of long ones over your head for touchdowns."

"Yeah, I know," said Joe. "I didn't get it and still don't."

"It's called being wrong, getting beat long," Hansen replied and walked out.

"Don't sweat it," whispered one of the analysts. "The guy's an asshole. Truth and justice will prevail. You aren't wrong; you were just early."

"Being early is same as being wrong," said another analyst, with a snide grin. Joe knew that unfortunately the guy was right.

As it turned out, Parton's stock price was to soar to 500 in late 1999 to over 700, then fall back a few weeks later to 500 again, only to rocket

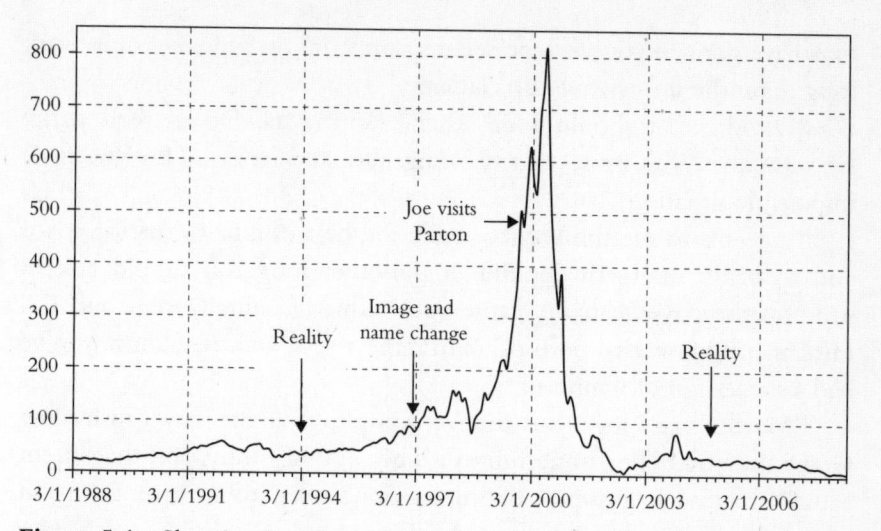

Figure 5.1 Shooting Star Goes Thud—Parton

to new highs. In July 2000, Parton hit 870. King's magic had worked, and Joe's skepticism was wrong.

Since Grant Investment Management didn't sell stocks short and since Joe had no money to invest, the stock's Icarus-like ascent didn't affect anything but his pride. But, as the tech and telecom bubble exploded, as Figure 5.1 shows, Parton turned out to be one of the era's great busts. Turns out Joe was right.

Fortunately, for Joe he wouldn't have to listen to the unpleasant gloating of his nemesis Hansen as he would no longer be at Grant.

Meanwhile, one Monday morning, Dawes was frank with Joe, explaining why his wife was unilaterally opposed to the relationship continuing. Joe listened respectfully.

"I understand," Joe said, calmly. "As I said before, I'm not going to give up Emily. What we have is too precious and it's the most important thing in my life."

"I understand," Dawes told him. "I respect your point of view."

"But I *am* going to resign from the firm immediately."

"No, you're not," said Dawes firmly. "That's just being dramatic. It would be embarrassing for all of us, including Emily. By now, Marlene may have guessed you've been seeing Emily. If you suddenly quit every tongue on the floor would be clacking."

"David, what should I do, then? With Mrs. Dawes feeling the way she does, you must see my being here and working for you is an impossible situation."

"It seems to me the way to make the best of a bad situation is for you to begin discreetly looking for another job. You should talk to some of the guys from the game you know, like Jim Donley and Bill Hickman. I know that both of them respect you, and they know you've had a succession of winners."

"Maybe," said Joe, "but they're going to wonder why I'm leaving Grant and you. They might guess it's because of Emily, and that might cause Greenwich gossip. I definitely don't want to involve Emily in any of this."

Joe paused for a minute and then continued, "The whole thing feels so uncomfortable. It seems disloyal and ungrateful. I've really liked working for you, David, and you've been wonderful to me. I guess I'm really not sure I want to work for another big investment management firm."

Dawes's affection for Joe welled up. "You've been a great addition, but we are where we are. Maybe you should be thinking about a hedge fund—they're the place to be for a smart, young, ambitious guy. You can use me as a reference, and I promise I'll give you rave reviews."

"Yeah, I have thought about a hedge fund. I had a good talk with a guy named Mickey Cohen from Bridgestone after the Nortel visit."

"Bridgestone has a great record. I know Cohen. Good guy but has had a tough investment life. Do you want me to call him?"

"No," said Joe, "It's better if I approach him directly. He sort of told me to contact him if I ever decided to move. If you call him it might raise questions in his mind as to why you're trying to get rid of me."

"Yeah, you're right. But use me as a reference."

For the next few months, Joe worked ferociously at Grant & Company while he explored job opportunities. The other analysts and portfolio managers who knew nothing of his dilemma were friendly and joked with him, and Joe covered his industries as assiduously as ever. He confided in no one. Only Dawes knew that he was looking for another job. There were moments when he felt downright perfidious, but he also was convinced that leaving the firm was the right thing to do.

Meanwhile, in the summer and early fall of 1999, markets continued to surge higher and speculative activity was rampant. Huge amounts of wealth were being created on paper, but were being treated as permanent. The mood at the firm became increasingly euphoric as Grant's own stock price rocketed up (see Figure 5.2), as did the shares of other big investment banks such as Morgan Stanley. Grant's managing directors received roughly 65 percent of their annual compensation in cash and 35 percent in either restricted Grant & Company stock or options. As a senior managing director, Joe guessed Dawes had probably been getting a total compensation package of around $3 to $4 million a year, and with the stock price at 80, he must have options and restricted stock worth at least $20 million. He mentioned this to Emily.

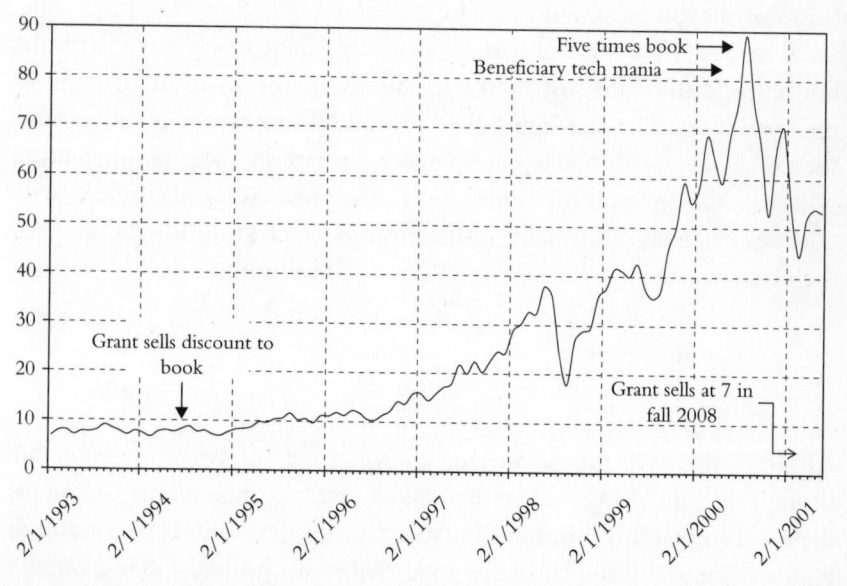

Figure 5.2   Grant Paper Money from 7 to 90

"It must be nice for Daddy finally to have some real money in his own name," she said with a big smile.

"Emily, it's just paper profits so far. I just hope he can sell some of it."

"But Joe, maybe it's too early. Suppose he did sell some now, and the price kept rising? He'd feel like a fool."

"Hey, you should hope he makes a bad sale. He would still own plenty of stock."

On one occasion in November, when Joe sat in Dawes's office with the door closed chatting idly about everything from the markets to the NFL, Dawes mentioned that several Grant investment bankers had recently purchased enormous, ostentatious, very expensive homes that were more like mansions in Greenwich. Others were shopping for ski houses in Aspen, Vail, and Sun Valley, and the older guys, the addicted golfers, were looking around Palm Beach and Lyford Cay. He said the chatter in the managing directors' dining room was now about the Nanny Bubble and whether you had to provide your nanny with her own car so she could get to and from your mansion on her own. "These days, *real* men with *real* wives in Greenwich, Connecticut, have four beautiful children, at least two Irish nannies, and five-car garages," Dawes said with a wry smile. It was a sign of the times or maybe an omen.

The largesse from the soaring price of Grant stock was distributed unevenly within the firm and particularly in the investment management division. The managing directors and a few senior investors were the only ones who had received stock as part of their compensation, whereas the younger people, both the analysts and Joe's former colleagues, owned virtually none. Instead of creating elation and joy, the price run-up was causing some envy and bitterness.

As all of this was going on, Joe didn't come up with any new buy ideas. For one thing, when he talked with company managements, they were beginning to mention weakness in new orders. For another, equities seemed just plain expensive. After all, he had been grounded in Graham and Dodd. He gradually evolved into being bearish on stocks in general and particularly negative on technology, telecom, and Internet stocks, but he continued to believe AIG and United Technologies would ride out the storm. They weren't tech, and their valuations were not particularly inflated compared to everything else.

Joe began to notice that except for the soaring technology sector, the rest of the market was going sideways (as seen in Figure 5.3). He worried the market was becoming a one-trick pony named *Tech*, which could be headed for huge trouble. In the fall of 1999, Joe began to gently urge Dawes and the investment committee to sell the Cisco position and to dramatically underweight tech, telecom, and the Internet sectors in all the firm's portfolios. Cisco was trading at 60 times earnings, and they had almost tripled their money.

Tech and telecom combined were now a huge 30 percent of the S&P 500 index that Grant's portfolios were judged against. The 100 largest stocks in the S&P 500 had a median valuation of 30 times earnings and were half technology companies, whereas the next 2,000 stocks had a median multiple of 13.4 times. The Internet mania was now certifiably insane with initial public offerings (IPOs) of companies with minimal revenues and no earnings tripling on their

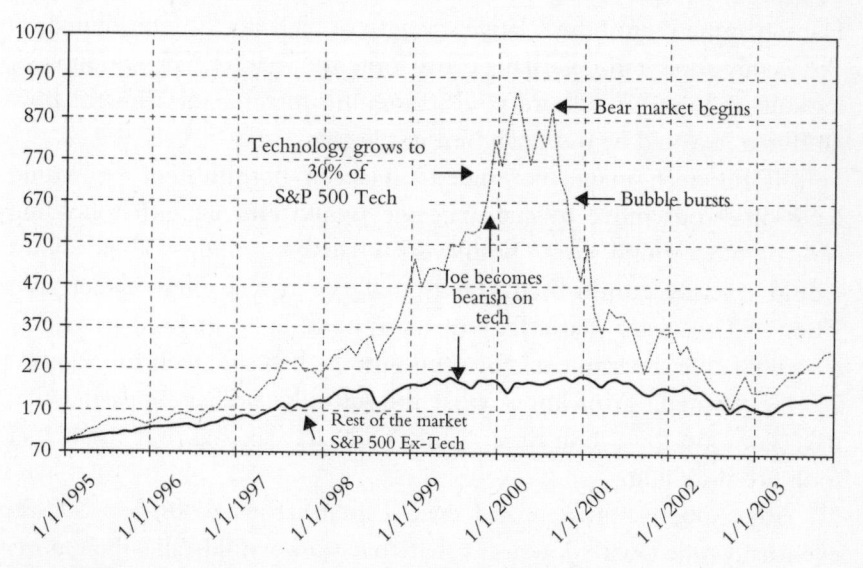

Figure 5.3   S&P 500: Ex-Tech and Tech, 1995–2003

first day of trading. Joe argued that history showed that courageous, counter-consensus sector allocation decisions could be powerful performance drivers.

He did some digging and pointed out that in late 1980, energy stocks had been by far the strongest group in the market for four years as oil prices rocketed higher because of the Iraq-Iran war and worries about future oil supplies. The chairman of one of the largest energy companies declared that the oil price—then $40 a barrel—would be at $100 a barrel in 12 months. Instead, it collapsed to $30 a barrel less than a year later. The energy sector's weight in the S&P had reached 26 percent in the midst of the euphoria, but now, 20 years later, it was a mere 5 percent of the S&P and the oil price was still hovering around $25. Staying with energy in 1981 had been disastrous investment inaction, while cutting exposure to energy stocks had resulted in huge portfolio outperformance rewards. The same dramatic swing also had occurred in the so-called consumer discretionary sector, which had reached 24 percent of the S&P 500 in 1986 and 1987 and was now a mere 6 percent.

The skeptics on the investment committee, however, pointed out that reducing tech now was a dangerous decision because they would be *fighting the tape*, selling strength and momentum. They should wait, Hansen argued, until the relative strength of tech stocks deteriorated.

"Only fools and charlatans try to time the market," he announced, looking at Joe. "Which are you?" Listening to him, Joe thought how satisfying it would be to punch him in the face.

"If the tech mania continued," Hansen pontificated, "it would be a disastrous move to cut since we would end up either holding cash or buying dull stocks with weak relative strength." Their clients would severely punish them, he argued. There was huge career risk. They had all heard that a famous Swiss bank had just fired its greatly respected chief investment officer because he had sold tech too soon.

He warned, "You know what the Japanese say about parties that have gone on for a long time. 'Only fools are dancing, but the bigger fools are watching.'"

After much animated and even cantankerous discussion, Dawes eventually sided with Joe and ruled that they would take their portfolios down from 40 percent in technology and telecom to 20 percent over the next two months. They decided to sell Cisco outright, and the trade was completed in October at prices from 35 to 37 a share. A number of accounts questioned the decision, and two ominously warned Dawes that he "had better be right." Several other clients asked why he hadn't done it earlier.

To Joe's horror, and the investment committee's dismay, technology stock prices continued to soar. No sooner had they finished selling Cisco than the price of the stock rocketed up (see Figure 5.4). (At year-end it closed at a new high of 53.61. Four months later, it almost touched 80. As for technology as a sector, the NASDAQ Index soared from 1,500 in early October of 1998 to over 4,000 at the end of 1999. (It hit over 5,000 on March 10, 2000.) The clients' reactions ranged from rage to sympathy. Two clients closed their accounts. At an investment committee meeting, Hansen gloated, "I told you so. It's a new world. The Internet is the transforming invention."

Dawes replied, "We all agree with that. The issue is the price that we as investors are having to pay for the stocks. I'm convinced valuations are insane, and that we did the right thing by selling and reducing our exposure, although clearly we were early."

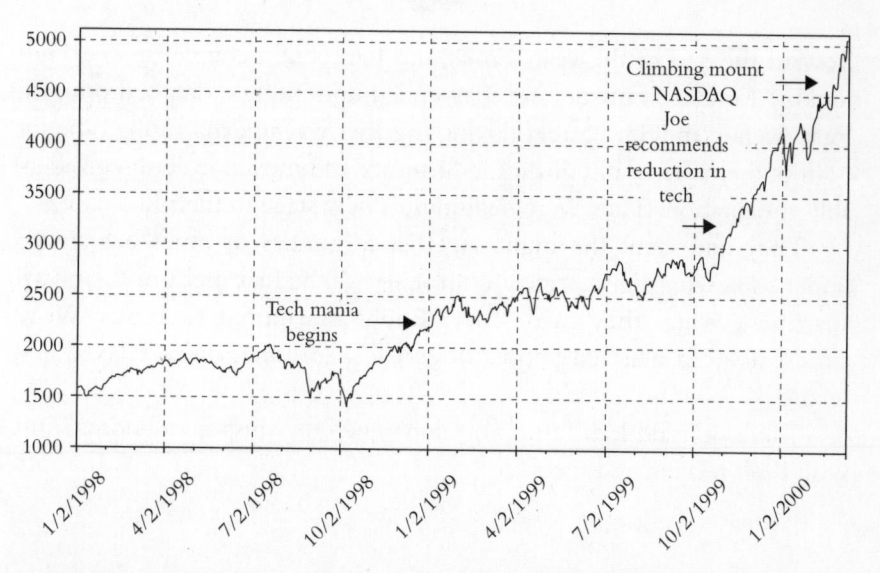

Figure 5.4 Being Early Is the Same as Being Wrong: NASDAQ Composite

"Tell that to the clients," Hansen said smugly.

"I intend to," replied Dawes rather grimly.

"David, the truth of the matter is that in our business being early is the same as being wrong." Heads nodded. Hansen was right. Joe squirmed.

After the meeting Dawes called Joe into his office.

"Look, Joe, I know you feel terrible, but you've got to shake it off. You've had a lot of good calls that have worked out well, but no investor is always right. Forget about it! You have to react like a professional athlete who has a bad game. The good ones learn from it but maintain their composure and confidence. Michael Jordan misses shots; Brett Favre throws interceptions, but they go right back out there and keep shooting. You've got all the right characteristics of an investor. You work hard, you're smart, you've got the tools, and your instincts are good. Keep your head up."

Joe thanked him but nevertheless he was depressed. Not only had he given Dawes horrible advice, but he made this dreadful investment mistake at a crucial moment in his life. Would he be able to get another job? What would happen to his life with Emily?

Toward the end of the year, Emily and Joe spent a couple of weekends looking for an apartment, and they ended up renting a one bedroom on First Avenue and 83rd Street. Living together was an exhilarating time for both of them. They bought some furniture and moved in with considerable anticipation. They were beginning a new stage in their life.

They had spent the night together a number of times but always under somewhat clandestine circumstances. The first night in their own apartment when they made love, Emily murmured to him: "We're almost like old married people now. I feel so much more relaxed and secure."

"I know," said Joe. "But, you don't need to whisper anymore. I just wish I felt relaxed and secure."

Chapter 6

Moving On

J oe had told no one but Emily and and her father about his plans to leave Grant, including Doug Scott. By coincidence, Doug himself was thinking of moving on. He angrily told Joe that at year-end he had been screwed by the firm and his warlord on compensation. Grant had taken a big hit on a fixed-income trade, but that had nothing to do with him. In addition, some of the other prop traders, including three in Doug's group, had been too bullish, and with the market selling off into year-end had pierced the drawdown limit and had been shut down. Doug had sat out the fall, and as a result booked an $8 million profit for the year. He was pleased with himself and expected under the 12 percent formula to get paid $960,000, which was *decent*.

However, when Doug's warlord sat down with him to discuss performance and compensation, he had been very complimentary on the former but had told Doug his payout was going to be only 9 percent, or $720,000. He explained the shortfall by a smaller overall compensation pool because of the poor performance of the firm's prop trading in general and the other members of the warlord's group in particular.

Doug was furious. "You told me the payout was going to be twelve percent, come hell or high water. You never mentioned it had anything to do with what the firm or what other prop traders did. You're reneging on our deal!"

The warlord was defensive. "I said *about* twelve percent. There was no guarantee."

"Bullshit," said Doug. "We had a definite arrangement, and you and the firm are violating it. Why should I be penalized because other guys screwed up?"

"I could probably find another fifty thousand for you. Will that make you happy? We like what you're doing, Doug. Your returns and your Sharpe ratio are good."

"No, it won't make me happy! What about next year? What's the payout going to be? Are you going to increase my line?"

"Sorry, but I can't commit to either, yet. The firm is rethinking the size of its allocation to prop trading. It's the usual senior management story. They love prop trading when she's pretty and hate her when she's ugly."

"That's reassuring," said Doug. "Thanks a lot," he said as he angrily stomped out of the warlord's small office.

"It really pisses me off," Doug told Joe. "He painted me a picture. I thought prop trading was going to be fun and exciting. It's not. It's grinding, scary stuff. Last summer, when the shit hit the fan I was pretty fully invested and the pressure practically ruined my life. Day and night I was agonizing over every tick. It's not investing; it's fucking mindless day trading with your career and family's survival at stake. It stinks."

He sighed. "One night this summer when Susan and I were out to dinner, I got physically sick at a restaurant. Every night like clockwork I was waking up at three in the morning hallucinating from nightmares to check Japan and Asia. Try going back to sleep when your positions are going the wrong way! I was taking Tylenol PM to sleep, and then I would wake up with that crummy, lousy, hungover feeling. While I was on vacation in August, I actually couldn't get it up either because of the Tylenol or because I was freaked about what was happening. And then after I survived all this trauma and booked good money for them, they cut my payout and I earn a lousy seven hundred twenty thousand."

Joe shook his head. The anxiety was bad but the money sounded good to him. He expected to get paid $270,000. "That kind of stress must be horrible. Doug, if prop trading is that bad, why don't you go back to sales?"

"Unfortunately, it doesn't work that way! It's a dog-eat-dog world. They've reassigned my accounts, and I'd have to start all over with new accounts. I can't afford to do it. I've put on some heavy overhead what with a wife, a baby, and another on the way."

Now, Doug said, he was looking at other situations. The deals at other investment banks and commercial banks were about the same as the original Grant arrangement. However, he was worried about these banks' commitment to the business since investors were increasingly unwilling to pay much for prop trading earnings, as profits from this source was viewed as low quality and volatile. Lehman Brothers had actually moved three of their biggest and best prop traders to their investment management division, hoping investors would pay up for earnings from that source. But was that really going to fool anybody?

Over the last few weeks, Doug told Joe, he had been talking with Hadron, a huge hedge fund complex in New Canaan, Connecticut. Tom Hadron was a legendary hedge fund figure from New Orleans who made his first big money 30 years ago trading cotton. He now had a successful, multistrategy hedge fund complex whose product lines include prop trading. He had perhaps 20 to 25 prop traders around the world.

"Tommy is regarded as a fair and honest man," Doug told Joe. "He's a good old Southern boy who likes to hunt and drink beer with his buddies."

"Yeah," said Joe. "I read he owns a whole island off the coast of Georgia to hunt on and raises tens of millions for his charity for poor kids every year."

"Tommy Hadron," Doug explained, "runs a much more enlightened show than the investment banks. His firm intensely interviews potential traders and insists they have had some experience under fire. If a trader is hired, he gets a draw of three hundred thousand and is given a two-year lease on life. He is allowed a loss limit of up to twenty percent compared to the ten-percent rule enforced at most banks. Measures of volatility and risk, such as the Sharpe ratio, are used to assess performance. The payout starts at fifteen percent, and the traders are given a line of fifty to one hundred million."

Joe responded, "It sound like a good deal with a lot of potential."

"But like I said," Doug interrupted, "prop trading is a tough business and you can't escape your batting average. Hadron's sweet, South-mouth talk doesn't mean a thing. He hasn't become a billionaire with hunting preserves and a major charity by carrying prop traders who don't put up big numbers. We're all hired guns. Personality and team spirit don't count for anything. It's make Tommy money or a not-so-fond farewell."

"So why are you going to do it?"

"Because I'm thirty-eight years old, with no capital to speak of, and with no visible, fungible skills. I need the money. Besides prop trading is like gambling—it's addictive and I've got the blood lust. Why don't you come with me? Hadron will pay two hundred thousand for one guy to work with me, and I'll give you twenty percent of what I make on the carry. You be my partner. How about it, buddy?"

Joe scratched his head. "Hey, I'm flattered. Let me think about it. I've been talking with Bridgestone."

"You'll disappear into the body of that beast," said Doug. "It will be years before you get a shot running real money like I'm talking about."

As Joe thought about his options, he and Emily were discovering the good and the not so good of their new life together. Her job at the Council was prestigious but not particularly demanding and the pay was meager. She began taking courses at Columbia University, with the objective of getting her master's degree in European history. Joe was finally finishing up at Stern and what with business dinners and some travel they didn't have much time together during the week.

On weekends, their small one-bedroom apartment was cramped. They were primarily living on Joe's pay as Emily was loath to draw on her trust fund. As a result, they didn't really have the money to enjoy New York or go away on vacation. With Emily estranged from her parents, they weren't about to go to Greenwich.

"I'm sick and tired of being poor," Joe said one late December afternoon. "I want my share of Wall Street's filthy lucre."

"That's a good word," Emily told him, "but for now you've got to be satisfied with your full share of my riches." They both laughed.

They began to go out to dinner with other people. Twice they went to restaurants in the Village with Doug and his wife, and they saw quite a bit of Emily's older brother. Her older sister Jill was in her second year of law school and she also visited them several times that winter but she and Emily had an edgy relationship.

They joined the Equinox health club on 72nd Street, ran around the reservoir in Central Park, and mostly stayed in the city on the weekends. After they had gone to the gym and exercised, they sat in the apartment and read on Saturdays and Sundays. It was a little claustrophobic, surrounded by Joe's endless stacks of research and company reports and Emily's nineteenth-century European history reading. Twice they went out with Ann Barnard, another girl from the Council, who had befriended Emily. She was a true foreign policy geek, and babbled endlessly about arcane complexities and State Department blunders. Joe found he didn't have much to say to her, nor she to him. In fact, he thought she was boring and he suspected the feeling was mutual.

As for Emily, she was concerned that Joe had become completely stock market–centered to an extent that was far more intense than her father had ever been. It was all he talked about, and he read nothing but business stuff and the sports page. They didn't seem to have as much to talk about as they used to, and they often ended up wanting to do different things in their spare time. She urged him to go to the theater or to a museum with her, while he wanted instead to read or work out. This troubled Emily.

As for Joe, he was increasingly focusing on Bridgestone.

In early 2000, Bridgestone was a 10-year-old, $35 billion multistrategy hedge fund complex, which was and is huge in hedge fund land. The firm managed seven different funds ranging from the $15 billion flagship multistrategy fund to smaller event-driven, convertible arbitrage, and equity market neutral portfolios. Bridgestone had been built by its two founding partners, Jud Spokane and Dan Ravine, in a rags-to-riches story that is the stuff of Wall Street dreams.

Spokane is the charming extrovert and a very shrewd marketing rainmaker, while Ravine is the intellectual powerhouse that creates the performance numbers. One couldn't do without the other; it's a highly symbiotic relationship, but not necessarily a loving marriage.

Spokane and Ravine grew up in the dingy hinterlands of New York City and actually knew each other as teenagers in the Bronx. They maintain they have always been close friends, but in retrospect it seems a little unlikely because they are so different now. How could they have been close friends then? Regardless, through some mysterious synergy, they have been linked together in their astounding business careers.

Spokane, 52, is a fit, bon vivant charmer, who joyously flaunts his wealth and physique. His custom-tailored, made-in-London suits cling to his broad shoulders and bring out the thinness of his waist. One-hundred-sixty-dollar Hermès ties hang from his strong, bronzed neck. Spokane is very proud of his neck and sometimes he looks almost like a great wild turkey as he struts around, projecting it forward.

For a number of years, Spokane has cut a broad swath in the hedge fund–nouveau riche layer of New York society. However, when all is said and done, this milieu is a little tacky. Too many uncouth loud-mouths unhappily married to plain old childhood sweethearts living in ostentatious modern buildings. Recently divorced again with bigger aspirations and more money, Spokane is focused on cracking the Upper East Side Gold Coast that lives in the great buildings on Park and Fifth, the old money that belongs to the really exclusive clubs, the high-powered social wattage of the city.

Hedge fund wealth is definitely *new* money, but if you want to make a splash and have enough money to give away and to spend on elaborate dinner parties, you can break into the big time with the right people. Also, having a reputation as a winner enhances credibility. Spokane understood all of this and knew what he had to do. He has worked and given his way onto the boards of the Robert Wood Johnson Foundation, the Sloan Foundation, and the New York Philharmonic, all of which are fancy, expensive seats to squat on because great New York organizations do not cheaply embrace arrivistes on their boards. He also has a box at the opera and seldom misses a society fund-raiser or a celebrity golf event.

Since real estate is a prime adornment for the ascending hedge fund beautiful person, he bought a somewhat rundown South Hampton mansion in 1997. This gargantuan house, located on East End Lane, was built in 1920 and in its prime looked like San Simeon. It is nestled on four acres of great, green lawns a hundred yards from the beach, and has 30 rooms. He has spent millions restoring it to its former grandeur. Other adornments included a ski house in Vail and a villa in Palm Beach, and he has been talking about buying a house on Eaton Square in London.

On the linenfold mahogany walls of his New York office are photographs of himself—playing basketball with Michael Jordan, with his arm around Mayor Giuliani, and schmoozing with a smiling President Clinton. He frequently lunches at the Four Seasons with big shots ranging from Henry Kravis to Tiki Barber, and he has shot quail with Dick Cheney and Dan Rather. Spokane is the smiling, virile face of Bridgestone who bedazzles prospective investors and pours oil on troubled client waters. Despite the ravages of some rather ugly divorces (two of the first Mrs. Spokanes did "not go quietly into that good night"), he must be close to being a billionaire.

Daniel Jehovah Ravine, 51, works down the hall from Spokane's spacious, light-lit, open office. Unlike his partner, he always keeps his door closed and the shades drawn in his Spartan quarters that are dominated by computer equipment and six screens. The shelves are stacked with books, and there are piles of reports and computer printouts stacked on low tables. There are no photographs or personal artifacts as there are in Spokane's digs.

Ravine is literally allergic to noise and refuses to respond to distractions such as phone calls and e-mails. In fact, he is as introverted as his partner is extroverted, but he is a tough, no-bullshit manager with a sharp pencil. Although he is without a high-powered mathematics education, Ravine is a respected quantitative intellect. While studying physics at the State University of New York, the longtime computer geek discovered an eighteenth-century physicist named Jean Fourier who had invented the mathematical formula that described the frequency of heat waves. Ravine used Fourier's formulas to calculate the distance between peaks and troughs in individual stock prices. From that revelation he developed trend-spotting software to find profitable trades. The only adornment on his office wall is a magnificently framed but crude wood block drawing of Fourier.

Unlike Spokane, he avoids publicity, meetings, and confrontations with his portfolio managers, preferring to do his own work, immerse himself in the data, and run his Statistical Opportunities Fund. He belongs to Club Kosher, a closely knit network of Orthodox Jewish professionals who are committed to keeping kosher and to Israel.

In the 1980s, Spokane and Ravine were a successful broker team at Bear Stearns that relied principally on technical analysis—charts and price momentum signals. Ravine developed the strategies and Spokane delivered the mumbo jumbo to their clients. These strategies resulted in heavy trading and big production numbers for the two men, but not much wealth for their clients. In 1989, they left Bear Stearns to form Bridgestone. At that time, nobody cared and they initially raised a mere $20 million. Performance the first two years was indifferent, as their technical programs seemed unable to overcome the burden of transaction costs and market impact.

Then in 1991, they changed their spots. No more technical analysis. Ravine began to concentrate on convertible arbitrage, using his analytical and computer skills. It worked, and merger arbitrage was the next step. By 1993, both funds had great performances. As Spokane began to spin his magic, their assets under management began to grow. By 1994, Bridgestone was at $700 million, and then in 1995, they shot the lights out with their multistrategy fund posting a 52 percent net return year. The money poured in and they added more new funds. The next three years were good, not great, but it didn't matter. They were the talk of the town—the charismatic golden boy and the Jewish stat/arb intellectual. A deluge of capital flowed in. By January 1, 1999, total assets under management reached $35 billion.

However, as so often happens, a hedge fund starts small, does well, gets big, and slips on its own banana peel. In 1999, five of the firm's seven portfolios had underperformed their respective hedge fund benchmarks, and three of the biggest funds had gains of between 2 and 5 percent after fees. The two funds that did reasonably well, the

Bridgestone Long/Short Equity Fund and the Bridgestone Technology Opportunities Fund, were up 22 percent and 28 percent, respectively, which was acceptable, but not spectacular in a year when many long-only managers posted fantastic results. For the firm as a whole, the year 2000 hadn't gotten off to a rip-roaring start either.

As a result, redemption notices were coming in. It wasn't a deluge, but there was unpleasant gossip that the firm was losing its momentum. Furthermore, in recent months, a number of managing directors with direct portfolio responsibilities had either quit or been fired. No one seemed to know what exactly had happened to whom or why. Also, the chief administrative officer had left for unexplained reasons, and the former head of product strategy had departed to join another hedge fund. Replacements for these positions were being recruited from other funds, but turnover of top portfolio managers is viewed with a very jaundiced eye by the big funds of funds and the hedge fund consultants. On the other hand, if performance is lousy, investors want to see somebody walk the plank attached to cannon balls.

After he made the decision to leave Grant, Joe had been very circumspect in his job search activities. He didn't want word to get back to people at Grant that he was looking for a new job, because it would be embarrassing for both Dawes and himself. Because of his contact with Mickey Cohen, he had focused on Bridgestone. He liked the guy. Mickey was perceptive, irreverent, and a value investor like he was. *A good combination*, Joe thought. By the end of 1999, Joe had been interviewed by three Bridgestone fund managers and the research director. He had shown them copies of the reports he had written, and in general he felt the interviews had gone well. However, he had heard nothing definite about a job, and he was beginning to get nervous. He worried that they had heard about his ill-fated technology call.

One morning, Mickey asked Joe to come to Bridgestone's elaborate glass offices at 900 Fifth Avenue. He assumed it was just another interview, but when he arrived, Mickey told him, "Hey pal, you're making progress. Today you're going to be interviewed by the omnipotent ones. Spokane's first. Don't get put off by his office bullshit. He just got it decorated by the newest hot *society* decorator, and he loves to brag about it."

"What's a society decorator?" asked Joe, making conversation.

"A rich, connected woman who decorates offices for very rich, smart men with no taste, and who egregiously rips them off in the process. This one is emaciated, but beautiful with two-hundred watt eyes . . . if you like eyes and emaciated, which I don't."

Without further preamble, Mickey ushered him into Spokane's office. Spokane gestured toward an armchair. His face was strong, swarthy, and shrewd, yet he smiled at Joe with closely set white teeth. The blue eyes looked at him intently, noticing the big, strong-looking hands.

"That's a Henry VI piece you're sitting on," Spokane told him. Joe shifted nervously as the elegant, delicate chair creaked. "The table there, that small antique one, is from Napoleon's office. So you were a big-time football player for AU?" Spokane said, eyeing Joe appraisingly. Joe shook his head.

"Well, I wouldn't quite . . ." but Spokane cut him off.

"I was a star running back in high school," Spokane told him, ostentatiously flexing his bull neck that welled up from a shirt made of lustrous Sea Island cotton. "Should have been All City, but I played for a lousy team. No one could block; had to make all the runs work by myself. Was a great receiver too, soft hands but the quarterback was a wussy. Then in college at Pace they didn't even have a real team. I definitely could have played college ball. Love the game. Do you play golf?"

"Growing up I played with my father some, but I haven't played much in the last five years."

"Yeah," said Spokane, "I started very late. I've got my handicap down to nine. It took a lot of work. You know, I've played with Tiger, and Phil's a good friend."

For the rest of the interview Spokane babbled about himself, dropped names, and told Joe what a great firm Bridgestone was.

"We'll have seventy billion in four years and then we'll go public. If you sincerely want to be rich, this is the place to be. Do you *sincerely* want to be rich?"

"Yes, sir, I do. I've been poor forever."

"Do you pay much attention to technical analysis?"

"Well, I'm sort of a value investor . . ." Joe started to say, but Spokane interrupted him.

"That's okay," he said. "I take my dog with me when I go hunting but I don't let him shoot the gun." He grinned at Joe, pleased with himself.

Spokane glanced at his watch with casual insouciance. "Hey, Joe, listen, good to talk to you. I got Monica coming in two minutes. Old girlfriend of mine. Maybe we'll play golf sometime." He rose and stretched inside his beautifully made gray-worsted suit and flexed his $1,200 English leather shoes from Robertson and Reeves of Shady Lane, London, as though he were about to sprint somewhere wonderful and exciting.

When they were outside, Joe murmured to Mickey: "That was an unusual interview. I barely said anything."

"It doesn't make any difference," Mickey told him. "He's always that way. It's a personality dump. His judgments are all very intuitive. Sometimes his instincts are good, but he puts a lot of emphasis on golf, which makes no sense to me. He's obsessed with what he calls 'grace under pressure.' Must have read Hemingway. It all seems a little weird, but, look, the guy is a winner and has made it big."

"Do you like and trust him?" Joe asked.

"No to both," replied Mickey. "He doesn't care much for me, either. I'm Jewish. I'm one of Ravine's boys from the temple, and I'm what is known in the firm as an investment shithead. Maybe even a shithead geek."

"What?"

"I'll explain it to you later. We gotta go meet the other big man."

Mickey took him down the hall to the other senior partner's office. As usual, Ravine's door was closed, and his assistant told them that Mr. Ravine was in his "monk mode." She hoped he would be with them shortly. They stood in the reception area gazing at the walls that were covered with colorful, incomprehensible abstract art.

"What's his monk mode?" Joe asked.

"He's a very intense, obsessive guy," Mickey told him. "You'll see. He believes in hiring people who are smart, curious, and irreverent. Irreverence is important because he's convinced it's in what he calls 'the fertile conversation of disagreement' where the best ideas come from or at least are tested."

"He sounds formidable," Joe said.

"He's also always looking for evidence in your background that you would death march before you would fail to complete something to perfection or accept defeat. It's very important to him." They were about to leave when the assistant's phone buzzed and she told them to go in.

Ravine was sitting at a Mission-style work table in front of four screens. He was thin and pale, almost pallid, and was wearing blue jeans and a faded polo shirt. Incongruously, the jeans were held up by red suspenders with black skulls and crossbones on them. A similarly dressed young analyst stood behind him, looking distraught.

"Impale thyself," Ravine said to the analyst. "The algorithm just doesn't solve. Doom loops. Run the equations again your way and come back in thirty minutes. I'll do the same."

He turned to Joe. His enthusiasm about having to interview someone in the midst of his research was imperceptible. "Here I am, an old man in a dry month, being read to by a boy, waiting for rain. Were you at the hot gates, knee deep in the salt marsh, heaving a cutlass?"

"What?" said Joe. "I beg your pardon?"

"So you've brought me another illiterate, Mickey. Doesn't recognize T.S. and the first lines of perhaps the greatest poem of modern times."

"*Here I am an old man . . . A dull head among windy spaces*," replied Mickey.

"Ah, thank you," Ravine turned to Joe. "Anyway, you're the guy we're about to hire. What are you going to do to lead us out of this performance wasteland we're in?" Now for the first time he seemed to focus as he stared intensely at Joe.

"I don't know about that," said Joe. "I'll try to work hard and hope to figure something out."

"Do you know where that 'old man in a dry month' quote came from? It says here you majored in literature and accounting. An unlikely combination."

"I'm afraid I also majored in football. No, I'm sorry but don't know where it's from."

"Well, it's from T.S. Eliot's *Gerontion*. A good investor must have an eclectic mind. Tell me, Mr. Hill, do you believe in God?"

Joe was dumbfounded. "Yes," he said. "I believe there is a God up there somewhere. My mother took me to church as a boy, but I'm not very religious."

"Do you agree that trying to unravel the stock market as a quant is like playing chess with God?"

"Come on, Daniel," Mickey interrupted. "Just interview him. Don't freak the guy out."

Ravine smiled faintly. "Yahweh is a quant. Did you know that?"

"No, sir."

"Do you know who Yahweh is?"

"I think so. He's the old-time Jewish God."

"What are the last two nourishing books you've read?"

Joe, grasping for names, stammered, "*History of the American People* by Paul Johnson and *Reminiscences of a Stock Operator* by Lefèvre."

"History and trading. Interesting. Did the Founding Fathers believe in God?"

"Not really—according to Johnson, they were mostly agnostics."

"So you actually did read Paul Johnson," said Ravine. "Take him away, Mickey. I hereby authorize you to hire another shithead."

Afterward, they went to Mickey's office.

"You did good! We're going to offer you a job in research as an analyst," Mickey told him. "We like your work and your thinking. What are they paying you at that sweatshop?"

"I made two hundred seventy thousand last year and I'm guessing it will be three fifty this year. But it's not so much the money. I want the opportunity."

"I can tell you for sure they'll guarantee to double it. If you make the firm some money, they could make it much more. We pay big for performance."

"That's wonderful. I'm very excited," said Joe. "But how can Bridgestone afford an offer like that? I don't understand hedge fund accounting, but I'm told that after last year's losses, Bridgestone overall is well below its high-water marks so you won't earn the incentive fee until you make back your losses."

"That's true," replied Mickey. "In the five funds that are under water nobody is going to make big money this year, but our fees are two and twenty—two percent of assets and twenty percent of the profits. Let's say we lose five billion of assets and go from thirty billion to twenty-five billion and the market is down again—assets for the year only average twenty billion, which is not inconceivable. Two percent of twenty billion is forty million dollars. Presumably just like this year a couple of funds will earn incentive fees. We have probably twelve million of back office, support, space overhead plus thirty investment and marketing professionals. We can pay you seven hundred with no problem."

"What did Ravine mean by that shithead comment?"

Mickey smiled faintly. "Around here there are three kinds of investors. *Growthies*, guys who love growth stocks, don't care about valuations, and only buy stocks with strong price momentum; *geeks*, who are quants and invest off computer models; and *shitheads*, who are value investors. In other words, they buy the stocks of dirty, shitty companies because they are cheap."

"I see. I guess I *am* a shithead. In the long run, value has beaten growth by around two hundred basis points a year."

"True, but in the last five years, it's been totally a growth world. But by the way, are you going to accept the offer?"

"It's a great offer and I'm very flattered. Let me think about it and I'll get back to you in a few days."

Joe walked back to his Upper East Side apartment through the light drizzle of a cold spring morning in a quandary. He liked the people he had met at Bridgestone with the possible exception of the two principals. Spokane appeared to be an egomaniac who talked rather than listened, while Ravine seemed very bright but weird. It sort of sounded like he was going to be working for Mickey. The gossip on the Street was that the firm was in trouble. He talked it over that night with Emily as they lay in bed.

"Joe," she finally said. "You've got to trust your instincts. What about Doug?"

"I'm not a prop trader; I don't want to be a prop trader. I'm an analyst and then an investor. The trouble is, I can't really explore the job market without it getting back to the people at Grant. Any other firms I approach are going to want to check me out and not just with your father."

"Then do it," said Emily. "You don't really have much choice and it's not the end of the world if it doesn't work out."

The next morning, he called Mickey and accepted the job and then went to inform Dawes.

"I hope Bridgestone is okay," Dawes told him. "What does Emily think?"

"She's for it."

"Okay. Well, it's done. It's over." Dawes shook his head ruefully. "Let's make the exit here short and sour. Your last day will be next Friday. You can move your stuff over the weekend. I'll announce it at the investment committee meeting the following Monday and say something nice about you, but also act like I'm a little pissed off. Good luck, Joe!"

They shook hands. "Keep in touch," Dawes added. "Let's have lunch when the dust clears. As for playing in our game next season, we'll cross that bridge next fall, but we need you!"

Chapter 7

Bridgestone

B ridgestone's headquarters were located at 900 Fifth Avenue, a
building overlooking the park and overwhelmed by sunlight. At
the height of the firm's glory, it had been furnished by one of
New York's most revered decorators who, according to his brochure,
specialized in "space, light, functionality, and congeniality." The firm had
two floors, which were joined by a curving stairway—Spokane's, Ravine's,
and the investors' offices were on the 37th floor; marketing, client
relations, operations, and an extensive fitness center were on the floor
below them.

The investors' offices were interspersed with reading rooms, and at
the core of their floor was "the cabaret," which opened at seven in the
morning and closed at eight in evening and offered a broad variety of
gourmet, cooked-to-order food. In one corner of the cabaret, which
overlooked Central Park, there was a long table that was reserved exclusively for the portfolio managers, the decision makers. It was understood
that no analyst or anyone from marketing or operations was permitted
to sit there.

Next to the cabaret were three smaller dining rooms for private meetings with clients. The one across the corridor from Spokane's office was reserved for his use, and it had the casually cluttered effect espoused by Spokane's decorator. In the center of this dining room was an opulent Louis XII table that was surrounded by six Chippendale wing chairs. On one wall there was a built-in mahogany bookcase with slim glass doors and elaborately bound, showcase volumes of Trollope, Kipling, Tennyson, and Dante. However, the real center of attention was a working wood-burning fireplace with an antique carved mantel that Spokane had bought in Scotland. After reading an article in the *Wall Street Journal* that stated that the head of Private Wealth Management at J.P. Morgan had such a fireplace, albeit somewhat more mundane, Spokane became enthralled and was determined to have one in his office. The installation of the fireplace, its flue system, and the mantel had cost a quarter of a million dollars.

Far down the hall from all this grandeur Joe had a small, glass office with a magnificent view of Central Park and the immense gathering of buildings that surrounded it. His office had a large, modern, teak workstation with high-tech curves at the corners and matching file teak cabinets with the ubiquitous four computer screens mounted on it. Sheer, filmy but opaque curtains could be drawn to ensure the utter privacy Ravine insisted on for all his investment professionals. He would say, "You can't concentrate if you can see people walking by in the hall."

When Joe arrived that first morning, there were also two stark but sleek and curved upholstered chairs in his office. There was a note on one saying: "Call Extension 2043 Immediately." When he did, a woman answered the phone and told him she would be right there. When she arrived she painstakingly adjusted the chairs to his body and posture.

"Mr. Ravine believes if you're going to spend half the day sitting, you'd better be in a fitted chair," she told him. "If you have any distress, you are obligated to call me." Joe had to admit the chair was very comfortable.

Joe quickly settled into the Bridgestone life. He arrived at the office at 6:30 in the morning and went to the superbly outfitted gym. On the treadmills, he watched CNBC and Bloomberg TV. On the days he lifted weights, headphones and a Walkman were supplied, which held a cassette full of economic and market material that the research director believed was particularly worthwhile. By 7:45 he was in the restaurant reading the morning newspapers and eating a quick breakfast. Then he checked his e-mails, and at 8:30 attended the morning meeting in the Yale Bowl—so called because the large conference room in which the meeting was held had a huge oval table in the shape of the Yale Bowl.

At 8:28, a bell chimed throughout the Bridgestone offices signaling that the meeting would begin in two minutes. The morning meeting was mandatory for all the analysts and portfolio managers in the office that day. The portfolio managers and the head traders sat around the conference table, and the analysts, junior traders, and marketing people (the "smile and a shoeshine gang," as they were called) perched in chairs, otherwise known as the "cheap seats," on an elevated platform that ran around the circumference of the table. There were between 30 and 40 men and women in the room. The meeting was run by the head trader, Sal Macri, a thin ascetic-looking Italian from Chicago. As time went on, Joe learned to respect his market insights.

Promptly at 8:30, one of Macri's lieutenants, who had started work at five o'clock in the morning, would run through a stapled handout summarizing overnight news events, both market and fundamental, from around the world. During this recitation, the portfolio managers often asked questions or made comments, but the analysts in the cheap seats never spoke up unless they were called on. Sometimes Ravine attended but said little. Spokane seldom came. It was understood he had business breakfasts at the Regency, where the great and powerful of New York hobnobbed and checked each other out.

As time went on, Joe found he got a lot of market color and news commentary at these meetings, but sometimes the atmosphere was intimidating and stultifying. There seemed to be an undercurrent of negative, not positive, competitive tension that verged on dislike and mistrust among certain portfolio managers seated around the table. Jibes were exchanged, and Joe sensed that the growth managers were not averse to taking shots at guys who, as they put it, "still didn't get it" and were fighting the price momentum of the tech and telecom equities in general and the Internet stocks in particular. Mickey Cohen seemed to be on the receiving end of a number of these hits, but he would just grin and good-naturedly throw up his hands. Yet, he never conceded anything and occasionally would point out what he called "the incredible dream premium" priced into technology. Joe, with his strong value-investing orientation, found himself empathizing with Mickey.

In general, Joe liked the atmosphere at Bridgestone. He didn't get any sense that the other professionals resented him. Just as at Grant, the men identified him as a football player. At the gym, he knew he got some admiring glances from a couple of the young female professionals. In the café at breakfast and lunch he made a point of sitting with the other portfolio assistant and analysts.

In this way, he met people in the firm, and he soon became friendly with Joan Liebowitz, a portfolio assistant who worked for Tom Leiter, the firm's growth stock specialist, on his hedge fund. She often seemed to choose to sit next to or adjacent to him.

Liebowitz was a slim—verging on skinny—long-legged woman about Joe's age, with jet-black hair and an interesting and pointed but not particularly pretty face. She was hyperactive, animated, and vibrant and was continually squirming and moving her arms and hands. She had good shoulders and the overall effect was sexy in an unusual way. As Cohen once put it, "She looks as though she wears out her clothes from the inside out instead of the outside in." Joe found her attractive and a kindred spirit.

"How come," he asked her one day, "there are a lot of female research and client service people but no female portfolio managers?"

"Because," she responded, "the two guys who run this place believe one, that women are too emotionally unstable to manage money well, and two, that the genetics don't work. Women are diverted from being obsessed and successful investors by either being mothers or by becoming old maids."

"How will they assess me?" asked Joe.

"You've got a lot going for you, babycakes. You're a big-time jock, and like most guys, they're jock lovers. Also, you're considered a minority, and legally, they are required to have a certain proportion of minorities on staff. At least I assume you are," she looked at him quizzically.

"Yeah, I'm half and half."

"If I were you, I'd work on my suntan and get even darker. Ravine in particular is a bleeding-heart liberal."

"How about Spokane?"

"He's a powerful, pompous asshole, in my book. Do you play golf?"

"Yeah, a little."

"Then work on it. He believes playing winning golf under pressure is the mark of a good money manager." She shook her head. "What macho bullshit."

"Whenever I see Ravine, he always seems unhappy," Joe remarked.

"Absolutely," she replied. "He's a hypochondriac. He complains to his friends that he suffers from what he calls *chronic diffuse despair.* The story goes that one of his friends told him that he, the friend, had a great shrink who could cure him, and that he would set up an appointment. 'No I can't do that,' Ravine told him. 'My depression is what makes me a successful businessman and investor.' You know what? He's probably right."

At the end of Joe's second week, the research director, a lean, ascetic man named Dennis Bogan, called Joe into his office. Dennis told Joe that his primary assignment would be to work as an assistant to Mickey Cohen, who would be running his own long-short equity hedge fund.

"Mickey is a friend of mine, and he says you've got a strong value orientation and are tech skeptical. Seems to me the right place for you is with Cohen. Good luck."

He went by Liebowitz's office and dropped in. "Joan, tell me about Cohen. I know him a little but not really well, and I've just been assigned to him."

"Well, a lot of guys around here think that in this new era he's a hopeless loser shithead. I'm not so sure."

"Is he a dead end?"

"No, I don't think so. He's one of Ravine's guys. He got to know him from the temple so Spokane probably is skeptical, but he'll definitely get a shot."

Joe was pleased with this assignment. From the beginning, he had liked the guy. Mickey Cohen was a tall, Jewish man in his mid-40s who had gone to Brown and the Harvard Business School. He had restless, blue eyes, steel-gray hair, a round open face, and a big grin. He was also developing a substantial paunch. Mickey was convinced investing was all about value, and Joe knew he had developed a fairly complex quantitative value model to identify cheap and expensive stocks.

However, Mickey had come to believe that the timing of putting a position on should be determined by price momentum. Raw valuation by itself was not enough, and using it as the sole criterion often resulted in being marooned in what became a value trap. He determined he would not act to buy a stock that was cheap until it began to show *positive upside momentum*—in other words, until the price of the stock began to go up. Similarly, he would not sell short a stock until its price momentum turned down, no matter how expensive it was or how negative the story.

After Joe was assigned, Mickey left him alone. "Get acclimated," he told him. "Take your time. Figure out how things work around here. Then I want you to take a look at America Online (AOL). I think it could be a great short sale. Let me know what you think."

At the time, certain value investors believed that Internet stocks in general and AOL in particular were grossly overvalued and were compelling shorts. Bearish investors opined that AOL's stock price was a misrepresentation because the company spent huge amounts of money promoting its services and in effect *buying* subscribers who paid a monthly fee. These so-called *customer acquisition costs* were capitalized and then written off over the expected life of the customer relationship, which, of course, the company said (hoped) was years. Thus, argued the bears, the reported earnings were grossly inflated.

With his accounting background, Joe immediately recognized that AOL's accounting did not comply with generally accepted accounting principles (GAAP), which required that costs be written off as incurred.

When he talked to Joan about these conclusions, she argued it was not that simple.

"You should work out the net present value of a subscriber by comparing the initial cash acquisition costs to the payments the customer will make over the duration of his or her expected relationship with the company based on historical experience."

He immediately recognized her perception and ran the numbers. His conclusion was that the true economics of the business were magnificent. Although AOL's real earnings per share were lower than what was being reported and the price-to-earnings ratio was very high, the company was adding so many new customers that its future growth justified the evaluation.

They talked about it. "Competition for customers almost certainly will increase," he told her.

"Undoubtedly, but on the other hand, babycakes, new sources of revenue such as advertising will also develop. I don't think it's a compelling short. Everybody knows the accounting fraud story."

Joe liked the clarity of her thinking, although he didn't much like being addressed as *babycakes*. It was very helpful to have someone to talk things over with. At Grant, the other analysts were, in a sense, competitors, and he had never felt comfortable opening up to them on important investment judgments. Having an investment confidante was a new experience.

He wrote a two-sentence conclusion to his report: *Internet stocks are grossly overvalued, but AOL is not a prime candidate for selling short. We should short the junk and the frauds rather than a company with dynamic growth potential and a compelling business model.*

Mickey appeared to be impressed with his conclusion and pleased with his analysis. By chance, 10 days later, AOL announced a massive write-off of its capitalized customer acquisition costs, stating that these costs would be expensed as incurred in the future. Earnings per share would be considerably lower in the future as the result of this policy. After the announcement, the stock price faltered briefly and then soared. Joe's judgment—and Joan's, for that matter—had been vindicated.

As the days passed, Joe could feel Mickey watching him, studying him. That was fine with him. He was observing Mickey too and his interaction with people, especially the other investors, and he liked what he saw. Mickey was an extrovert—warm and outgoing. He was a friendly, touchy-feely person, grabbing arms and slapping backs. He had been around so he was opinionated, but he was nevertheless open-minded and listened. Toward the end of Joe's fifth week, he invited Joe out to dinner. "We need to have a real heart-to-heart. I want to get to know you better. We're going to be all over each other, and you gotta know where I'm coming from. Like Ben Franklin said, we gotta hang together or we'll all hang separately."

Mickey took him to Smith & Wollensky on Third Avenue. As they entered the bedlam of the fashionable steak house, he tipped the captain and asked for a booth.

"This place is so noisy that we'll have complete privacy," Cohen told him as they sat down. "But the food's great. The joint is famous for its red meat, but I always get the sea bass, which is even better. That okay with you?" Joe nodded.

Mickey ordered two sea bass plates with side orders of sautéed spinach and home fries, plus a bottle of Russian River chardonnay.

When the wine came, Cohen said, "First, let me tell you about me and how messed up I am. I know you're an all-American half-black guy from nowhere, and I think it's great. But I want you to understand me."

He paused and took a deep breath. "My parents sent me away to Deerfield when I was thirteen, and some of the boys in my dorm beat on me because I was Jewish, fat, and uncoordinated. The girls, particularly the homely ones, felt sorry for me and liked me because I was smart. They were my friends. I like women." He then went on to tell Joe that after Brown and the Harvard Business School, he had not found a real home in the investment business. "I've had more horses shot out from under me than the Lone Ranger," he ruefully told Joe.

After business school, he had been hired as an analyst by the prestigious but hierarchical Magnum Capital firm, which managed large institutional and mutual fund portfolios. Magnum Capital employed a team approach in running its huge amount of assets. All of its portfolios were run by six to seven portfolio managers and analysts with different areas of expertise, each of whom had his own segment over which he had complete discretion. This ensured diversification, and equally important, guarded against hot and cold spells from individual managers. It also partially eliminated the risk of individual stars rising who then could hold the firm hostage. Segment performance was kept track of, but *the team* and *the firm* rather than *the individual* were the overriding values of the firm.

Mickey had done well as an analyst at Magnum. After eight years, he had been given a segment to run. He got itchy as time went on, though, and realized that he didn't really fit in to the very collegial atmosphere of the firm.

"Working at Magnum was like living in a benign, egalitarian, state," he said. "It was okay, but it was socialist. You got stock in the firm, but in order to get rich you had to stay forever. I want to get rich now, not when I'm sixty-five years old."

Also, Magnum had a profound growth stock bias, whereas Mickey believed very strongly in a deep value approach.

"They had a different religion from me," Mickey told Joe. "Magnum was and is a growth stock house. Their portfolios were stuffed with growth stocks, and they really had no interest in buying value much less my kind of deep value with hair and dirt all over it. I would continually argue with the head guys that it was nuts to be so one-way, particularly since all the data shows that value beats growth in the long and intermediate run, but they're growth-stock fanatics."

In 1995, Mickey left Magnum to join a small two-man firm that had been rapidly growing assets. Their style, like his, was deep value. Unfortunately, over the next two years, growth stocks had one of the great performance spasms of all time and value languished; it "stunk to high heaven," as Mickey put it. "We were a pure value shop, didn't own a single tech or Internet stock name, despised them as either outrageously overvalued or as frauds, when everyone was nuts over them. We never had a chance. We were out of business before we knew it."

"I was crushed," Mickey told him. "So then I brilliantly stepped right back into even deeper shit. There was this guy who I had known at Magnum. He was their great health care analyst, and he had left three years before me. He was clearly smart but a very intense and compulsive guy. He ran very concentrated portfolios. After he left Magnum, he started a hedge fund named Copperfield, which specialized in pharma, biotech, and managed care. Since its inception, it had shot the lights out and was up to two billion dollars. He hired me because he thought the growth mania was getting silly and wanted to diversify by starting a value-oriented fund. By this time I was desperate, so I signed on with him even though he made me nervous.

"The first year I was there, the firm totally blew up. Turns out the guy was a control freak and wouldn't let me buy or sell anything for my portfolio without his specific approval. Then in June, his two biggest short positions were total disasters—one-product companies with no earnings that were acquired at gigantic premiums. His major long position was Merck, which went from eighty-eight to forty-three; the other big one was Pfizer, which also got crushed. Copperfield was down fifteen percent for the year in a roaring bull market, and as you would expect, the clients bailed in one great tsunami of redemptions. In a flash, assets were down to three hundred million, there was all kinds of overhead, and the high-water mark was somewhere up in the sky. Basically, he was out of business, and I was out of a job."

Ravine knew Mickey from the temple, and had followed his misadventures. Mickey wasn't into the big-time Jewish and Israel stuff, but Ravine liked him as a kindred investment spirit. He hired Mickey with the understanding that he would be given a small fund, one assistant, and full access to Bridgestone's resources. Ravine made it clear it was strictly on a trial basis; it was an opportunity to battle-test his value theories.

But remember, it was early 2000, and the great speculative technology and big capitalization growth stock bubble was still in full force. The technology and Internet stocks stumbled briefly in the first couple of weeks of the new year, and then soared again. Stock picking, said most of the hot portfolio managers at the daily meeting, was all about growth and momentum; few cared about valuations, much less value investing. A few even openly mocked Mickey.

As they sat at dinner Cohen bared his investment soul to Joe.

"I can't fuck up this one," Mickey told him. "I've already swung twice and missed. One more whiff and it's three strikes and I'm out of the business—unemployable. I can't afford it. Ravine likes me, but I'm not Spokane's kind of guy. Things aren't great between them and this place is full of factions and jealousy and politics." He sighed. "The firm has had two mediocre-to-lousy years back to back, and there's finger-pointing and back-biting. Few do grudges as well as hedge fund guys. But in this business, performance is everything. They're going to give me some money, and if we can deliver, we'll be fine."

"So here's what were gonna do, pal. Ravine told me that the head guy at Grant gave you rave reviews and told him chapter and verse on your picks. And I, personally, have seen you in action, defending your value orientation at the Parton meeting. And you did great work on AOL. I need you! It's going to be like we're investment married. We swim or sink together."

Joe nodded. He didn't necessarily feel great about swimming or sinking or hanging with this guy he barely knew.

Mickey went on. "But Joe, believe me! Being a good stock picker is not enough. For years, I've been developing and refining a long-short program that will screen the universe of the two thousand biggest U.S. stocks. It compares each stock to three different constituencies: all stocks in the universe, those within the same sector, and finally those with the same capital deployment and earnings quality characteristics. The unbiased output is an expected return for each stock.

"I've also included a factor to identify changes in price momentum. It's the ultimate refinement that no one else has. Like I said before, we're not going to act until the price momentum of a stock reverses, telling us that the market is starting to smell change. We don't want to own inexpensive stocks where nothing is happening . . . no matter how cheap. Positions like that become value traps. What we want are inexpensive stocks in the most attractive value quintile where the fundamentals have begun to improve and price momentum is turning, but the analysts and the consensus remain skeptical.

"Nor we do want to short growth stocks—no matter how wildly expensive they are—whose prices are still soaring. Trying to call tops in sky-rockets, in blow-offs, is a game for fools and egotists. My failure models are designed to spot expensive stocks whose price momentum is diminishing and are poised to underperform the market."

He leaned back in his chair. "There's one more thing. Our four basic building blocks—valuation, market reaction, capital deployment, and earnings—are not similarly correlated across market cycles. We have to assign changing weights to them, depending on the market environment. Right now, valuation should be the most heavily weighted component at just under forty-three percent, which suggests that valuation discrepancies are extreme at this point."

Mickey looked at Joe quizzically. "You following me?"

"Yeah," said Joe. "I'm a rookie, and I'm certainly no computer whiz or quant jockey, but I am totally convinced value investing is the way to go. Still, what you say about being more than just a pure value model and avoiding value traps makes sense. At Grant, they developed quant models that screened for pure value alone and they didn't work."

Mickey nodded. "Yeah, you've got to combine value with momentum and give at least a passing nod to fundamentals."

"Sometimes it seems as though these quant models only work for a short time until other quants figure them out or the market mood changes," Joe said.

"In the back tests that I've run," Mickey went on, ignoring the implied question, "covering the last twenty years, the stocks identified by the program in the top and bottom quintiles beat the benchmark by about nine percent over one year, seventeen percent over two, and twenty-five percent over three. In the past five years the annual alpha of the top quintile was seven percent and the deficit of the bottom was six percent."

As the waiter placed the white fish and fresh spinach down on the pristine tablecloth, Mickey continued talking as if he didn't even notice that his food had arrived.

"We'll use a lot of leverage, maybe four or five times our equity, and most of the time run a moderate net long position. I mean, if our investors' equity is a billion dollars, we go long two point three billion in cheap stocks whose prices are perking up and we are short one point nine billion of expensive shit that is not just expensive but is rolling over. Our net long therefore is only four hundred million on our equity of a billion, so we're forty percent net long. We listen to the market, and if we get really bearish, we reduce the net long to ten percent, but basically we're going to make money because our longs are going up and our shorts are going down. We'll have low market risk and volatility, and we'll commit to our clients that we won't ever deviate from it. If our volatility as measured by our value-at-risk ratio [VAR] starts to increase, we'll pare back the size of our gross book. In effect, we're offering returns five, maybe six hundred, basis points better than the market, and suggesting that though some years may be better than others, we shouldn't ever have a down year.

"I've back-tested the whole model until I was blue in the face and it works like a charm. The consultants and the funds of hedge funds will love it because of its low risk and value quant orientation. Being part of Bridgestone gives us respectability and credibility, and if we perform, we could get a load of money. But let's not fool ourselves. Above all, we have to stick to our model and put up numbers for the first couple of years."

"Sounds good!" Joe said. "But what's my role going to be?"

Mickey impulsively reached out across the table and grabbed Joe's arm and squeezed. "You're going to be my partner, dude. You're going to be involved in the portfolio and digging into the analytics. If a position or a sector starts acting weird, you're going to find out what's going on. It's a quant thing we're doing but there's judgment too. You're going to cover me and I'm going to cover you!"

Joe grinned. He couldn't imagine anything better! And that *cover me* stuff was what Emily had said to him way back when. "Hey," he said. "I'm just a rookie, but I love it. I'll bust my ass!"

"Joe," Mickey said. "Let me tell you something enormous, gigantic! Reversion to the mean is the most powerful trend in our business. Excesses always get corrected—eventually. Michael Goldstein at Empirical Research is one smart guy. He maintains that driven by this insane Internet and technology mania, valuation spreads of growth over value have never, ever, been this extreme in modern times. Not even in the 1950s madness or the early 1970s during the small-cap growth and then the Nifty-Fifty bubble."

Mickey then reached into his briefcase and handed a piece of printing paper to Joe. He said, "Take a look at this relative performance chart I printed out" (see Figure 7.1).

Joe stared at the chart. It was stunning. He was right! There had never been anything like this growth stock madness as long-lasting or as big as this growth bubble. Mickey was passionate. It wasn't just the wine and his usual ebullience, Joe thought, he really believes his own bullshit.

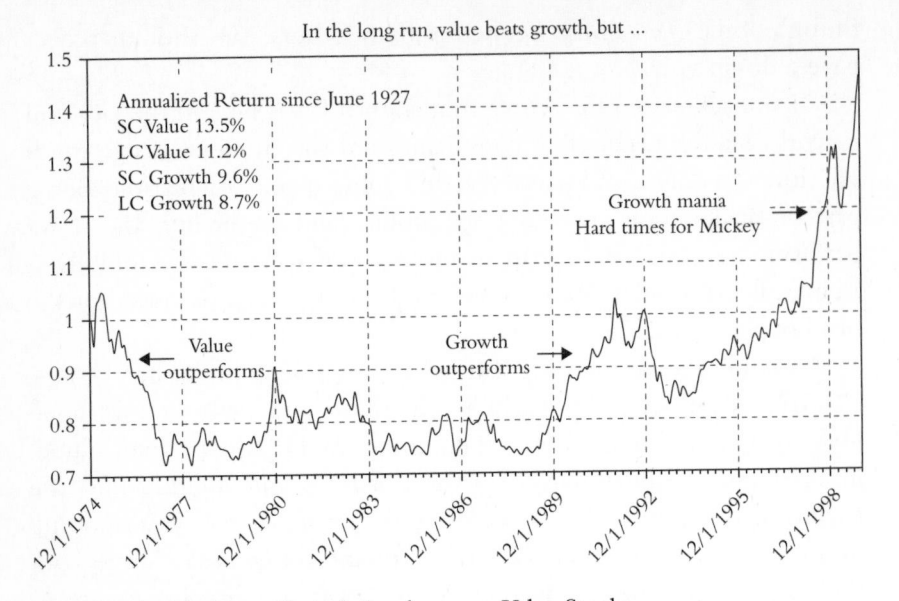

In the long run, value beats growth, but ...

Figure 7.1 Madness: Growth Stocks versus Value Stocks

"Furthermore," Mickey continued, "although you wouldn't know it from this chart, value beats growth big in the long run. This is my shtick so I know the numbers. Since 1927, large-cap value has had an annual return of eleven and a quarter percent and large cap growth of eight point seven percent. Small cap value has done even better— thirteen and a half percent a year. Large-cap value has returned two hundred and fifty basis points *a year* more than large-cap growth. This is an enormous differential when compounded over a decade, much less half a century. Why would any right-minded investor buy and hold growth stocks?

Before Joe could even answer the question, Mickey excitedly continued. "It's a golden moment. The exciting thing is that it looks as though the tide has begun to turn and spreads are beginning to close. The trend is our friend. We don't have to be early; we just have to be there and be awake. The gains in alpha over the market will be fucking stupendous for seven quarters if history is any guide. And guess what, pal, history is the best Sherpa!"

Joe responded, "So what you're telling me is that with your algorithm we're going to be geek shitheads with a whiff o' momentum."

Mickey stared at him. "Geek *momentum* shitheads! You're right, Joe. I hadn't thought of it that way but that's what we're going to be."

"Why does Buffett say, 'Beware of geeks bearing formulas'?"

"Because he doesn't understand the analytical power of computers, and besides, he's an old-time guy. He disdains geeks as black-box guys and says black boxes never worked in the past. [A *black box* is investment lingo for a computerized model–driven investment program.] That was just one of his smart-ass one liners."

Mickey abruptly changed the subject. "One last thing, Joe. We've got to be pure. The really pure, good hedge funds put in their Articles of Agreement that the managing partners will reinvest eighty percent of their earnings in the fund and that they—and their immediate families—won't own individual equities in their own accounts. It's to make sure there's no distractions for the managers and that there can't be a conflict of interest. Is all that okay with you?"

"Hey," replied Joe. "Of course it is. I haven't got any money to begin with. I like the idea of putting most of what we make back into our own fund."

After they walked out of the restaurant onto Third Avenue, Mickey hugged Joe and pounded him on the back. Somehow Joe sensed that everything he had laid out was true, was right. Joe went home throbbing with excitement, but when Emily asked him what had happened at the dinner, he was tongue-tied.

"Tell me!" she pressed him.

"It's such a long, complex story," he said. "I can't explain it, but it's going to work. You wouldn't understand. It's like the waning of the moon and the ebb of the tides."

"You've got to tell me. It sounds mysterious and mythical, like poetry. I want to know."

It had been a long day and an even longer dinner. Joe had drunk almost a bottle of good Russian River chardonnay. He was tired. He simply couldn't summon the intellectual energy to go through the whole thing with her. He sighed.

"Sweetheart, I'm exhausted. I'll tell you in the morning. Let's go to bed."

"Wake me up before you go," she said. "I want to understand what you're doing, and I've got to go to a dinner at the Council tomorrow night."

At six the next morning when he got up and showered, Emily was still peacefully sleeping. Joe was loath to disturb her and besides, what was the use of explaining such complicated things to her anyway? She wasn't going to get it.

Chapter 8

Revenge of
the Geeks

Two days later, Mickey Cohen was scheduled to meet with Ravine and Spokane. He told Joe, "Hey pal, you're coming with me to see the big guys. We're a team."

Joe was flattered. This was the opportunity he had always wanted.

Ravine's assistant called and told them to come on over.

When they entered the conference room, Ravine smiled wanly at Mickey and stared at Joe from his bottomless eyes.

"Spokane can't make it," Ravine said. "Wanted to reschedule until tomorrow but couldn't. Tell me in five minutes what you have."

In a detailed paper, Mickey had outlined their model and its rationale and had given it to Ravine's assistant yesterday for his review. Ravine obviously had studied the paper and understood the thesis. He asked Mickey to synopsize it in his own words and now he listened intently. When Mickey was finished, Ravine said, with just the faintest hint of cynicism, "Ah, a *black box* with a couple of bright, shiny, new formula ribbons hung on it. Sounds plausible. Of course, they always do. That doesn't mean it will work, but we need some new products."

"It *will* work!" Mickey told him enthusiastically. "We've back-tested our model every which way under every conceivable situation. In a negative value versus growth environment it may produce less alpha, but negative alpha is virtually inconceivable because of the number of names and the momentum and fundamental adjustments."

"So you have found a new computer-driven formula that has unlocked the secret soul of the market. Sounds good," Ravine said reflectively. "Maybe too good to be true."

He shook his head and continued, "It will work until it doesn't work. We'll give you one hundred fifty million. A hundred million is the firm's money. The other fifty is from clients who have given us discretion. If you get down more than ten percent, I've got to shut you down. When we were on top of the world, I would have made it twenty percent, but we're licking our wounds. Another hit this year, even a flesh wound, could really cause a hemorrhage."

"How do we get paid?"

"You each get a draw of four hundred thousand. The firm keeps the two percent fixed fee on the fund and pays your expenses. You get ten percent of the carry. This first stub year we'll waive the formula."

"How much time we got?" Mickey asked.

"Two years to raise another four hundred million."

"Fair enough," said Mickey.

"You can christen your fund Bridgestone Alpha. Internally, we'll call it BA."

"Thanks for everything," Mickey said, rising.

"Two things before you go," said Ravine. "Your start-up year is crucial. Don't bet the ranch. Watch your VAR [value at risk]. Remember that to finish first, first you have to finish."

"We know. The first year for new hedge funds is live or die. We're going to tell potential clients we absolutely will not violate our VAR target. If we even get close, we're going to reduce exposures and positions."

Ravine nodded. "Second, aren't you in your quant arrogance assuming that the long period of growth beating value is about over? Aren't you trying to time a huge secular bottom in value and top in growth?"

"Sure," said Mickey. As he waved papers in the air, he continued, "but this time the stars are aligned. I got the charts here that show that growth stocks have never been this extended both in momentum and valuation compared to value. This is a seven- or eight-standard-deviation event bottom."

"Yeah, yeah, yeah," said Ravine. "I've heard that before. People that go around picking bottoms usually end up with smelly fingers." Then he murmured. "May Yahweh watch over and keep you."

Mickey ran his models again, and they poured over the reams of output. Ever since he played *Running Back,* Joe had loved the purity of manipulating and analyzing numbers—be they baseball batting averages, football statistics, or stock valuations—and searching for the hidden messages in them. Now it became a magnificent obsession. The computer could unlock what was happening deep within that great churning mass that was the stock market and find the best stocks to own and to sell short. If Renaissance could find a magic formula, why couldn't they?

With almost a religious intensity, they stuck to their basic model: Buy and hold cheap stocks whose fundamentals and price momentum were improving and be short the opposite. They had to be sure that their buys had solid balance sheets, strong free cash flow, low leverage, and, hopefully, upward earnings revisions. Since it seemed they were approaching a change in the market weather and maybe a bear market, they would maintain a low net long position but be sensitive to potential opportunities. In addition to dissecting the data, it was Joe's job to check out the fundamentals of the companies that were showing up on their screens either as longs or shorts. Analyst controversy and a large dispersion between earnings estimates had to be investigated. He did this by calling and intensely questioning the relevant industry specialists at brokerage firms and by using Bridgestone's own analysts and extensive research library. In some cases he called the companies themselves.

It was hard, time-consuming work, because there were 150 stocks in their long and short portfolio, with some positions being substantially bigger than others. However, as he got into it, he learned how to use Bridgestone's immense power. As one of the 10 largest sources of business for brokers, he had access to every analyst on the Street simply because he was calling from Bridgestone. Furthermore, he got involved and took an active interest in Bridgestone's somewhat casual order allocation system, and he and Mickey made sure their primary sources got paid quickly and lucratively. Joe would send a trusted analyst a list of stocks (in the sector he or she covered) that he was interested in. Then, the analyst was asked to initiate calls to him *first* when the fundamentals changed. The unspoken implication of contacting him first was that information would come to him before the analyst told his sales force or other clients who could move the market. Joe knew, from what Doug Scott had told him at Grant, that the analysts often tipped (wittingly or unwittingly) their own prop traders first. In any case, analyst responsiveness was immediately rewarded with business.

As time passed, Mickey and Joe found 14 traits that distinguished losing stocks that could be counted on to underperform compared to the market. These characteristics changed from month to month, but weakness in fundamentals, a wide dispersion of analyst earnings estimates indicating uncertainty, low gross cash flow yields, and high price-to-earnings ratios were the strongest signals. Although their intensity varied from month to month, they tended to persist throughout the bear market.

These same indicators worked best in identifying stocks to own, but high capital spending and strong balance sheet growth were traits that enriched results as well. Both on the long and short side, rapid share turnover and an idiosyncratic trading pattern raised the odds that something was happening. Price momentum and volume were important signals.

For Mickey and Joe, collecting and analyzing all this information was a massive organizational task.

"There's no use having all these data if we don't have the time left to understand it and identify the opportunities," Mickey said. "We have to be investors, not just quants."

"Yeah," said Joe, "what we really need are a couple of quant analysts to collect the stuff and run the models."

"Well, we ain't going to get them from Bridgestone until we put up some good numbers and get some assets. This place is leaking assets and the two big guys are at each other's throats."

This worried Joe. "Are you concerned it's going to fall apart?"

"Not really. The asset base is so big it can absorb more redemptions, and Ravine and Spokane have always had a love-hate relationship."

In the third week of February 2000 they made a presentation in the Yale Bowl after the morning meeting. About half of the other invest-ment managers and analysts stuck around, and all of the client service and marketing people were there in the cheap seats. The idea was that maybe some of the marketing people could come up with some more money for them.

Mickey believed in extemporaneous presentations, but Joe thought he seemed nervous and said *you know* a lot. Joe had repeatedly rehearsed his relatively brief part of the presentation, and Mickey deferred to him on several of the questions that followed. To Joe, the audience seemed to listen with a jaundiced ear. Skepticism oozed. The buzz that Joe heard at the café was that people were turned off by Mickey's less-than-sparkling record and wondered how a value investor was going to fare in a growth stock market.

By the end of February, they were ready to launch. Mickey and Joe took down their $150 million of captive firm capital and put it to work as of March 1. Their initial portfolio was 110 stocks with $350 million long and $320 million short for a net long of $30 million, or 20 percent of their equity. The performance clock was now running on Bridgestone Alpha, otherwise known as BA.

Joe and Mickey were scared to death. As Mickey had pointed out at their dinner at Smith & Wollensky, at no time in market history had growth and low-quality speculative stocks been so grossly overextended on all conventional valuation measures compared to value. It was like a four-standard-deviation event. Theoretically, their portfolio fairly bristled with alpha on both the long and short side. However, the animal spirits, the "mo" of the market, was as powerfully toward growth and away from value as their models had ever recorded. They had begun running a model portfolio as of the beginning of the year, and it was down 2 percent in January and 4 percent in February. At that rate, unless the headwinds of momentum changed, they would be closed down by Ravine's 10 percent edict in three to four months.

They had vowed in blood to stick to their strategy, but to mitigate the risk they initially chose to run a very low, 20 percent net long. To their horror, in their first week of existence, the initial week of March, the NASDAQ Index surged 3 percent and they lost 2 percent as their shorts soared and their longs went sideways.

That weekend Emily had to attend a Council retreat in the Catskills. With the market going against them, Joe spent a weekend of despair and agony, much of it at the office checking their analytics. When Emily returned Sunday afternoon she sensed his depression and insisted they walk to Broadway and find a movie. They went afterward to a simple restaurant, The Pig and Whistle on 45th Street, for dinner and tried to talk. Emily found herself searching for things to say and ended up telling him about the issues raised at the retreat, which to Joe were hardly the stuff of fascination, much less distraction. It was not a fun or satisfactory evening.

When they got back to the apartment, Emily took his hand.

"I'm going to take a shower and then let's lie down."

He barely smiled. When she came out of the bathroom, he was on the phone with the night trader at Bridgestone. Then he called Mickey and they talked for a long time about whether to reduce their net long further. When he hung up the phone he looked at her.

"I'm sorry, Emily, but I'm just not in the mood. I'm so distracted. And I'm tired and discouraged. I can't stop waking up at two in the morning. It's like I've got an insomnia factory inside me."

She sighed and turned out the light.

As he lay there in the darkness he thought about his life. He'd gone from obsessing about Emily's sneakers and insomnia about the future of their relationship to obsessing about the portfolio. He thought to himself, *I'm so consumed with the anxiety of work that I can't make love to the woman I love. What's happened to my life and to me? Am I completely screwed up?*

The following Monday, for no discernible reason the NASDAQ Index plummeted for five trading days only to rally again, climbing to just short of its previous high. (That turned out eventually to be its last gasp.) In the last week of the month, the tech and Internet stocks fell precipitously. For the month of March, Mickey and Joe's portfolio gained 4 percent, with their longs up 0.5 percent and their shorts up 3.5 percent. The violence of the market's gyrations and the huge moves in their stocks had begun to take its toll. Mickey's back was giving him wrenching pain, and Joe had a very queasy stomach and a bad case of diarrhea.

"This always happens to me when the serious heat is on," Mickey told him. "Don't worry about it. All our aches and pains will go away if our stocks start behaving."

In early April, their ailments miraculously cured as markets collapsed in a wave of manic selling (see Figure 8.1). After the markets closed on Wednesday, April 3, Mickey stormed into Joe's office. "Fucking unbelievable!" he shouted. "We've made six percent in three days! I've never seen anything like it. We're up ten percent."

Joe was speechless. Even after winning a big football game, he had never felt such elation. Mickey babbled on, "Dude, we've found our yellow brick road! Like the Munchkins said, 'Follow the yellow brick road' and you'll eventually get to Oz."

"Yeah, but the Wicked Witch of the West is still out there looking to do us harm, and she has powerful magic."

"But we got the ruby slippers."

He called Emily at the Council and told her he was taking her out to dinner to celebrate. He asked her to meet him at The Four Seasons restaurant on 52nd Street. Joe had been there once for lunch and he had been overwhelmed with the ambiance, the space between the tables, the service, and the food. He knew it would be wildly expensive, but they had something to celebrate.

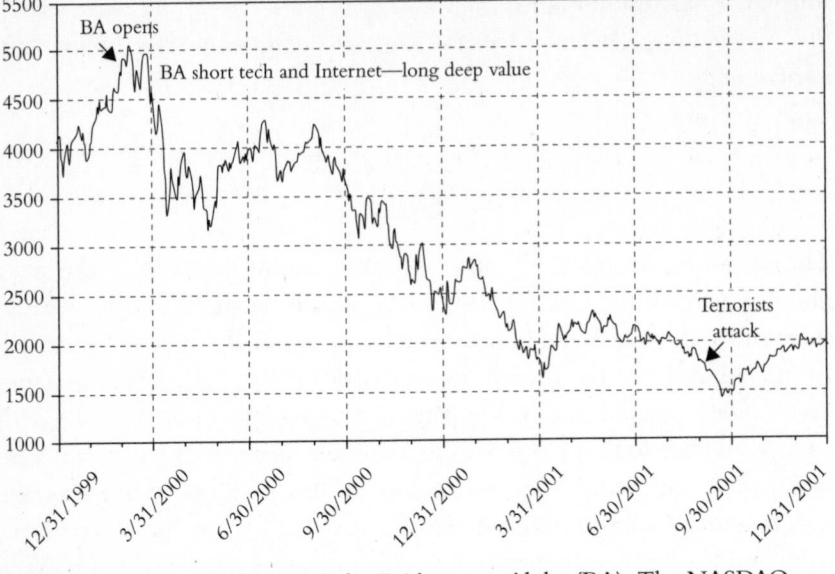

Figure 8.1 Two Golden Years for Bridgestone Alpha (BA): The NASDAQ Index—Sick unto Death

Emily looked wonderful when he met her at the entrance to the Four Seasons. Her hazel eyes were shining, and her clean, dark looks had never been more appealing to him. When they sat down at their table overlooking the fountain, he took her hand and murmured "I love you."

"I love you, too," she said. "Now tell me what we're celebrating."

"First, let's order something to drink. I'm in a spending mood."

He ordered her a glass of champagne, the Tattinger, which he knew she liked, and he asked for a bottle of Far Niente chardonnay. The price was appalling.

As they waited for their drinks, she said, "You're a changed person in the last few days. Suddenly, you're so happy. Now tell me what happened so I can understand."

"We got it right!" he said jubilantly. "The model is working. We're going to survive—and maybe even prosper."

"How did you do it? I still don't really get what it is that you're doing."

He began to explain the model. Before he knew it he was talking so fast and with such complexity that he could see he had lost her. Abruptly, he paused.

She looked at him quizzically.

"It almost sounds as though you and Mickey are gambling, betting your jobs, your lives, on the market changing its spots. It all sounds so dangerous. Like a war, a battle."

"Yeah," he said as he sipped his chardonnay, "you're right. We are gambling. It is a battle—Mickey and me against everybody else. It's like building a sand castle on a beach with big surf. You know the tide has been coming in for a long time and that it is about to crest, and when it does it will go out for a long time. We're betting that the high tide of tech has peaked and that we've built our sandcastle in the right place and the other guys haven't."

"Not exactly a consoling and comforting image."

"I explained it wrong. It's much more scientific than that. The quantitative model tells us where to build the sandcastle just as the tide tables tell you when high tide will occur."

"But Joe, the battle, the uncertainty about the tide—it has made you sick. Your business has separated us. I don't see you much anymore. You're obsessed."

"I know. I'm sorry."

"Will it get better now? Will there be less stress? Will we have a life together again?"

Joe grimaced. Somehow, this celebratory dinner was not going the way he planned. "I hope so, sweetheart. I hope so. But we, Mickey and I, are not out of the woods yet."

In an effort to appeal to Joe's love of literature, Emily responded, "You know what Robert Frost wrote: 'The woods are lovely, dark, and deep. But I have promises to keep and miles to go before I sleep.' I have a feeling that's where you are. You love being in the woods. You love having miles to go before you sleep."

But the metaphor was lost on him, "Who knows?" he said. "All I know right now is that we're winning. Now let's order some food."

Of course they didn't know it at the time, but the summit of Mount NASDAQ had been reached. At the same time the S&P 500 Index was entering what would turn out to be a brutal *secular*, not *cyclical*, bear market that saw the index fall from 1,540 in mid-2000 to a low of 775 by the fall of 2002. There was a steep break after the World Trade Center tragedy, a year-end rally, and then another even more severe fall in 2002.

Joe and Mickey had built their sandcastle in the right place at the right time.

BA was prospering. The fund's short portfolio of ridiculously high-priced Internet stocks and the so-called New Nifty Fifty group of big capitalization, high-quality growth stocks that had done so well and whose valuations were so inflated was now under panic liquidation as the hot money, terrified by the carnage, fled. Moreover, the broad market of relatively cheap industrial value stocks, which had missed all the previous speculative fun, was drifting sideways to up. BA owned the best and the brightest of these beleaguered beasts. Market momentum was violently turning toward value and brutally away from growth. For Mickey and Joe, it was the perfect environment for their strategy as long as they faithfully worked and executed their algorithm.

The conventional wisdom that most investors stubbornly clung to, however, was that the weakness in the old leadership was only temporary and that it was a buying opportunity. As a result, there were periodic, violent countertrend rallies. The American and European economies now were beginning to slow, and the advocates of growth adamantly maintained that it was insane to buy shares of ugly, dirty, cyclical companies and be short growth stocks in such a deteriorating economic environment.

As the overall market suffered in April and May, BA posted returns of 5 percent and 3 percent as its technology and Internet growth stock shorts went down substantially faster than its deep value longs. June, July, and August saw the markets churn back and forth. BA made money in June and July but then lost 1.5 percent in August. They were now up 14 percent since inception and their net long had risen to 35 percent.

"It could have been a lot worse," Mickey told Joe, punching him lightly on the arm. Nevertheless, they sweated out every position every day. They were determined not to trade their basic positions and to stick with their disciplines of valuation, momentum, and fundamentals. They acted to reduce the size of a short position only if the price abruptly broke 20 percent or more without any new incremental fundamental deterioration. The same applied to their long positions.

Joe was frantically busy throughout this period checking the fundamentals when any one of their stocks, long or short, misbehaved. He consequently spent long hours in the office. When he wasn't in the office, he was compulsively fixated on his BlackBerry. He was checking it day and night for e-mails.

"I hate that damn Blueberry thing!" an exasperated Emily said to him at one of their rare meals together. "It's ruining our life together. You have to turn it off. Otherwise, I refuse to sit here with you."

"I know it's an obsession," he told her. "But the market never sleeps."

"I don't care. I deserve your undivided attention once in a while."

"But it's life or death."

"If that's the total case, then make love to your fucking algorithm and sleep hugging your BlackBerry!"

"Come on, Emily."

"I'm serious. You give me all this crap about I'm your soul mate when your real soul mate is your portfolio." She continued, "I gave up my relationship with my mother and my trust fund for you, and you can't even spend one minute away from your damn portfolio or BlackBerry."

Emily subsequently calmed down, but now it was seldom that the two of them had dinner together during the week. There were days when she was in bed asleep by the time he got home in the evening and barely awake when he rolled groggily out of bed at 5:30 in the morning. But it was all worth it—well, at least for Joe. Although their performance that summer kept them humble, BA's strategy was working. In late July, Joe and Emily went away for nine days to Fisher Island off the coast of Miami. They needed some time together and had bought a cheap package deal.

They read books, played some tennis in the early mornings when it was a little cool, and swam in the ocean. The second day there, Joe asked Emily if she wanted to play golf. He knew she had played growing up in Greenwich, and he was pleased when she agreed. They rented clubs and went to the sweltering driving range. Then they got a cart and played 18 holes on the empty Fisher Island course, not even pretending to keep score. The heat was intense and sweat poured off them, but they thoroughly enjoyed themselves. Joe marveled at Emily's easy, graceful swing and natural athletic ability; while Emily was astounded at how good he was. The muscle memory from all those years of playing with his father was still there.

"If Daddy knew about this, he'd have you signed up for the Member Guest no matter what Mom would say," she teased. During their vacation, they played every day, with him giving her a stroke a hole. They returned to New York rejuvenated, but Emily still harbored a nagging worry about the intensity of his job.

One morning, in the third week of August, Joe went to Mickey's office, closed the door, and said, "Although the economy still looks good on the surface, the company calls I listen to and the analysts are telling me that something bad is beginning to happen out there. We could be on the brink of a recession. If so, the earnings for tech and for the rest of the market are going to be very disappointing for a while. Investors aren't ready for it and valuations are still way too high. The leadership groups of the past couple of years, tech, the Internet shit, and the big cap New Nifty Fifty are losing price momentum. What do you think about reducing our net long to plus ten or even zero and relying completely on alpha?"

"Yeah," Mickey replied, "but the technicians are saying the market is oversold and a lot of smart guys are very bullish here. They argue this correction is about over."

"I think they're missing it. Price momentum has switched from growth to value and the junk Internet stuff is collapsing. The IPO market has dried up."

"So we stay where we are. Forty percent net long."

"If the U.S. and the world are on the brink of a recession, earnings are going to be disappointing for the rest of the market as well. We could see a real serious bear market in everything."

Mickey shook his head doubtfully. "We've had a great start and I would hate to blow it by getting caught with no net long if the markets did rally."

They chewed on it some more, but Joe was passionate and insistent. He argued that when an entire asset class goes to wild excess, the history of markets is that a break in the weakest link in the chain often deals a decisive blow to the whole system and even the entire economy. He explained, "The bubble analogy works here. When the thinnest part of the membrane bursts, the gas gushes out and a little later the whole balloon collapses. The bursting of the tech and dot-com bubble would undermine the U.S. economy and the entire stock market!"

Although not entirely convinced, Mickey agreed and they reduced their net long to 10 percent of their equity. Markets fell steeply in September, and BA made another 4 percent for the month.

But manias die slowly. Many sophisticated investors and most of the unwashed investment public still believed in the dot-com mania and that the stocks were just experiencing what one market guru described as a "healthy correction." After all, weren't they using their PCs and the Internet more every day?

Joe knew David Dawes agreed with him on the tech bubble and was still very underweight tech in Grant's institutional portfolios. Thus, in early September, he was shocked to learn that Grant was gearing up to sell what was being advertised as the largest new tech fund offering in history. The fund would be managed by a guy who had been a brash, somewhat uncouth, young analyst when Joe was at the firm.

Joe called Dawes and said, "David, what's going on? I thought you were bearish on tech. What am I missing?"

"Nothing! I am bearish. The bust has just begun, but our retail brokerage system says there's a ton of a demand out there for a tech fund. They don't care what I think. It will be a big payday for them. Lambs to the slaughter."

"Who's going to run the money?"

"We are. We have a boy genius who has no fear and who the brokers love."

Joe just shook his head. "I'm sorry," he said. "I feel bad for the poor guy. A couple of years from now the buyers of this fund are going to crucify him." As it turned out, Joe was right. In the months and years that followed the offering, the value of the Grant tech fund plummeted, and its unfortunate manager was deluged with hate e-mails and even threatening phone calls. The poor guy took it personally and developed an uncontrollable twitch.

Mickey and Joe kept worrying about their exposure. They could still identify plenty of expensive stocks that were losing momentum and where the fundamentals were deteriorating—but that wasn't the problem. The problem was that it was becoming more difficult to find stocks to buy whose sales and earnings weren't suddenly falling out of bed. The underlying companies were cheap on value metrics—such as intrinsic value, free cash flow, and price to sales—and their price momentum was turning up, but they wondered if the stocks were going to go up if their earnings were way below current expectations.

Joe argued no.

"I think we ought to go net short," Joe argued. "Guys are getting really discouraged and down. Maybe even a little scared. You should hear the talk in our café. There could be some serious regurgitation."

He continued, "It's market timing to some extent but if we're ever going to play that game, now is the time when we've got a big lead. As Druckenmiller likes to say, 'It takes courage to be a pig.'"

Mickey agreed and they went from 10 percent net long to 20 percent net short. Now with the firm's other more growth- and momentum-driven hedge funds struggling, Bridgestone's marketing group discovered BA as a hot new product to sell. Suddenly Mickey and Joe found themselves in front of prospective investors and being listened to with respect and interest. Their spiel worked. In spite of the general malaise, $350 million of new money came in on September 30.

Of course, not everything was peaches and cream and high fives. Being net short twisted their psyches. You were abruptly rooting for bad things to happen to the economy and the stock market. Joe still anguished over his individual positions. He knew he had to think of himself as just *renting* stocks, not owning them, but he had a soft spot for AIG. With his prior knowledge of Sun America and AIG, he had originally put the stock in their long portfolio with a rare double weighting. It qualified as value, it was certainly not tech, and it had positive momentum. The day BA started, he got lucky and bought the shares at 59. As the overall market struggled and tech got crushed, the price of AIG's stock rose steadily and hit 90 in late September (see Figure 8.2).

Joe was beginning to suffer from acrophobia. The price of AIG obviously was elevated, but the stock seemed reasonably valued compared to technology and other large capitalization growth stocks. AIG was a far more complex company than Sun America, was covered by 20 different analysts around the Street, and Joe had to rely on the official company guidance that prophesized continuing strong earnings. He called Scooter, who was still at Sun America. Scooter lugubriously bent his ear about the unfairness of his treatment by the Chargers but had no insights on AIG. He said the variable annuity business was still very strong, but Joe wondered how long it would be if the bear market continued.

Joe decided to hold on to the stock for a while longer. For one thing, its price momentum was still very strong. *It was possible*, he thought, *that the financial stocks would be the new leadership of the market now that the momentum has been drained from tech.* In late December, AIG surged over 100 and for the 11 months (ending on December 31) was

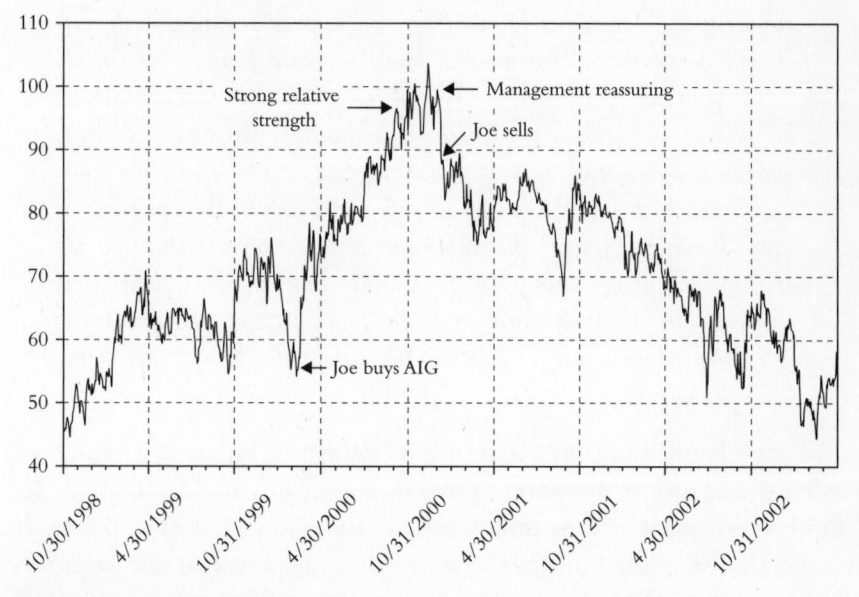

Figure 8.2 Narrow Escape: AIG
Note: On March 5, 2009 AIG sold at 7.

one of the three best longs in their portfolio. Then to Joe's horror, the price of AIG suddenly dropped over 20 points to 83 by January 12. As best as Joe could determine, the fundamentals were still excellent, as management had stated that guidance for earnings for the year would be on target, but the change in price momentum was a warning. Joe sold the position on January 20, getting an average price of 86. When the shares rallied to 90 over the next two weeks, he felt sheepish but then steep declines and bad news followed. He had dodged a heavy caliber bullet. Both Mickey and Joe were elated. Their model worked on the sell side as well.

"There's an old Japanese saying: 'Fallen blossoms do not return to trees; a broken mirror does not reflect again,'" Mickey intoned.

"What does that mean?" Joe asked.

"Busted stocks stay busted," Mickey replied.

In the years that followed, they used AIG as an example to describe their investment process to potential new investors. Their spiel went something like this:

> On our kickoff day, March 1, 2000, AIG, a company we knew well, a stock with sound fundamentals, cheap valuation, and good momentum, was added to our long portfolio as a major, high conviction position. Eleven months later, in early January of 2001, AIG's fundamentals were still good but with the stock up almost 50 percent from where we bought it, valuation was now extended, and price momentum was deteriorating fast. As a result, we made the decision to sell the position and realized an average price of 86. Obviously, it was disappointing to have missed the top tick of 103, but the position had been a big winner in a tough environment. In the long run, we avoided the collapse that followed. AIG has never again reached the heights of the year 2000 or the price that we sold it at.

They handed out the chart of AIG shown in Figure 8.2. The consultants and the smart young guys in suits from the funds of hedge funds loved the story. As time went on, their story got even better. In 2006, the SEC filed charges against AIG, alleging that the company had used sham transactions to inflate earnings. As a result, the stock collapsed even further. The BA model seemed the ideal—no, the perfect—combination of quant, technical, and intuitive investing.

Joe now attended the portfolio managers-only session that followed the morning meeting, and he relished the intense and sometimes acrimonious discussions that flourished, particularly when Ravine was not in attendance. Not surprisingly, especially in a competitive shop like Bridgestone, Mickey's and Joe's success inevitably engendered jealousy as the bear market continued and the performance and the assets of most of their colleagues diminished. There were snide comments, and sometimes tempers flared.

"How can you buy that deep value shit? How can you be proud to own it?" the growth stock guy Tom Leiter asked Mickey one morning. "I'd be ashamed to go to a client meeting and describe the businesses of those rusty, obsolete, old-world companies you own."

Mickey just smiled—a friendly, warm smile out of that jowly, fleshy, good-natured face. "Tom, the market's momentum has turned to value and away from growth and tech. I'm willing to bet this value orientation is going to last for a long while—maybe for years. It's not a question of being proud or ashamed."

"That's nuts. The Internet is a transforming, disruptive creation that's going to change the world forever. As an investor, you should want to participate in the growth of the new world, not be short of it."

"I agree," Mickey replied, "but we're talking about stocks—not companies or inventions. Stocks that are outrageously overpriced. You guys don't get it. Remember Hans Christian Andersen's famous children's fairy tale 'The Emperor's New Clothes'? The ending is not so happy. Eventually everyone in the crowd who was watching the emperor's parade was shaking their head and tittering, 'But he's got nothing on.'"

Mickey looked around the room. "Then even the emperor, deluded as he was by his courtiers, realized that he wasn't splendidly dressed—that he was naked. He thought to himself, 'I must not stop or I will spoil the procession.' So he marched on even more proudly and the courtiers continued to pretend to carry his invisible train. Soon everyone was laughing and the emperor was no longer the emperor. But the stock market is no fairy tale—there's no moral at the end of the story. The bottom line is that growth stocks are still priced for perpetual growth they can't possibly achieve. This mania is going to end terribly badly."

"Are you suggesting I'm like the asshole emperor in this investment fairy tale?" Leiter asked. "Actually, I do feel like I have no clothes on recently."

"Well," said Mickey calmly, "before this is over, either you or we are going to get stripped naked in public."

"You've been running around bare-ass naked for years, Cohen. You just didn't know it."

"I knew it all too well! Believe me, I knew it."

"Fuck you and your fairy tales," Leiter snarled with a wry smile that took some, but not all, of the sting out of the epithet. "We'll see next year whether you geek shitheads are just a flash in the toilet or not. As Bart said to Homer, 'It ain't over until the fat lady sings.'"

Mickey had had enough. "And as Homer replied, 'Is that NASDAQ lady fat enough for you, son?'"

After a feeble rally in the S&P 500 and NASDAQ in early October, both markets plunged again through the end of the year. Value was dramatically beating growth. BA had a huge quarter, gaining 12 percent and finishing the 10 months up 30.4 percent gross or 22.1 percent net after fees. Their relative performance radiated, because for the year the S&P 500 was down 9.10 percent, MSCI EAFE (the world ex the U.S.) was off 13.7 percent, and the NASDAQ fell 39.3 percent. Since BA started on March 1, the relevant declines in the popular averages were even more enormous. The NASDAQ, for example, was down 50 percent for their 10 months. For the full year, the average hedge fund after fees gained 4.1 percent. The composite of Bridgestone's other funds was down 4 percent—not awful, but hardly inspiring.

At year-end, Joe got a Bridgestone check that brought his compensation for the full year to $1.7 million. Mickey told him he was paid $3.5 million, which Joe did not think was unfair. After all, it was Mickey's algorithm, even though Joe figured he was an equally important factor in the risk management and stock-picking process. They figured Bridgestone had grossed about $40 million on their fund from the fixed fee and carry. The payout to them of just less than 13 percent seemed reasonable. After all, it was the firm that had seeded them, sponsored them with potential investors, and provided the infrastructure.

When Joe told Emily about his compensation, she was stunned. "My God!" she said, "That's amazing. Let's look for a better apartment and go out to dinner at fine restaurants."

He hugged her. "Not so fast on the apartment," he cautioned. "This is a very volatile business and we're not out of the woods yet, but it sure feels good to score. And we are going to upgrade our eating for sure. I'm sorry I've been such an obsessive geek."

She looked at him gravely. "I'm beginning to think that in your business it takes being an obsessive geek to score."

Chapter 9

Life Its Own Self

Joe and Emily agreed to spend the holidays apart. Emily went home at her father's very specific reconciliation request to be with the whole family in Greenwich, and Joe spent the long holiday weekend in Big Neck. They had agreed to meet in Palm Beach after Christmas.

His time in Big Neck was a little grim, and he couldn't help but contrast it to Emily's hectic social schedule of meeting old friends and rushing from one opulent cocktail party or dinner to another. Where had his life and human connections gone wrong, he wondered, but did he really wish he was with her, enduring her mother's relentless hostility and engaging in disjointed snatches of conversation with nameless people he would never see again? On the other hand, he did know the guys in the football group, and he would enjoy being with them. For sure, there would be other hedge fund guys at those parties. How come there were no holiday cocktail parties in Big Neck?

Joe spent Christmas Eve with Big Joe and his half-sisters. Big Joe looked good, but he was definitely the strong, silent type. Except for sports, Joe had very little to talk to him about. His half-sisters were loving and sweet but he had nothing in common with them. He spent Christmas Day with his mother. She basted a turkey while he watched football games. Her biggest worries were if he was eating well and when was he going to get married.

He walked down to Churchill's Bar & Grill after dinner, where the lively townies always went for a nightcap. The old, dilapidated tavern was crowded with a noisy mixture of what looked like high school guys and older men. One of the bartenders greeted him loudly, calling him by name, and he saw heads turn. He ordered a beer. Immediately a large, fat man about his age came up to him. Joe knew his face was very familiar but the total effect was somehow so different he couldn't connect it to a name.

"Joe, it's me, Tom Terry," the man said, and shook his hand warmly. "Remember me? I was your center the last two years. You must have put your hands on my ass four hundred times."

"Dude, of course I know you," said Joe, realizing that he hadn't immediately recognized Terry because his face and body had blown up like a balloon. Tom Terry now must weigh close to 300 pounds, whereas when Joe had known him seven years earlier he weighed maybe 190. The weight made him look older and had distorted his appearance into almost a caricature of his former self.

"You were All-State our senior year, Tom. You protected me real good all those games. You just look different, hoss," Joe replied, slipping back into the down-country Virginia patois.

"Yeah, I know," said Terry. "I'm as fat as a pig."

Other guys drifted over, but after a few reminiscences of old football games, the conversation waned. None of them even knew what a hedge fund was. Joe had another beer and eventually excused himself.

"Call me if you ever come to New York."

"Hey," said Terry. "Real good to see you, Joe! Sort of slow around here these days. All the guys with any gumption who went to school with us have moved on. Still, it's good living."

Joe had dinner the next night with Josh Gibson at McDonald's, which was the only open restaurant in town. Josh was as garrulous as ever. He told Joe he had calculated his investment returns from 1980 to 1999. The S&P 500 averaged, including dividends, almost 15 percent a year over that 20-year span. Despite his focus on investing, his return had been about 8 percent, or about half of that of the S&P.

Joe looked at him, genuinely surprised. "Why was that, Josh? You had some good stocks."

"Because I listened to that damn broker and their strategists and technicians and tried to time the market. I was always too bullish at the tops and got too bearish at the bottoms. Plus, those transaction costs burned up a lot of money, and the selling created capital gains on which I had to pay taxes. I should have just bought an index fund. No market timing, no transaction costs, minimal taxes, ten basis points a year of investment management fees. For a sucker like me, it's the way to go."

Joe was interested. "Yeah, the right way to look at it is your return after all costs, including taxes, but most people don't."

Josh then proceeded to query him intensely about BA. Joe pointed out to him that transaction costs were high because they traded a fair amount, and so far they had generated mostly short-term gains. He went through the fee calculations. Josh was obviously shocked by the size of the investment management fees.

"What a sweet deal," he said in his soft Virginia drawl. "Nobody with the talent and brains should flat out do anything else." He shook his head. At the end of dinner he asked what the minimum investment was in Bridgestone Alpha.

"Five hundred thousand dollars," Joe told him.

"Okay, pal, will you send me the documents? I've finally learned I can't do it myself and index funds are almost against my religion; seems like giving up. I want to be with you."

Joe promised to do so, and they embraced and walked into the chill Virginia night to Josh's car. When Josh had left, Joe stood in the street, feeling the cold and looking at the half moon and the stars—a frozen arc overhead in the dark sky—wondering if Emily had called him. They had agreed he would not call her because she would be surrounded by her family and her entourage, and calls from him would just piss her mother off.

Suddenly, standing there with the light of the gibbous moon lying in a pale, sulfur haze over the old town, a wave of insecurity and anguish seized him. He had little experience with either emotion, but recently he had been feeling very uneasy in his relationship with Emily. These emotions were heightened when she was with her mother, who was continually, consciously trying to undermine their relationship and to introduce her to *suitable* men. It made him feel uneasy.

Joe and Emily had talked romantically—but never seriously—about marriage, but he guessed it must be on her mind. Two of her best friends from Princeton had announced their engagements, and she had been pressing him to go to their weddings. But her mother was right. He was not suitable. And it didn't help that her grandmother, that pretentious, phony old bitch, loved to remind her that "you're not getting any younger, dear."

Her older sister, Jill, he knew, was no fan of his, either. Jill had always been competitive with Emily, and she sometimes teased her sister by referring to her as "live-in Emily" and once or twice even as "the live-in body." Joe knew the jibes rankled with Emily. Now he wondered how it would work if they were married. Their jobs were so different; their passions didn't seem the same now. Would her family—with the exception of her father, of course—ostracize him?

But he loved her. He checked his phone. She hadn't called. In fact, she hadn't called the entire time they had been separated—not even on Christmas Day. What was going on?

Joe walked the five blocks to Dolores's house engulfed by a pervasive miasma of loneliness that verged on despair. Was Josh his only friend in the town? What had happened to all his high school buddies? This was the town he had grown up in and yet he felt estranged here. It had started to snow. *Happiness is like a snowflake*, he reflected. *Catch it in your hand and suddenly it is gone.*

That night when he finally turned off the light and went to bed, he couldn't sleep for a long time. Then, once he did fall asleep, he woke up at three in the morning with the Black Dog of depression on his chest. For some middle-of-the-night reason, he began to think guiltily of Pat. Had he used her? Dark, dismal thoughts about his inability to create stable, enduring relationships plagued him until he finally drifted back to sleep.

Early the next morning Joe drove his rental car to Richmond for his flight to West Palm Beach, where he was to meet Emily. As the day progressed, he began to feel better, and soon the Black Dog was gone.

He had booked a room at The Breakers in Palm Beach. Joe had been to the beautiful, baroque hotel right on the ocean for a Grant conference, and he loved the ambiance. The Dawes family had flown down after Christmas to their house at Sea Island, and Joe was anxious, even desperate, to see Emily. Had her family's onslaught of hostility to him frayed her love? He couldn't help wondering and worrying.

As soon as he was in his room, he called her on her cell phone. She said she would drive down and be at the hotel by mid-afternoon and come directly to his room. Their greeting was awkward, but they changed into their bathing suits and went to the hotel's beach savoring the smell of the salt air. They walked up the beach in the wet sand, talking aimlessly. Yet, Emily still seemed restrained to him. Then they turned and went back to the Breakers' beach. Fighting through the churning Atlantic surf with just a hint of danger into the swells of the sea was exciting and invigorating. Joe thought he could almost feel the stress washing off him. He sensed Emily felt the same way.

When they got back to his room and closed the doors, he put his arms around her and kissed the back of her neck. Her smooth skin, and firm body felt wonderful against him. In a moment, they were out of their bathing suits and lying next to each other in bed.

She turned toward him, held his face in her hands, told him how much she had missed him and how inconsequential the men her mother threw at her seemed. Then he told her about Big Neck and his loneliness. As they talked, he thought how lying like this, confiding utterly in each other, was the ultimate intimacy. He had never felt anything like this before. Suddenly, his fears about their relationship, his worries about the BA portfolio, evaporated, and he felt completely at peace.

After they made love, they had dinner at the Sea Grill. Her cell phone rang. She listened and then turned to Joe, putting her hand over the phone, "It's Daddy. He wonders if we want to play golf with him tomorrow at Seminole."

Joe's whole face almost exploded into a smile. "Yeah, I'd love to. Seminole is a legendary course and I haven't seen your father in such a long time."

"Joe," said Emily softly, "I thought you and I were going to play tennis. Then we could swim, walk on the beach, and have lunch together right here at the Breakers—maybe take a nap!"

"Sweetheart, golf is the hedge fund game. I need to get grooved a little. And the big hedge fund guys play Seminole. Besides, you're playing, too."

She made a face at him.

The next morning Emily and David Dawes picked Joe up early, and they arrived at Seminole a half hour before their tee time and went straight to the driving range. They were situated at the far end with their backs to 20 men who were hitting balls. Suddenly Joe felt a golf club nudging him in the butt. He turned around. It was Spokane, with a big friendly grin on his face.

"Hey dude, I been watching you. I didn't know my new investment genius had a great natural swing and can hit a six iron over two hundred yards. I'm impressed, Joe. What's your handicap?"

"I've never had one."

Spokane's eyes seemed to light up. "You honest-to-God don't have a handicap?"

"My dad and I just played for fun on the public course in Big Neck, Virginia, where I grew up. It was really just a cow pasture. No carts; we just carried or pulled. No real handicap system."

Spokane looked at David Dawes, who was taking all this in.

"Hey, Dave, you going to the Breeds' cocktail party tonight at Eagle Oaks?"

"Yeah," said Dawes.

"Bring me your scorecard, if you would. I want to check this stud out. No gimmes." He turned to Joe. "I have to go. Well, let's talk on Monday. I got some ideas for us."

After Spokane left, Dawes looked at Joe.

"You know, Joe, I hear he's a big success, but what an arrogant, hustling asshole that guy is."

"Why is he so interested in my golf game?"

"Because he wants someone from his firm who can really play to work into his golf games. Makes it easier to for him to write off the private jet that got him here as a business expense. And it's good client golf."

Nevertheless, as they played Seminole that day, Dawes faithfully kept the scorecard, and he made Joe putt out every hole. When he saw Spokane that evening he handed him their scorecard for the round. Dawes had shot an 83, Emily, 102, and Joe, 81.

"Wow!" said Spokane. "Not bad for the first time he's seen the course."

"He's a big strong guy, and he's an athletic natural," Dawes told him. "You should see him on the football field."

"The spooky thing is that maybe he's also an investment natural," said Spokane reflectively. "Or maybe he's just lucky and has had a hot streak. I've always thought the guy he's working with is a loser. Anyway, I have got to get closer to him."

Of course, Dawes told Joe about the conversation.

That night, a million thoughts ran through Joe's mind as he lay in his bed. *I wonder how he figures to get close to me*, Joe thought. He was also a little disconcerted by Dawes's assessment of Spokane and Spokane's appraisal of Mickey.

The conventional wisdom in the New York investment world was that Spokane was a superb salesman. His competitors didn't necessarily like him, but the legend was that he had "a great line of bullshit." Within the firm, however, there was some skepticism that he could sell anything but products with hot performance.

A prospective investor who had expressed interest in BA would come to the Bridgestone office and presumably be suitably awed by the opulence and majesty of the surroundings. The smile and a shoeshine guy assigned to him would then conduct a 50-minute tour through the BA so-called pitch book. The pitch book was actually a legalistic, dry document that reviewed such scintillating and romantic topics as portfolio construction and implementation, ongoing risk management, and monitoring. It also described the awful things that could happen from the use of leverage. Most prospects didn't pay much attention or ask any probing questions. They were only interested in performance.

The pitch book also covered the backgrounds of Mickey and Joe, their investment philosophy and an innocuous description of how their model worked, and laid out all the relevant statistical information on the derivation of returns and the *modus operandi* of the fund. Particular emphasis was put on risk control and stress tests. The stress tests measured how the portfolio would have performed in the October 1987 crash, the Russian and LTCM defaults, if the S&P 500 moved 10 percent, and if the U.S. Treasury bonds swung 50 basis points. The offering memorandum made a specific commitment that the fund's VAR would never exceed 7 percent, which meant that it was very unlikely that the portfolio would ever lose more than 7 percent in a single month. It was a legal, sanitized document.

"It doesn't tell how you used to howl at the full moon down there in Fat Neck," said Mickey to Joe after reading it, "or that I was a loser for years."

Joe laughed.

At this preliminary meeting, the smile and a shoeshine guy would assess whether the prospect was a serious buyer or just window shopping, and would also estimate what size investment he or she could be capable of. An investment of $1 million to $5 million pieces was welcome as long as the client didn't require handholding.

For investors with more than $5 million, after the initial run-through, either Mickey or Joe would spend half an hour or so of their precious presence with the prospect, describing their investment philosophy and how the fund was currently positioned. They could get away with saying things that the gang, bound by legal restraints, couldn't, such as "Our goal is to grind out annual returns of 12 to 15 percent after fees without a big drawdown" and "We're immune to market timing," whatever that meant. Joe found it effective as he said goodbye to murmur, "We would like to have you as a partner." Many people, particularly women and younger men, seemed to melt when he asked them to be his partner. A partner received bimonthly reports on performance by e-mail, the monthly letter, could listen to the quarterly investment call, and would be invited to the annual investment review and cocktail party at The Four Seasons.

If the prospect was an "Elephant," capable of investing really big money (in the $25- to $100-million range), he was then taken for an audience with The Great Spokane. Spokane had made it clear to the marketing people that he always wanted to be in on "the final kill" of an elephant. He reveled in his role as the guy who asked for the order.

When charming an elephant, Spokane never enunciated a specific view of the markets. That was a fool's game, he said. Suppose you were wrong in the short run. The elephant would be turned off. Instead, he showed the prospect his wall of photographs of the fast and famous and shared a few of his favorite stories. Then he sat the prospect down in front of his fake fireplace with the hundred-thousand-dollar crested antique London mantle. At this point in the act, he would get that faraway look in his eyes that made him seem possessed of a special vision (but which some cynics believed really came from gazing down fairways), and waxed eloquent about the world. He would then utter phrases like "when I saw *Alan* last week he seemed curiously withdrawn" or "*Henry* says the problem with Bush is that he doesn't know history." *Alan*, of course, being last name Greenspan and *Henry* being Kissinger. When Spokane had a hot fund to sell, this routine usually closed the deal. Yet, sometimes the less gullible elephants left shaking their heads and mumbling on the elevator to the lobby about clouds of fragrant bullshit.

After the Christmas holiday, Spokane appeared in the door of Joe's office. He was beautifully dressed as usual with a tight-fitting Thomas Pink shirt and tan Burberry slacks. *His tasseled, soft leather Berluti loafers*, Joe thought, *must have cost a thousand dollars—each.*

"Man, you dudes are still flying high. Everyone's fascinated that you're putting up those numbers with almost no market exposure. Clients love low beta funds. It's almost too good to be true!"

Joe gave him his most modest smile. "Unbelievable is the right word, Jud."

"Think you can keep it up?"

"Our models show that the spread between the top and bottom deciles are still extremely extended—like four standard deviations wide."

"Huh," grunted Spokane. He paused: "Joe, how about you and Emily fly down to Palm Beach this weekend with me, and we'll play some customer golf? I've been wanting to see your backswing close up under pressure. We'll leave Friday afternoon on my plane and come back Sunday afternoon. I'll put you and Emily up at the Breakers."

Joe couldn't help but be flattered. "Thanks a lot. It sounds good to me. I'll check with her. As far as I know, we have nothing going on."

"Okay," said Spokane. "You guys will be on your own Friday night, but Saturday night you're invited to a dinner party at my new place. We'll play some serious golf both days. Client golf one day; competition and money the other. As for Emily, I've got a sweetie, a new squeeze I'm checking out, and maybe they can hang out together."

Joe smiled and said "sounds great" but inwardly he winced. He knew Emily was not going to be thrilled by the exclusionary agenda.

When he told her about the trip to Palm Beach that evening, he made the mistake of mentioning Spokane's comment about his date.

"Wonderful," she said. "I suppose he thinks I'm just a live-in squeeze too who can be packed off to the spa to get my nails done and back rubbed while the big boys play golf. To hell with it! I'm not going."

Fifteen minutes later, after her tantrum had subsided, he had persuaded her that it would be interesting to observe the new hedge fund rich at play. Besides, Friday night it would just be the two of them, and he promised he would play only 18 holes on Saturday no matter what Spokane demanded, and that they would play tennis after the golf. She grudgingly agreed to go.

As it turned out, the weekend was certainly *interesting* and maybe even *enlightening*.

Joe and Emily left early Friday afternoon from Teterboro on Spokane's G-5. Neither Joe nor Emily had ever been on a G-5, or for that matter any private plane, and they were dazzled. Spokane reveled in showing everyone all the jet's amenities, including its ability to sleep six comfortably. He bragged endlessly about the G-5's speed and range.

"With this thing I can fly to anywhere in Europe nonstop. I could even get back from Japan in it. There isn't a woman in the world who can resist me after cruising on these wings. Even Paul Tudor Jones, Julian, and Druck don't have G-5s yet. It's the ultimate toy."

Spokane's sweetie turned out to be a rather demure, well-dressed, young woman with dark hair, an innocent face, and a pleasant manner. She was introduced simply as Robin. No last name. She was about

Emily's age. Also on the plane was Bob Schapiro, the chief investment officer of White Rock, a giant fund of hedge funds. Joe knew White Rock had a $400 million investment in three Bridgestone funds, of which $110 million was in BA.

Joe had met Schapiro in the middle of the previous year when he was checking out BA. He was a large, somewhat corpulent man in his mid-forties, and Joe's initial impression of him had been that he took himself very seriously. He knew he had the power to make or break hedge funds, and he expected to be listened to and revered. Schapiro greeted Joe warmly.

Also on the plane was Jimmy Brown, a member of Bridgestone's marketing gang. Brown was a lean, good-humored man about Spokane's age, a good golfer, and known to be a great favorite of the senior partner, although Joe had detected no flashes of brilliance. In fact, he was nicknamed "the playmate" or "the court jester" within the firm. He was along on this trip to facilitate.

On Friday evening, Joe and Emily played late tennis under the lights at the Breakers, had a fine dinner in the lovely, arched main dining room of the hotel, and went to bed early. On Saturday morning, Spokane had a 10:15 tee time, and since Joe knew he first should hit practice balls, he got to Seminole at 9:30. Their fourth was Bill Furlman, the chief pension fund officer of Georgia Teachers and another Bridgestone client.

It was a windy, slightly chilly, Florida January day. They played the front nine holes, had lunch, and then played the back nine. Joe was paired with Schapiro, who was a decent, 12-handicap golfer. Spokane said Joe should play to a 10 handicap. Spokane himself was a nine and Furlman, a big, strong Texan, said he was a three. They bet a hundred dollars each on the match.

Joe had played the course three times with Dawes, and he was beginning to feel comfortable with his game. All those rounds on the scruffy local course with Big Joe had left him with a smooth, natural swing, and his short game was accurate. When on the first tee he whistled a climbing monster drive 300 yards, Schapiro murmured his appreciation. As they walked the course, he questioned Joe about his background and his thoughts on the current bear market. Furlman also seemed interested.

At lunch in the Grill, Spokane held forth in usual braggadocio style with much name dropping. He seemed to know a number of the older members of Seminole, and he told his guests how difficult and expensive it was to get into the club. Joe wondered how he had managed it. Joe sensed that Schapiro was at first bemused and then irritated with Spokane's references to the rich and famous.

That afternoon they finished the back nine around 3:00. Joe shot a 77 and was very pleased with the way he had played. Schapiro was extremely competitive, and he openly celebrated when he and Joe won the match. He hugged Joe when the hundred-dollar bills changed hands.

The dinner that night was interesting. Spokane's villa—on a quiet road just down the beach from the Breakers—was Palm Beach sumptuous. The guests included Spokane, the quiet Robin, Schapiro, Furlman and his wife, and Joe and Emily. Robin was a puzzle to both Joe and Emily. She certainly didn't look like Spokane's flashy type of woman, and she seemed to retreat into her shell when Emily had tried talk to her at the spa that afternoon. Emily's heart went out to her.

"My God," she said to Joe. "The poor girl is embarrassed to be with that jerk."

"Easy," cautioned Joe. "You're talking about my meal ticket."

Upon arriving at the villa, Spokane took his guests on a guided, prideful tour. The provenance of every piece of art on the walls was described, and its price gleefully announced. Even the $75,000 cost of his massive four-poster antique bed was disclosed. The sheer lace curtains in the dining room had cost $50,000. The 200-year-old dessert plates with hand-painted faces of the prerevolutionary French nobility had been acquired in London for £8,000 each.

"I hope you don't put them in the dishwasher," Emily commented, dryly.

Spokane scowled, apparently irritated at the others' laughter. "I'll let you hand wash them after dinner," he replied. She grinned at Joe. He smiled ruefully. He definitely did not want to get her going. Spokane didn't have much of a sense of humor.

In the living room on an exquisite Chippendale table were the pictures in heavy silver frames of three beautiful women smiling benignly.

"My three previous wives," said Spokane proudly, waving at them as he ushered them along. "Each one of them a ten! No hard feelings."

"That's not what I've heard. Do you suppose any of them have a picture of him in their living rooms?" murmured Emily to Joe. Schapiro, who was standing next to her, stifled a laugh.

"Don't be a wiseass," Joe murmured as they moved on to the porch.

Spokane, with a martini in his hand, seemed oblivious to his guests and was clearly feeling exuberant.

"Somebody once described marriage to me as six months in heaven and six years fighting in the light heavyweight division. Actually, that's unfair because I never stayed married long enough to even know their bathroom habits."

Everyone laughed except Emily and Robin. "That stuff about bathroom habits is positively weird," she whispered to Joe.

When they got back to the Breakers, Emily said, "Let's have a drink and look at the ocean." They got two rum and tonics and walked out onto the deserted balustrade. The weather had cleared and the giant moon hung directly out from them, casting a long path of silver light over the sea.

"You know, Joe," Emily said as they stood there drinking in the salt air and the sight, "one of your two senior partners and the public face of your firm is a pompous, insecure, egomaniac asshole. That's not good."

Joe looked at her. She looked incredibly attractive, standing there in the moonlight. He reached out and took her hand. "You're right. He's somewhere between an asshole and a jerk. However, his money is green."

"How did he become so successful and rich?"

"I've asked myself that. I think it was a fortuitous combination. His sales drive, Ravine's investment performance, and being in the right place at the right time in the hedge fund boom were the ingredients. Success brought out the jerk and the asshole characteristics that were always there but were muted," Joe replied, feeling the rum and watching the surf break on the narrow beach and rocks in front of them.

"Well, anyway, we're going to get up and play tennis at seven o'clock since your stupid golf starts at nine thirty."

"Oh, man!" said Joe, "I wanted to go to the gym early."

"Forget it," Emily said. "I sat around here all day today, and I want to do something with you. We're playing tennis."

They played tennis early, and then Joe quickly got into the shower. She came in after him.

"Emily, you know I have to hit some practice balls and that I can't be late for the golf."

"Oh, of course not! So now my assignment for the day is to get us packed, checked out, and meet you at Seminole on the way to the airport."

He kissed her lightly. "You're a sweetheart!"

"Right," she said. "An unhappy one."

Later that day, when they met at the first tee, Spokane ordained that he and Joe would play Schapiro and Furlman. The stakes would be two hundred dollars each. The handicaps matched up well, and on the first tee Spokane murmured to Joe.

"This is customer golf, but play well. I don't like losing. I want to beat these guys. Schapiro pisses me off."

After 16 holes, they were all even on the match. On the seventeenth, a long par four and a stroke hole for Schapiro, he chipped his third shot from the fringe of the green to perhaps five feet from the pin on the undulating, difficult green. Joe was down in four, but if Schapiro made the putt, he would win the hole and his twosome would have a one-hole lead in the match with one final hole to go.

Spokane looked at the ball, the distance from the pin, and the rolling green. It was not an automatic putt by any means, and just the kind of putt it would be easy and embarrassing to miss. Joe knew Spokane loved seeing how people responded to this kind of pressure. However, to Joe's surprise, Spokane reached down, picked up the ball, and flipped it to Schapiro.

"It's your hole. Good playing."

"Thanks," said Schapiro, deadpan.

On the next hole, a difficult twisting, uphill par four over a stream, Joe once again had a par, while Schapiro and Furlman were down in five and with a stroke had net fours. The outcome of the match now rested on Spokane, who needed a par, which would give him a three with his handicap. He had hit a wonderful second shot that went 160 yards in the air and landed about 17 feet from the pin.

As they all stood there watching, his first putt rolled by the hole and was two to three feet long. They all looked at Schapiro, expecting him to concede the putt since Spokane had conceded his considerably longer and more difficult putt on the previous hole.

"Think I'm going to make you putt that out, Jud," said Schapiro with an evil smirk. Joe was astounded. It was incredibly crude of Schapiro.

Spokane just stared at him. Then he went and squatted and meticulously studied the contour of the green both from in front of his ball and behind it. He stood over the ball, took three gentle practice swings with his putter, squinted at the hole again, walked away, and then set up over the ball for what seemed like 30 seconds. Nobody moved. Suddenly, he violently swung his putter sending the ball rocketing across the green, the fringe, and far out into the fairway.

"Your hole and your match, guys," was all he said.

He handed Schapiro four hundred-dollar bills. "Here's your money. I got you covered, Joe."

They went in to the clubhouse and had quick drinks, lunch, and a shower before the cars took them to the airport. At lunch Schapiro was subdued, and the conversation was desultory.

On the plane back to New York, Spokane chatted with Robin and then put on an eye mask, tilted back his seat, and napped. Furlman cornered Joe and grilled him on BA while Emily sat in the back cabin and read the Sunday New York Times.

Monday morning, Spokane came by Joe's office.

"So you think I was pissed at Schapiro?" he asked. Before Joe could utter a word, Spokane answered his own question. "No, I wasn't. The guy is a jerk. But he'll never forget what I did to him. He's in my pocket forever because he's terrified I'll tell the world what a jerk he really is. I own him forever! It was the ultimate control move in customer golf."

Joe nodded. He guessed he understood. It was a very sophisticated form of intimidation.

In the months to come, Joe often played golf with Spokane, Spokane's supposed friends, and the firm's clients. During the course of these games, he wondered what it was about golf and business and hedge fund guys. As they got older, men seemed to become totally obsessed with the game and their handicaps. It was as though playing golf *good* (*good* was an adverb in sports talk), grace under pressure with your golf ego and money at stake, sinking the 10-foot putt, or blasting a 280-yard drive dead, solid perfect on the eighteenth hole was the defining test of their manhood. It proved a man had "the right stuff."

Once, a few years later, he asked Spokane why he put so much emphasis on testing golf with the money managers who worked for him. Spokane echoed the old baloney that you can learn more about a man's character by playing 18 holes of golf with him than you could by transacting business with him for years. When Joe looked doubtful, Spokane said, "Who would you rather have running money for you? A guy who can coolly curl in a long putt to birdie on the eighteenth hole, or a turkey who double bogies the big one when he's the only one with a stroke?"

Well, thought Joe to himself, *my answer would be neither one. What a half-assed way to evaluate investors. I would want the guy with good intuitions and the best and broadest quant model.* But Joe didn't say anything; he just sat there and nodded his head.

Chapter 10

The Halcyon Years

Bridgestone Alpha (BA) began its second year, 2001, with $600 million of capital and a flood of new money that was in the paperwork queue to get into the fund. Suddenly they were the talk of the town, or at least the talk of the hedge fund neighborhood. A year earlier there had been no interest, but by the end of their first year there were so many requests for introductory meetings with them that the firm assigned two of its best marketing guys full time to BA. The smile and a shoeshine gang became smooth, slick, and articulate experts on their investment story.

Because of the additional marketing help, BA was growing by leaps and bounds. January began with the economy and the markets showing increasing signs of serious illness. In early January, the Fed cut rates 50 basis points, and the markets' reaction, contrary to most expectations, was a steep sell-off. Furthermore, and far more important for Mickey and Joe, growth stock–oriented investing was collapsing. Their formula of shorting stocks with eroding fundamentals, a wide dispersion of earnings estimates, low gross cash flow yields, and high price-to-earnings ratios, and owning cheap stocks with improv-ing relative strength was working like a charm. Contagion was begin-ning to contaminate even healthy tech stocks, and greed was turning to fear. Mickey and Joe would jump from one dying horse to another that was just beginning to become ill. Meanwhile, they continued to collect small profits from their portfolio of value longs.

As Mickey inelegantly put it, they "were like pigs in shit." In a down market they were making big money on their shorts and a little money on their longs. Joe had checked it out. The consumer staples sector had a perfect record in recessions, outperforming the market every time, and they concentrated on this normally dull sector. Two takeover attempts further juiced their performance. Throw in 400 percent leverage and the brew made for spectacular returns. (To see what was happening, look at Figure 10.1.) The flight from growth and momentum to value had become a rout. They had a virtual hurricane at their backs. Although they didn't know it at the time, there had never been such a favorable environment for their strategy.

However, there were still a lot of bulls around who resolutely main-tained that the declines in technology were just corrections in what was

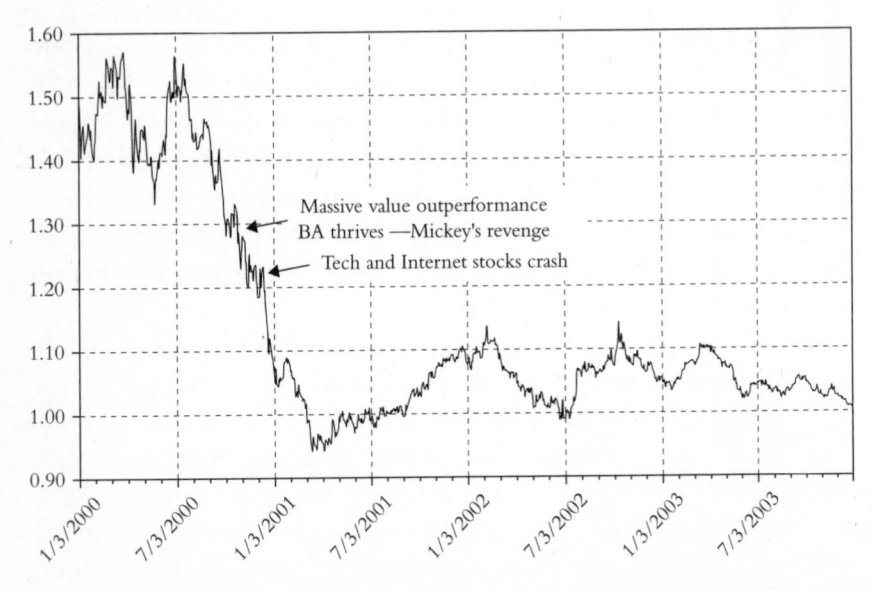

Figure 10.1   The World Turned Upside Down: Value Beats Growth

a bull market and were therefore buying opportunities. It was a new era, they argued. The intellectual heroes of the bulls were two supposed investment intellectuals, James Glassman and Kevin Hassett. Hassett had been a professor at Columbia Business School and a senior economist at the Fed. Glassman was a "scholar" at the highly respected American Enterprise Institute. They had written a best-seller published by Random House at the height of the bubble, titled *Dow 36,000*. In the book, they theorized that stocks should sell at one hundred times earnings. There was not even the decency of a question mark in the title of their book! They had provided academic respectability to the stock market bubble.

As Mickey put it, "Those two guys should be ashamed of themselves. This is highly toxic, inflammatory foolishness. But it's good stuff for us. Keeps the craziness going longer."

Meanwhile, the demands of Emily's master's program at Columbia were taking increasing amounts of her time, and she joked that she had almost as much reading to do as Joe. Her adviser suggested that she interact more with the other master's candidates, and the afternoon seminars often extended into the early evening. Since she was also still spending a couple of days a week at the Council, her schedule was very heavy, and she and Joe seldom met for dinner.

In early February, she was also charged with organizing a trip to Eastern Europe for a group of the Council's major contributors. She put together a 10-day itinerary that included meetings with political, business, and cultural leaders in Warsaw, Prague, and Budapest. The trip would last 10 days, and Emily told Joe that a number of interesting couples had signed up for it.

She passionately urged Joe to go with her on two counts. First of all, it would be good for him to take a break from Bridgestone, the stock market, and his usual work routine. Theoretically, he didn't disagree, but the thought of being away from the portfolio and the markets for almost two weeks terrified him.

"Secondly," she said, "it will be good for us to go away together with a group like this because we'll have a chance to see how we interact with them and they with us. We have to break out of this sterile cocoon we're in. Sometimes I question if we are socially compatible."

That last phrase got his attention. What was she driving at?

"What do you mean, '*Are we socially compatible?*'" he asked.

"Just what I said," she replied, looking at him seriously. "What's going to become of us, Joe? I'm getting tired of being good old *live-in Emily*. Are we capable of moving on in civilized society? Right now our social connections are dead ends." The words, fraught with meaning, hung in the air.

"Yeah, I know what you mean," said Joe. "Emily, I love you. I want to marry you and have children with you."

"I love you, too! But where would we live? Who would we socialize with? This is America in the twenty-first century, and interracial marriages are no longer a big deal. In fact, they're common. But we don't seem to be fitting in, to be making it."

"Yeah, I know. It stinks," Joe responded. "I am hedge fund–obsessed. Fine, I'll definitely go to Eastern Europe with you."

As the year wound on, much of the bull's optimism began to fade as it became clear that the U.S. economy and much of the world was in recession. Prices peaked in late January, and fell steeply through February and March. By the end of March, the S&P 500 was down 20 percent from its January 31 high and the NASDAQ was down over 40 percent. Nevertheless, for the first three months of the year, BA was up 14 percent gross. All was right with their world.

Spokane invited Joe and Emily for another weekend in mid-February, but Emily declined emphatically. Instead, Joe, Spokane, and two important clients flew down to Florida early Friday, and played golf that afternoon and on Saturday. Joe begged off on the Sunday game and flew back to New York commercial Saturday night. He and Emily played indoor tennis at Grand Central on Sunday, but the canvas courts were extremely fast and not very satisfactory. Joe knew he and Emily were still struggling.

Abruptly, following a selling climax in late March, commencing on April Fools' Day, markets rallied. By the end of April, the NASDAQ had soared 32 percent from its March low. Speculative and junk stocks (just the kind of names BA was short) jumped even more.

"Well, I guess we've learned dead cats can bounce," said Mickey.

"Yeah," said Joe. "I read today that at Fidelity sixty-two percent of all the money is still in the ten funds that are tech, Internet, and telecom-related. That's down from eighty percent a year ago but still far above the twelve-year average of thirty-nine percent."

"Even after they've sprung a leak and have been punctured, enormous bubbles take a long time to deflate. We have to hang in there."

At the same time, their longs were listless. It was a hurtful combination. For the month of April, BA lost 4 percent. Even more disturbing to their clients was the volatility of their returns. BA was not supposed to have swings of anywhere near that amplitude.

Suddenly, Mickey's and Joe's phones were ringing day and night. The questions were: "What in the world is going on?" "Is your algorithm broken?" and most worrisome of all, "If this kind of volatility is what we have to accept, then we're going to redeem."

The implied threat of redemptions particularly irritated them.

"Upside volatility is okay, but it's unacceptable on the downside. You would think they'd have some sense of trust and loyalty. What a bunch of bullshit," Joe growled.

Mickey just laughed. "Welcome to the NFL, kid. There's no trust or loyalty when the fee structure is two and twenty."

Nevertheless, the calls were upsetting, and they intensified as markets in general and growth in particular continued to rally. BA was now reporting its mid-month performance, and the fund had lost another two percentage points by May 15. Their performance and the need for hand-holding had particular immediacy because their investors could only redeem at the end of calendar quarters and were required to give 30 days' notice. In other words, to get their money on July 1, they had to send in their redemption notice by May 31. The May redemption notice date loomed ominously.

Mickey and Joe were sweating redemptions, scared that they would experience a massive outflow. Under these circumstances, Joe agonized that he couldn't go away with Emily on her educational European tour. Although Mickey wasn't putting any pressure on him, he knew Mickey needed him and that he shouldn't go.

Three days before they were scheduled to leave, he told Emily that he wouldn't be able to go with her. Angrily, she yelled, "Thanks a lot! You've been looking for an excuse ever since I first begged you to go."

"I have not. That's unfair! I have never been overseas and would have liked to explore Eastern Europe. And I really wanted see how we did with your group. It's just that this is an investment crisis, and I know I'd be distracted and not myself."

"Sure," said Emily. "Will you be too distracted to play golf while I'm away?"

"Come on, Emily, that's not fair."

She relented. "You can always change your mind if your precious stocks start going in the right direction again."

"I promise I will."

BA got through the May redemption notice with minimal damage, and the phone calls abated. Joe decided to join Emily, but by then her tour was in Prague and almost over. When he called to say he was coming, she told him it didn't make sense now. When she returned to New York, their reunion was frosty. Her first weekend back he did not play golf, and they went to a tennis club in the city and played both days. She tried to arrange a dinner with one of her college friends and her husband but they were busy, and they went instead to a movie. She was mollified but still not happy.

In the hot summer of 2001, markets churned sideways as optimism grew that an economic recovery was just around the corner, and that the bottom had been made. Mickey and Joe were skeptical. They argued it was hard to believe that such a gigantic speculative boom could dissolve into such a mild bust and that everyone was going to go happily on their merry way.

"That's not the way the world works," said Mickey. The global economy was now weakening, and they could find more high-conviction shorts than they could find longs. As a result, they were slightly net short. Under those circumstances, performance in June and July was okay with gains of about 2 percent in each month.

Sure enough, markets fell sharply in August and by September tenth, the NASDAQ was down 40 percent from its January high. Then came the September 11 terrorist attacks, and panic prevailed.

By September 21, the S&P 500 was down 28 percent from its January peak, and the NASDAQ had plunged almost 50 percent. Beginning in early October, both markets rallied into year-end, erasing much of the losses.

Overall, the year 2001 was a wearing, grinding bear market. For all 12 months, the S&P 500 was down 11.9 percent and the NASDAQ Index was down 21 percent. The J.P. Morgan Global Bond Index was off 3.6 percent, the Private Equity Index 4.5 percent, and Venture Capital lost 8 percent. There was no place to hide except in hedge funds, where the HFR Composite eked out a meager but still positive 2.3 percent return. Despite their double fees, the HFR Fund of Funds Index earned 3 percent. By contrast, BA, with its massive long value short tech bet, returned 38.1 percent gross or 28.8 percent net to its investors. They had shot the lights out!

However, other parts of Bridgestone were suffering. The concept behind the so-called *multistrategy* hedge fund firms is that management builds a diversified empire under the same roof by sponsoring multiple funds that are following different strategies. Bridgestone called itself a *multistrategy* firm but it really wasn't. In 1998 and 1999—in the full flush of the speculative mania—Spokane and Leiter had brought in and funded young tech and Internet analysts and traders who appeared to be *savants* of the new world. These hired gunslingers prided themselves on being fast—fast talkers, fast buyers of hot stories, and fast sellers if a stock wavered. They were essentially gossip, quasi-inside information purveyors, and momentum traders who were speculating with the House's money. In the glory days of the bull market, they swaggered with immense arrogance, had no fear, and used massive leverage.

As a result, they were massacred when the bubble burst, so 2001 had been another rough year for the firm. Four of Bridgestone's main funds finished down more than 5 percent, and five of the smaller ones were down more than 15 percent and were basically in liquidation. Only Ravine's big global macro fund was up for the year after fees. The hedge fund magazine, *Absolute Return*, ran a story whose title was "What's Gone Wrong at Bridgestone?"

With this background in mind, Mickey and Joe sat down and did some simple arithmetic. It was January 5, 2002, and they had received their final figures for 2001. Their assets at year-end were $2.5 billion, but average assets for the year were about $1.5 billion. Thus the firm had earned a 2 percent fixed fee of $30 million on those assets. BA's incentive fee, after the fixed fee was subtracted, was roughly $108 million (36 percent of $1.5 billion = $540 million and 20 percent of $540 million = $108 million). In other words, the total profit for Bridgestone from their fund was $138 million. The formula Ravine had mentioned indicated they would be paid one half of the firm's take on the incentive fee. Fifty percent of $108 million was $54 million. At that level, Bridgestone had earned $84 million less expenses and overhead, which couldn't be much more than $10 million. They wondered what would they be paid.

In mid-January, Spokane and Ravine called them into the small conference room off Spokane's office. As they entered the beautifully appointed room, they were greeted by Spokane, who was sipping sparkling water with a slice of lemon and exuding *bonhomie* while Ravine sat ramrod straight in an antique, wooden chair.

"So we're going to pay you geniuses exactly what we agreed to. Fifty percent of the incentive fee, or fifty-four million. We suggest twenty-nine million for Mickey and twenty-five million for Joe."

"That's what we agreed to and that's very fair," said Mickey with enthusiasm. "How about a performance bonus?"

Ravine just laughed while Spokane scowled and flexed his neck. "You're lucky we didn't cut you back," Ravine said. "After all, if you guys were out on your own, you would never have raised all that money. Not a chance! We gave you respectability, a platform to stand on, and a great marketing machine. Actually, you've sucked money away from our other funds."

For the first time Joe spoke up, somewhat surprised at his own boldness. "If we keep doing well and growing assets, at what point can we look to becoming partners of your firm? We want to be owners, not just hired guns." Both Ravine's and Spokane's heads spun around to look at him.

Spokane answered. "No chance. The two of us are the only owners of this firm. We created it and we have no plans to share the profits, the management, or for that matter, the risk. If something goes wrong, we're the ones who get sued."

"Yes," added Ravine, "we don't think a business like Bridgestone—where performance is the whole game but is so volatile—works in the partnership form. What happens if a partner gets fat, lazy, and happy and has lousy performance? A multistrategy hedge fund firm has to be a benevolent and sometimes a not-so-benevolent dictatorship, like Lee Kuan Yew's ruling of Singapore. We're committed to paying guys like you huge money when you perform but not to getting married to you till death do us part."

"I understand," said Joe.

Mickey interrupted. "Okay. We love and cherish you two dictators, and we appreciate the fact that you seeded us. If you don't mind, we want the deal for next year signed and notarized."

"Oh, thee geek shitheads of little faith," murmured Ravine.

"Look," said Mickey, "no offense, but now we're talking about serious money. You know we could walk tomorrow."

"And probably only half to a third of your money would go with you."

"Yeah right, and if we performed, the next year it all would come and so would loads of new money."

"We'll get a memorandum of understanding prepared by the lawyers and we'll all sign and notarize it. Your compensation will continue to be half of the firm's profits on the incentive fee."

"Why not half of your total profits from both the fixed fee and the incentive fee?" Mickey asked.

"Because that's not the deal. We provide the house you live in and we pay for all your noninvestment overhead. The fixed fee is our compensation for that. And by the way, you guys need to add some more research firepower."

Joe shook his head. He had played golf the previous weekend with two guys who ran a successful, $2 billion fund for Rextun, a big multistrategy hedge fund complex. They told him that Rextun charged their clients 2 percent fixed and 25 percent of the profits. They, the fund managers, got half of the fixed fee, or 1 percent, and 15 percent of the profits of their fund. In other words, Rextun got 1 percent and 10 percent. He thought now was a good time to mention this arrangement.

"Well, we're not hot-shit-Rextun able to charge two and twenty-five," Spokane said, his voice rising. "We're charging two and twenty and our proposal stands. We keep the whole fixed fee. Take it or leave it. You guys are greedy, ungrateful fucks. Don't forget two years ago you were nothing. We backed you and put you into business."

"Yeah," said Ravine. "Mickey, two years ago you were a career loser. Joe, you're lucky we hired you. You were about to get fired by Grant because you'd been screwing around with the guy who runs the place's daughter, who, out of the kindness of his heart, rescued you from the coal mine of the back office. Apparently, you'd knocked up some woman there."

Joe was appalled. They really had checked him out. Mickey looked sheepish, too.

"Okay, okay," Mickey said. "We accept your offer."

Ravine stood up. "Onward Christian soldiers, go forth to war." He turned and walked out of the room.

As they left, Joe said softly to Mickey. "Nice bunch of guys we're in business with."

"Yeah, but we knew that from the beginning. They're shits but at least they're *our* shits."

Bridgestone is a New York State and City corporate entity, and under its structure, Joe's and Mickey's pay was ordinary income. After all taxes, Joe figured he cleared $14 million. His accountant told him he could give $12,000 tax-free to anyone, but he wanted to give some real money to his mother. Dolores couldn't believe it when he told her he was opening an account in BA for her with $1 million in it. He didn't tell her that the gift tax was going to be another $600,000. He did the same for Big Joe, who was left speechless, and sent checks for $12,000 to each of his three half-sisters. His capital account had been $1 million at the beginning of the year, and it was now a little over $8 million. That felt really good.

For some reason he couldn't even explain to himself, he didn't tell Emily about the stunning extent of his largess. He simply said he was happy with what he got paid, and she didn't press him for particulars. A new and much bigger apartment was the logical next step but he was hesitant about committing to the city.

However, he did go to Spokane, whom he knew was a member of the Lone Tree Club, which had a very beautiful and challenging golf course, a brand-new baronial Tudor clubhouse, a luxurious locker room, a magnificent oak-paneled bar, and superb service. It was a relatively new club and not particularly difficult to get into as long as you were in the investment business and recommended by the ruling clique. A lot of hedge fund guys were members.

"So you want to join Lone Tree?" Spokane said with a knowing smile that bordered on being an evil grin. "You know, it's not a country club at all. No swimming pool, no tennis courts, no spa, no ladies' locker room. Every one of my ex-girlfriends mentioned how much they hated it."

Joe laughed—a little weakly.

Spokane told him he would be glad to help, and furthermore, he knew the man who had created and controlled Lone Tree, John Spencer, the president of Merrill Lynch. Spokane talked to Spencer, got three other members who had played golf with Joe to write letters, and sent in the application form. Joe was in two months later. The admission fee was $500,000 and the dues were $2,000 a month. He was in the big-time golf world overnight.

It was 2002, a new year, but the same old bear market. Mickey and Joe stuck to their guns. They let their formulas, their *modus operandi,* identify the expensive and cheap stocks they should be looking at, and waited for the sweet combination of their momentum shifts and their fundamental analysis to trigger their actions.

With $2.5 billion under management, they expanded the number of positions in their portfolio to 300 to keep the average position size manageable. This meant more work to research the qualitative factors, and they added two more analysts, bringing the total that worked exclusively for them to four.

Mickey liked having analysts around, but Joe found two of them to be a distraction because of their apparent need for extensive face time with him. The other two he respected and related to. However, the continual parading of analysts in and out of his office was distracting. He and Mickey eventually implemented a strict rule that all reports from the analysts had to be submitted in e-mail form. This practice also created a written record that they could refer back to. If an analyst had something to tell them, he sent them an e-mail. If they wanted to talk to an analyst, they called him. Basically, they wanted to minimize the distraction of office traffic.

By June 30, they were up 11 percent, and with the appreciation and new money, BA had about $3.3 billion under management. With more and bigger positions, their sacred alpha was becoming more difficult to earn, and Joe came to believe they needed more firepower. He decided to recruit Joan. Joe had come to know Joan well over the years. They had either a quick breakfast or lunch in the café together a couple of times a week. She was smart, quick, and perceptive, and he enjoyed being with her. He also knew that the man she worked for, the arrogant Tom Leiter, was down for the year and was now at least 10 percentage points under his so-called *high-water mark*. Since Leiter's fund had lost money in 2001, he was in the tough position of having to make back his losses before he could earn any incentive compensation to pay himself and his people with.

After Joe told Joan that he was interested in recruiting her to his team, she asked, "What's my job description going to be?"

"You're going to be working with me and running the analysts we've brought on. They're good but they need direction, and I really value your insights and instincts."

"Joe, you know I want to run money. Am I going to be able to pull the trigger on stocks?"

"I don't think so, initially. You'll be more like an assistant portfolio manager."

"Then the answer is a definite no. Thanks, but no thanks." She waved her shapely arms. It was strangely sensual. "And by the way," she added, with a grin, "fuck you, Joe, and the horse you rode in on!" He hypothesized the horse that she was referring to was Mickey.

He didn't blame her and he liked her feistiness. He talked to Mickey about it, who was also sympathetic. They agreed to give her discretion over 10 percent, or 40 names out of the 400 that they were long and short. She would have to work within the restraints of their system, and they would track her performance, but it would be her portfolio.

"Sounds really good!" she said, her dark eyes flashing, when he told her of their decision. "Thank you both! Now, what are you going to pay me?"

"We'll pay you like us. You get a draw from the firm of six hundred thousand and at year-end we whack up the profits."

Joan looked a little doubtful. "Sounds a little nebulous to me."

"Hey," said Joe. "We can't afford to screw you. You'll be part of our team."

"Okay," she said. "But I like formulas. Mickey is tougher than he talks."

Leiter was pissed when Mickey told him about hiring Joan, but he had no ammunition, and Joan started her new position on July 1. She fit in from the beginning, and she was not shy about running her portfolio—her segment was what they called it—of 40 stocks. Operations tracked her performance, and since she had adopted their religion, it was virtually the same as that of the total portfolio.

By this time, Mickey and Joe had developed the habit of meeting in Mickey's office right after the firm's daily morning meeting to discuss any investment developments that might require action. There was almost always something to talk about as they debriefed each other. They invited Joan to join them, and at first she was subdued and reticent. Joe missed her usual, outspoken animation and was surprised by her reluctance to contribute. He gave her time to open up, but after a month he told her. "Listen, we didn't think we were making a dumb mute our partner and co-portfolio manager. I know you've got opinions and ideas. Speak up!"

She looked at him with a serious expression. "Okay, I will. Thanks for the heads-up! Participate!" And she did.

In July, Joe invited Big Joe and Josh to come up to New York. He wanted to make it a special weekend, and, he had to admit to himself, to flaunt his new wealth a little. He had a car and driver meet them

Friday afternoon at La Guardia Airport and take them to the Four Seasons Hotel. Emily joined them for dinner, which was a big deal since she hadn't met either of them before. Although the conversation flowed, Big Joe didn't have much to say. Joe knew Emily was genuinely curious about both men who had played such an important part in his life, and he was very pleased when she joined them on Saturday to play the back nine and for dinner at the Lone Tree Club. He could sense his father becoming more and more at ease with her.

Sunday night after Josh and Big Joe had left, Joe told Emily how he wished they could do something with her family, particularly her mother. David Dawes had joined him to play golf at Lone Tree several times, and Emily had even played with them once.

She responded, "It would just be too awkward with my mom. She is such a hard-ass."

"Then nothing has changed in her attitude toward me?"

"Not really. You're not what she had in mind for me—or for her. It's as simple as that."

"Yeah, I know," said Joe resignedly, but inside he felt a deep sense of discouragement that almost verged on despair.

She reached over and squeezed his hand. "But I do sense some softening. To be crass about it, the fact that you're a successful hedge fund manager helps. To be even crasser, the realization that you've made a lot of money helps even more."

"Suppose we had children? Would she accept and love them like they were her grandchildren?"

Emily paused for a full minute before she answered. "I think she would—as long as they resembled me. But look, don't get bent out of shape. Daddy is very proud of you."

"Great. I'm proud of him, too. So what?"

Back at work, Joe now had a group of analysts at brokerage firms whom he felt he could trust, and, of course, he had his own BA analysts to assign projects to.

He also spent considerable time on the phone gossiping with his widening circle of hedge fund friends that he had developed through golf. Joe knew he had to be careful with them. A guy could be your buddy, but you couldn't count on him not to sandbag you. In fact, he knew guys who wouldn't hesitate to screw him at the first chance they got. It was a dog-eat-dog world. You wanted your competitors to buy the stocks you owned and sell the ones you were short, but having the other fast money in your positions was a double-edged sword.

Mickey and Joe kept their net long position at close to zero throughout the year and relied on stock selection. The spreads between the most expensive and the best values in their stock-picking universe had narrowed, but they could still find high conviction longs and shorts by using their qualitative factors. The NASDAQ Index— with its heavy orientation of Internet, technology, and lower quality stocks—fell relentlessly (except for a brief but sharp surge in early March) until climaxing with a real selling panic in early October. On October 9, the Index, which had at one time touched 5,000, hit 1,114. Through their short positions, Mickey and Joe rode the free-fall all the way down, which periodically required selling more shares short as their existing positions fell.

As for the general market as epitomized by the popular averages, there was a brief interlude of optimism about the economy and equities early in the year, but by the end of March the S&P 500 Index and the Dow Jones Industrial Average were in steep falls. By now, doom and gloom were everywhere. There was much chatter about a double dip in the economy, and criticism of the Fed and its chairman was rising. It was truly darkness at noon. The first selling climax and bottom in the S&P came in July and was followed by a rally that by mid-August had carried almost 20 percent. It aborted, however, into another cascading decline that climaxed in the second week of October. The steep rally that followed petered out in December. All year, Mickey and Joe kept their net long position close to zero and did not attempt to trade this volatility.

By the time 2002 was over, the S&P 500 had declined 21 percent on a total return basis and NASDAQ had fallen 32.1 percent. Considering the carnage in the general markets, hedge funds did fine, but the illusion that they could consistently make money even in bad markets was fading. For the very first time, the Equity Hedge Fund Index was down 4.7 percent for the year—although certain sectors, such as Distressed and Emerging Markets, posted small positive returns—and the HFRI Fund of Funds Composite Index eked out a mere 1.02 percent gain after all fees. Almost everyone else had struggled, except for the short sellers. The Short Bias Index posted a 29.7 percent gain, but there was only tiny money in these funds.

Nonetheless, BA ground out a good year, even though it was not as magnificent as the previous two years. As their longs went sideways and their shorts went down, returns were positive every month except November. Although they had individual positions that went against them, their broad diversification helped, as did their very substantial leverage. Figure 10.2 tells the story.

Nevertheless, in an extremely poor year for the indexes and disappointing results for the hedge fund industry as a whole, BA was up 19.1 percent gross and 13.6 percent net to investors. On December 31, BA had $4.4 billion in the fund, and for the full year averaged $3.4 billion. They ran the numbers. They were startling.

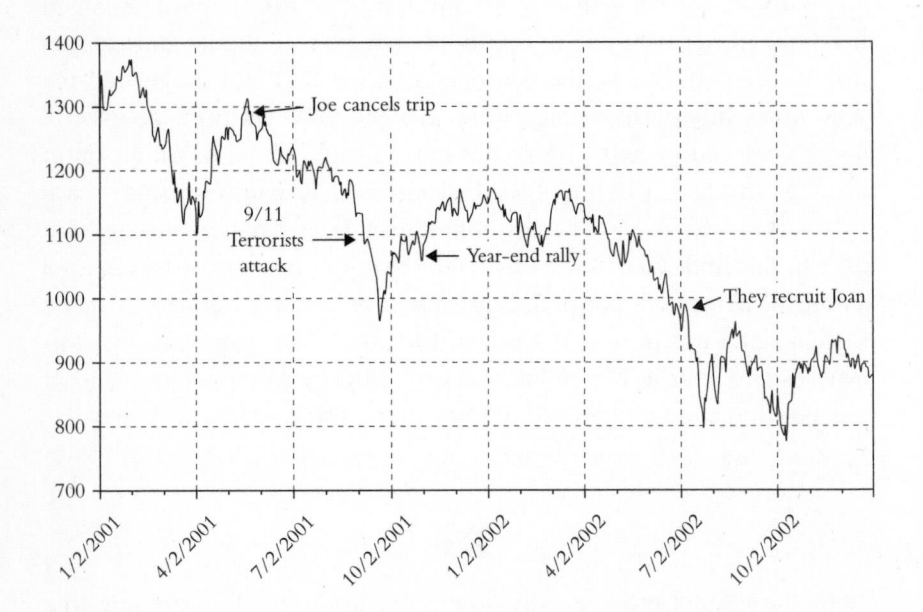

Figure 10.2 Bridgestone Alpha (BA) Prospers in a Bear Market: S&P 500, 2001–2002

Bridgestone, the firm, in the form of Spokane and Ravine, received $68 million from the fixed fee. The incentive compensation for the firm (20 percent of the profits) worked out to $120 million, of which Mickey, Joe, and their team got half, or almost $60 million. In total, Bridgestone had earned $184 million simply for managing the fund. A large mutual fund for a global mandate of similar size would charge 50 basis points and would have booked fees of $17 million. Of course, there were no large funds in 2002 that returned 13.6 percent net, and, in fact, few funds of any size had similar gains.

Mickey and Joe determined to pay Joan $3 million for the less than six months she had worked for them; they paid their two good analysts $2 million each, and gave the uninspiring other two $750,000 apiece but told them they were going to be replaced and to start looking for new jobs. They asked themselves whether they should pay the two good ones more. There was the risk of spoiling them, and as it was, their compensation would be far above almost any of the other analysts at Bridgestone or almost anywhere else. After they had finished, Mickey tapped Joe on the arm and said warmly, "Look, we've got about $51 million left. It's an obscene amount. I say we divide it equally. It's been another great year and we're partners." Joe was surprised and stunned. When they shook hands, Joe's eyes were misty.

"The other thing we need to think about," Mickey said to him looking serious, "is that the total compensation from our little baby, BA, was one hundred eighty-four million, of which we got sixty million, and our friends in the front offices got one hundred twenty-four million. Seems a little disproportionate, huh?"

Joe had done the math, too. "They gave us a shot and put us in business, but it strikes me that we've more than paid them back over the last three years."

"I would definitely say so. It's not that I'm greedy or don't know I am a grossly overpaid, incredibly lucky guy, but we are where we are. We could walk with half of the money easy."

"Yeah, but the administrative job of setting up our own fund would be a killer. We'd have to hire operations people, traders, compliance, and a client service staff. It would a nightmare. All kinds of legal stuff to get through, like registering with the SEC. Then there's the money-raising. The whole process would take four to six months and be very distracting from investing."

"We could get a really high class chief operating officer–type guy who would hire the people and some lawyers to do the agreements for us," Mickey replied.

"And who's going to contact the clients? Are they loyal to Bridgestone or to us? Spokane would sue us. We'd have to resign from the firm. What are we going to do while we're setting up?"

"The clients are only loyal to performance, but you're right. It would be a fucking monumental pain in the ass. But let's at least demand a better deal here."

Joe and Mickey arranged for a meeting with the two partners. When they entered Spokane's conference room, Joe noticed with amusement that it had been redecorated again. Now it had the aura of a distinguished men's club like The Brook—leather easy chairs that almost seemed to suck you into them and a lot of Sheraton and Hepplewhite English furniture.

"I wondered how long it would be before you two wolves would be snapping at our heels," Spokane said sourly. "Don't waste our time with the numbers. We know them. I don't feel like haggling. Let's raise the fee structure to two and twenty-five. We'll give you seventy percent of the carry instead of fifty and twenty-five percent of the fixed fee."

"Come on!" said Joe, almost angrily. "You know we can't raise our fees like that in the midst of a killer bear market! We're not established enough. It would be suicide if we then stumbled."

"You're right," said Spokane. "Greedy . . . but right."

"Pride goeth before destruction and a haughty spirit before a fall," Ravine murmured.

"Come on," said Mickey. "After all my wanderings in the wilderness I'm no haughty spirit, and you guys are the greedy ones. Let's not waste time. Pay us seventy percent of the carry and leave the fixed fee structure the way it is or we walk."

"After we got you two deadbeats started now you want to take money right out of our pockets," Spokane snarled. "Get the hell out of here. We'll get back to you in a couple of days."

Two days later, the response, of course, was acceptance of the offer. Like it or not, BA was the only real engine Bridgestone had going, and its loss would have been catastrophic to the firm.

As the new year began, Joe recognized two things—one good and one bad. First, 2002 had been a marvelous investment year for him. He was now a rich man who was regarded as a new, bright shining star in the hedge fund firmament. He liked being wealthy and esteemed. Three good years back to back and no one could say he was just a flash in the pan. Furthermore, now, finally, he had developed real confidence in himself as an investor.

Joe decided to put his newfound money to good use. He gave more money to his family, and contributed $65,000 for new lights on the Big Neck High School football field. Josh, Big Joe, and the new head coach wanted him to come down to turn on the lights at midfield before the first game of the new season. The *Big Neck News*, the local weekly, had run a story about his gift and how he had made good in the big city, but somehow the notoriety left him feeling very uneasy. When he told Emily about the lights ceremony, she was enthusiastic about going. "I've always wanted to see where you grew up, see the whole scene at the game, the town. It's such an important part of you."

He was appalled. What would she think? What would Big Neck think? He finagled an invitation to a member-guest tournament at Winged Foot, and told Josh and Big Joe he couldn't make it. They were very disappointed. Emily was positively pissed.

"What! Are you ashamed of me? Afraid that all your old high school buddies will think you've gone Greenwich?"

He tried to shrug it off as a joke.

"Don't give me a lot of grief about my mother. You're almost as bad as she is."

He dropped the subject.

The second thing he knew was that 2002 had not been a great year for Emily and him. He knew he had become a workaholic and a golfaholic. His precious BA portfolio had become his obsession, and she was a demanding mistress. She was never boring, and she didn't have tiresome friends. However, if you didn't spend endless time with her and pay her the constant attention and accord her the homage that she required, she would quickly and with ruthless cruelty punish you. There was always something going right or something going wrong somewhere in the nooks and crannies of the portfolio companies, and the ebb and flow was infinitely fascinating to him.

It was the greatest game of all, and the world kept score. You were in a life-or-death competition with everyone else. He now spent so much time reading, thinking, and talking about investing and stocks that he knew the rest of his intellectual life was barren. He also recognized that although he might be intriguing for another investor to talk with, for normal, ordinary, people with a variety of interests, he had become something of a one-track bore. Maybe even more than *something*. An outright plain and simple bore.

The result of all this was that he and Emily had less and less to talk about. He occasionally found himself almost dreading going out to dinner with just her because they would sit there in the restaurant like two old married people staring at the walls with almost nothing to say to each other. When they went out with her friends, he knew they found him hard to talk to and, in fact, he was bored by them.

He tried to reach out to Emily by buying—or rather his personal shopper bought—an antique Vacheron & Constantine wrist watch for $85,000. Although she seemed touched when he fastened it on her wrist, he noticed that she hardly ever wore it.

"Too fancy for Columbia," she told him. "People there will think I'm a kept woman."

The opposite social situation applied when the circumstances were reversed. Sometimes now he and Emily were invited to dinner Friday or Saturday night at a club or a hedge fund guy's home. Such events didn't work for Emily. She made it clear that she found these social occasions where the dinner-table conversation was dominated by endless babble about investing and golf extremely tedious.

"I don't know what's more boring," she once said to him. "A stroke-by-stroke recount of the fourteenth hole or an animated argument over whether Apple's third quarter earnings will disappoint."

On the other hand, she wasn't a soccer mom with a Mercedes SUV, so she didn't have a lot to say to the hedge fund guys' upwardly mobile and nubile wives with their smooth, bronzed arms, glittering jewelry, and child chatter. The truth was that she was engrossed with her work at the Council and her studies at Columbia, and the historical and geopolitical subjects that interested her did not much interest them or him. Emily and Joe knew they were doing less and less together. Their sex life was also deteriorating.

The other problem in their relationship was Joe's addiction to golf. He knew he had become compulsive about the game. His handicap was falling slowly but steadily. He was now a solid four. Spokane had introduced him to a number of other serious golfers, most of whom were in the investment business. Joe's idea of perfect weekend relaxation had become to go the gym in their apartment building first thing in the morning, work out, shower, take a car service to the Lone Tree Club or some other club, and read the papers on the way there, hit balls, and then play 18 holes for money with three other investment types. He loved the Lone Tree Club. It was the first club he had ever belonged to, and he was very proud of it. The discreet but perfect luxury, the obsequious service, the sitting around in the wood-paneled bar after a golf game talking shop with the guys. It made him feel rich and part of something.

The final thing that bothered him was Joan. He hadn't thought of another woman with even the faintest flicker of lust since he had met Emily, but now he found himself looking at Joan with her tough, prickly personality and her restless physical energy and wondering what she would be like in bed. He knew she went out occasionally with some man, but he sensed that she felt the guy was not very bright, and just company. Joe liked her passion and the way she challenged him in investment conversations, and their conversations were always animated. Sometimes in the evening now they would stop in at Delmonico's for a drink before going home. He still loved Emily but what was happening to them? Or was it nothing? Maybe there were other distractions.

Chapter 11

Dinner at the Perots

A s time went on and their outstanding performance became more widely known, the financial media discovered Mickey and Joe. The media attention began when the Columbia Business School invited Mickey to speak at its seventieth-anniversary celebration of Benjamin Graham's and David Dodd's seminal classic, *Security Analysis*, which is considered the bible of value investing. Graham had taught at Columbia, and Dodd had been dean of the school. Furthermore, "The Natural," Warren Buffett, their most renowned disciple, had graduated from Columbia. In fact, 19 years earlier, at the fiftieth-anniversary celebration, Buffett had given his famous speech, "The Superinvestors of Graham and Doddsville," that had directly attacked and dismantled the so-called *random walkers* and the efficient market hypothesis (EMH).

The EMH believers, led by Burton Malkiel, a Princeton professor, argued that anyone who consistently outperformed the stock market was no different from a coin flipper or a lucky monkey throwing darts at the stock page listings. At the famous anniversary debate, Michael Jensen, speaking for the random walkers, said that if enough people flipped coins, a few of them would flip heads over and over because that was the way randomness worked. Buffett then got up and argued that while this might be so, the string of heads would not be random if all the successful coin flippers came from the same town and had the same religion. He then produced the records of nine great value investors, all of whom came from what he called the village of Graham and Doddsville.

The Columbia Business School cherished the idea of itself as the creator—the hotbed of value investing—and the dean of the school was intrigued that a new breed of value investors using computer algorithms was rising from the ashes of the madness of the tech bubble. Although he knew the master, Buffett himself, was skeptical of computer geeks, in mid-2003 the dean asked Mickey to speak at the school's annual investment forum. Mickey was flattered by the invitation and eagerly accepted.

"It's almost like getting an honorary degree," he told Joe. "In a way, it's vindication for all the shit and abuse I've taken over the years from growth stock investors."

"It's a huge invite," Joe said. "We'll send out your talk to all our clients."

Mickey labored over his speech for weeks, and it turned out to be a great success. Legally, he could not in any way mention their performance or seem to be promoting BA, but there was still plenty he could say. Although not revealing the details of how their model and algorithm worked or the actual factor weightings, he did describe their approach in plain English.

Please recognize that these models are not esoteric constructs but rather just thoughtful, intuitive, systematic approaches to choosing stocks and constructing portfolios. We acknowledge our intellectual debt to Cliff Asness of AQR Capital Management and Michael Goldstein of Empirical Research, both of whom are great and original thinkers about methodical value investing.

We, my partner Joe Hill and I, think these are good long-term logical strategies (own cheap, good-quality, and improving companies and short the opposite) that have worked for many years because people's behavioral biases go the other way. We believe many of these effects occur because of what is most commonly referred to as "behavioral finance," which encompasses a series of biases investors have, that in the aggregate, affect stock prices. Our approach seeks to profit from these biases systematically. For example, we are betting that the glamour stocks will continue to receive multiples that are too high based on reality and vice versa (this is the value factor), that firms with weaker earnings quality will continue to fool some investors, and that investors like to buy and sell what's been working and not working lately (momentum). I will present some formal evidence that these biases remain intact and that we can measure them using what we call the value spread.

The speech was well received, and Mickey enjoyed hobnobbing with the academic heavyweights at the reception that followed.

Over the following couple of months, Joe was interviewed by both *Barron's* and by Kate Welling of *Welling at Weeden*. The lead-in to both interviews highlighted his Arizona Union background, his football career, and his entry into Grant through the back office. The *Barron's* piece was the feature story of that week's issue, and it was titled "A Star Is Born." After the interviews ran, CNBC and Bloomberg television began calling him for appearances on their shows. He was a new and different kind of Wall Street hedge fund guy who had not gone to a fancy college or the Harvard Business School, and they loved his rags-to-riches story.

Suddenly, Joe was a mini-celebrity. He was The Kid. The Kid from nowhere who had made it in the major leagues. The rookie who was putting up the big numbers and who was being accepted by the veterans into their privileged company, the penumbra of the inner circle. It was heady stuff. When he went to investor meetings, he sensed guys looking at him. "That's him," they were whispering. "That's him, The Kid, Joe Hill."

BA's success and the surrounding publicity certainly had raised the profile of quant value investing. There were plenty of newly minted quants who aspired to be rich, and they began to hear of new funds starting up.

One afternoon in early June when Mickey, Joe, and Joan were sitting in Joe's office babbling at each other, Ravine came in. They were surprised as he seldom walked the halls. For once, he was friendly, but, as always, serious.

"Are you guys sure you're not making a mistake telling the world about how wonderfully quant value investing is doing?"

"I hope not," Joe replied, surprised. "We want to appear like we're serious quant students of value, and we hope to become respectable and legitimate."

"Yeah," said Mickey. "Our clients seem to like the publicity."

"From what I read, a lot of new funds are being created and money raised," Ravine said.

"We think we could easily run a couple of more billion. Liquidity hasn't become an issue."

"Maybe," replied Ravine thoughtfully.

"Imitation is the sincerest form of flattery," Mickey said.

"Yeah, but the imitators are going to be competing with you. Seems to me there's a new risk factor in your world and it's you. Anyone and everyone can data mine just like you, and you're even telling them how you do it."

"Our edge is not that we have a proprietary database or computer model. It's that we have the experience and judgment to interpret and adjust the data."

"I hope you're right. Will cheap stocks with good recent momentum continue to beat expensive stocks?"

"Yes, at least most of the time," Joe answered confidently.

"The Sermon on the Mount said size is the mortal enemy of performance," Ravine replied.

"We aren't there yet. Wouldn't you like another two or three billion under management?" Mickey asked him.

"As Cliff Asness says, strategies are often alpha when first discovered and not broadly adopted and then move slowly to beta or at least develop an 'exotic beta' component over time." Ravine looked at them reflectively. "In our business over the years I've seen a lot of guys die from overexposure."

When Ravine had left, Mickey delivered the benediction. "That was a little scary. He wasn't just giving us literary shit the way he usually does. He's a very smart guy. Maybe we should lay low for a while."

In late June 2003, Joe and Emily were invited for dinner in Greenwich by Jonathan Perot. Perot was tough, smart, and very rich, and Joe was curious to see his home and how he lived. He was a member of the Lone Tree Club, and he and Joe had played golf perhaps half a dozen times. Jonathan had been called John or Johnny until he had made it big with his health care hedge fund and had matriculated to a new, zippier wife. Joe had been seated next to the second Mrs. Perot at a dinner during a hedge fund conference a few months earlier, and had been amazed and intrigued. She had talked nonstop. He learned among other things the square footage of their new house, that she had grown up in Chicago, and was a former flight attendant. He was told they had two children, Joshua and Brittany, and three live-in servants, one of whom was a French butler who answered the phone, *"Bon soir."*

"It's so expensive to be rich," she told him. Joe wondered afterward if that was a very profound insight or was totally banal. He couldn't decide.

She also confided to him that she was now a Francophile, and that she and Perot had a *pied-à-terre* in Paris. "Touch of class in this snotty town, don't you think?" she had asked, rolling her eyes guilelessly.

For the dinner, Joe had arranged for a car to pick up Emily in the city and then come for him at the Lone Tree Club after golf. They wound through the winding roads of Greenwich that May evening with a soft spring bursting out on all sides of them.

Perot lived on Clapboard Ridge Road. Fine old houses every hundred yards or so faced the street. The houses were big and substantial and clearly visible from the road. Emily, who knew her Greenwich, told him that this was a two-acre zone and the resting place of the *haute bourgeoisie*.

"He's got a very tony address," Emily told him. "Can't wait to see the McMansion."

Unlike the other houses they had passed, the driveway of 148 Clapboard Ridge Road was sheltered by a thick hedge and the house was not visible from the street. They turned and drove in several hundred yards over a Belgian Block driveway and then abruptly broke out into a field on which three fine-looking horses were grazing. They could see a lighted tennis court, a large stone building that appeared to be a combination barn and stable, a long swimming pool, and an elaborate pool house. In the distance, they could see a gigantic but attractive stone manor house with large windows and a massive parking area.

"Well," said Emily, "my mother always says the real sign of Greenwich wealth is people who have long driveways. Your friend must have at least fifteen acres here and land goes at around two million an acre in this neighborhood."

"You gotta be kidding. So Jonathan has maybe thirty million dollars in land."

"It's crazy!" said Emily. "Crazy!"

"I'll bet land has been a great investment in this town. Greenwich is where successful hedge fund guys want to live. Land is diversification, a hedge against inflation, and something real instead of just paper and numbers. I've always wanted to own land. My own land to walk on and grow stuff on."

Now—as though in a flashback—he was suddenly remembering Virginia and walking with Josh Gibson on the land down by the river with the rich, loamy-smelling black soil and how in the spring the new corn—small, pale green, narrow-leafed plants—would suddenly after a few warm days be sprouting on fragile stalks.

"This isn't Virginia or Iowa. The soil is grainy and full of stones. The only thing that grows on Greenwich land is property taxes," Emily told him slightly disdainfully.

"And money! Can it be that I think I see a couple of golf holes?" said a dazzled Joe. He was right. They could see that were two par fours and a par three behind the stable and the riding ring.

The entrance hall of the main house arched high into a cathedral ceiling, and a curved staircase that was a replica of one at the Palace of Versailles floated upward. On a handsome oak table was a soaring arrangement of fresh flowers in a gilded crystal agate vase. They could hear the buzz of conversation, and almost immediately they were offered champagne or chardonnay from a silver tray by a tall, elegant waitress.

In a moment, Jonathan Perot greeted them. He was a tall, good-looking man, wearing a silk shirt with the two top buttons open, pale slacks, and tasseled loafers without socks. He had an open, Midwestern sort of face and you immediately sensed that what you saw was what you got. He was also unbelievably loquacious. Words, half-formed thoughts, insights poured out of his mouth in a disarmingly charming stream of consciousness. He was perhaps 45 years old. Joe liked him. He kissed Emily on the check.

"So glad to meet you at last! Joe's one of the most brilliant investors I've ever known. You grew up in Greenwich, didn't you?" he said.

"I did," said Emily. "Your grounds are spectacular. Wonderful views. May I ask how much land you have?"

Perot positively beamed at her. "Eighteen acres. I paid twenty-five million for it four years ago and it must be worth at least thirty-five now. It had better be. I got a giant mortgage."

"I'd love to look around your house."

"Of course! It's eighteen thousand square feet." He beamed with obvious pleasure. "I'm very proud of it. You know I grew up in a two-bedroom apartment in Cleveland. Never dreamed I'd have anything like this. *My Nancy* got a wonderful decorator. She did it all with great taste, don't you think? Picked out the art, the wallpaper, the works. Cost me five million, including the art, and I haven't even bought any big-time stuff . . . yet."

Perot shook his head like a dog shaking off water. "We've done nothing splashy or ostentatious like Harmon's or Petrowski's mansions. Those guys piss me off. Always bragging about their houses and how big they are and the special toys they got. Subliminally, the implication is that if you have a huge house you've got a huge penis. I'm just as rich as they are, but I don't flaunt it."

Emily couldn't resist any longer. "I'm reading a biography of Theodore Roosevelt and the so-called Gilded Age. Roosevelt said envy and arrogance are the two opposites of *the same black crystal.*"

Perot gazed at her quizzically. "*The same black crystal?* What does that mean? It doesn't sound good." He paused, then continued. "I'll spare you the ground floor game room. It's marvelous, though. A squash court, an indoor pool with miniature palm trees and a waterfall, a play room with a padded floor and walls where the kids can play real soccer, football, or lacrosse."

"Wow!" said Joe. "Sounds great."

"Great, but expensive as hell," Perot replied. "I'm just hoping my two young boys don't take up hockey. I'd have to build an indoor rink." He laughed. "Being really good at a sport, particularly an esoteric one like squash, is a great way to get kids into an Ivy League college. My first family didn't have those advantages. We helped 'em with their homework, and they ended up at UConn and Nebraska. But, *My Nancy's* heart is set on the Ivy League for our boys. I'm working like a dog to make money so I can endow some college with a building and get my kid in. Where'd you go?" he asked Emily.

"Princeton."

"Princeton! My God, Princeton! I'd give 'Old Nassau' a new science building if I could get a kid into Princeton. *My Nancy* would be ecstatic if one of our kids went to Princeton. Where'd you go to prep school?"

"Hotchkiss."

Jonathan gazed at her with only partly feigned awe. "And you're hanging around with this hick from rural Virginia who almost flunked out of Arizona?" He punched Joe playfully on the arm.

"I got into Hotchkiss and Princeton on their diversity program," Emily told him. "Us Greenwich girls are a rare and endangered species."

"Yeah, right," Jonathan said nonchalantly, leading them through a library paneled with antique wood siding and shelves stacked with books, some in frayed dust jackets, in studied disarray that looked as though they had been read.

"Yeah," said Perot. "See those books in there? The decorator bought from an estate a complete collection of the vintage twentieth-century American novels. I got the great novels of F. Scott Fitzgerald, Hemingway, Faulkner, James Jones, and Robert Penn Warren—all first editions. See, they're much more valuable in their dust jackets. I'm going to get around to reading them any day now." He laughed sheepishly.

They walked down a long hall with some obviously fine American art on one wall and Venetian tapestries on the other and wandered into a massive, high-ceilinged living room in which 30 people were gathered, chatting animatedly in cocktail party groups.

"This room," Perot told them with a somewhat embarrassed grin, "is an almost exact replica of the Green Room—you know, the main reception room in the American Embassy in London, which was commissioned by Andrew Mellon himself in 1928 and created by some guy named William Haines, or so the decorator tells us. The décor is called *Chinoiserie*, which is pastel furniture, waxed pine helmet boards and parquet floors." He paused.

"See that wallpaper?" said Perot. "It's hand-painted eighteenth century. I'm supposed to point out the jade background with the pink peonies and birds and butterflies."

He grimaced. "Actually, it's all bullshit. The kids hate this room because we have plastic covers on all this fancy upholstery most of the time. We never sit in here."

Emily agreed. The room was beautiful, impressive, and tasteful, with no stench of excess, but it didn't seem welcoming or look lived in.

"I see you have horses, a stable, and a riding ring. Your family must be into riding?" Emily inquired, making conversation.

Perot grimaced. "Aw, my God," he said. "What a farce. My oldest daughter Patti, by my first wife, became fanatical about riding after her mother and I split. Our shrink said it was a reaction to the divorce, and of course I felt terrible about it. Guilt trip! I'd never ridden before . . . except for motorcycles, but I took it up to be with Patti. Total disaster. I didn't like it; was scared; took me away from golf. Hurt my back when I fell learning to jump."

He shook his head, apparently waiting a response. Joe had no idea what to say. Jonathan went on almost compulsively.

"When we did this house, I built the stable, the ring, the whole thing. I bought a couple of half-a-million-dollar show horses and got a live coach for Patti. Then, one day when she was seventeen, Patti discovered boys and hasn't ridden a horse for over a year now. Says she's through with riding. So what am I going to do with all this horse shit, pardon the expression, I've accumulated? Especially those horses? Expensive playthings. Vet bills to pay and they have to be exercised. Not like some bad painting you paid too much for and you can hang on a wall in the back bedroom."

Joe and Emily were rendered speechless by this family tragedy. "Sell the horses, fire the groom," Joe finally said. "You know the drill. Just like with stocks. Cut your losses."

"It's a disaster," Jonathan went on, "my handicap went from eleven to sixteen while I was learning to ride. Here, I want you to meet *my Nancy*." Did she call him *my Jonathan*, Joe wondered. Somehow he doubted it.

My Nancy obviously had no idea who they were—even though she had met Joe before—and was only interested in talking to another couple. The engrossing subject seemed to be about how to get her son into the nursery school class at Regional Day the coming fall. In a few moments, Jonathan was swept away by other guests, and they wandered out onto the flagstone terrace where they sat on a retaining wall and sipped their chardonnay in the tender but dispassionate light of early evening. Young women with eager, poised faces and sleek bodies in bright dresses with wine glasses in their hands circulated among casually but stylishly dressed men. Green lawns gently rolled down to a stream bordered by a line of mature cherry trees in full spring blossom.

"Good looking bunch of squaws these guys have," commented Emily laconically. "Looks like they all hit the gym pretty hard."

Among the clusters of guests, Joe saw a couple of hedge fund guys he knew, but Emily knew no one.

"I've been away from Greenwich for a while, but since I grew up here I thought I would have seen *someone* I recognized," Emily said to him "Obviously, a different social circle!"

"Nevertheless, getting into Regional Day seems to be on everybody's mind," said Joe sardonically. "Is that where you went?"

"Nope! Daddy was a trustee of Greenwich Academy. Smart or dumb—everybody I knew went to Regional Day or Greenwich Academy." She looked at him appraisingly. "Now those schools are deeply committed to diversity. If we had children the Greenwich schools would be competing for them. The attractive offspring of a socialite and a star black hedge fund manager. What could be better?"

At the dinner, they were placed separately. Joe was seated between a woman from Argentina and the wide-eyed wife of the Perot family's tennis pro. The Argentine woman was tall, slim, with black hair and had a beautiful, very pale, almost ethereal face. As she stretched back in her chair, she exuded a languid sensuality. Joe guessed she was in her mid-thirties.

"Are you here by yourself?" she asked.

"No, my girlfriend is down the table."

"Which one? Show me." He pointed out Emily to her.

"Ah, so you have an Ivy League lover. Perot told me she went to Princeton. How exciting!"

Then she proceeded to extract from him exactly who he was, what he did, and how rich he was. Her questioning was shameless, penetrating, and artful. Joe was amused and for a while he actually enjoyed the interrogation. In turn, he queried her. She was at the dinner unescorted and was "one of Nancy's decorators."

"This house is decorated not just exquisitely, but relentlessly," she murmured. Joe grinned back at her, but he was wary and beginning to feel that she was very tough and out of his league.

They talked in this manner through the first two courses. As the plates were being removed, Jonathan rose, thanked them all for coming, and asked everyone to join Nancy and him in the living room for a séance with "the great magician."

Twenty minutes later, Joe was standing in the crowd watching the magician when the Argentine woman came up behind him and whispered.

"Here's my card. If you ever want to do some decorating, give me a call." She drifted away.

Emily came over and gave his shin a not-so-gentle kick. "Let me see that card!" She looked at it. "She's a brazen vamp, not a decorator. She's a no-fly zone for you, pal."

As he lay in bed that night in his rented Upper East Side apartment, Joe reflected on his visit to Perot's opulent house. In particular, he thought about his female dining companion whose inquisition had been interesting. Physically, her pale, ethereal look and her slim, white body were enticing. He reflected that Emily was the only woman he had ever really known; certainly the only woman he had ever been truly intimate with. Was he missing something? Was he emotionally and physically immature?

Chapter 12

Big Decisions

The following week, Joe took Emily out to dinner at Le Bernardin. Both of them now were picky about their restaurants and their food, and this was one of their favorites. The acknowledged purpose of the dinner was that the lease on their apartment was expiring, and they knew they had a couple of serious decisions to make. Joe had been thinking about them, and their future, steadily since that evening in Greenwich. The dinner at the Perots had kick-started his mind.

They ordered two of Le Bernardin's mostly raw fish courses and a fine bottle of chardonnay. Joe sat back feeling luxurious and enjoying the wine. He looked at Emily and thought about how much he loved and cherished her. What was he doing even thinking about Joan and that pushy Argentine decorator?

Seemingly from out of nowhere, he blurted out, "Emily, I want us to get married, start having children, and move to Greenwich. What do you think?"

She looked at him for a long moment. "I'll be short but sweet. Yes, yes, and yes," she said with a big smile. "I'm very ready for all three. And by the way, it's about time you asked that question!"

For the rest of the evening they talked about their future. Emily was animated, her eyes flashing. The wedding should be in Greenwich, she said, and it should be small and immediate—family only. She wanted a church service but no bridesmaids, no best man, no pomp and circumstance. Her family would send out an engraved announcement notice afterward. Her mother would not be thrilled, but it would be even more painful for her to be presented with the *fait accompli* of a totally private New York wedding.

"I'm not one of those girls who has always dreamed of a big wedding connected to a stream of parties," she told him. "Besides, for us to do that now would be phony. After all, everyone knows we've been living together for over three years."

"You're sure?" he asked.

"I'm absolutely sure. But what about your parents?"

"I know, it's a problem. We'll have to work them in. Maybe your father, Big Joe, and I will play golf the day before and we'll all have dinner afterward."

"Inevitably," she told him, "the reception is going to be bigger than just immediate family. There's going to be friends we're going to want to have. I'm thrilled just thinking about it. It will be a celebration!"

She went on to say that she was very excited about the idea of having children and thought she would continue to work at the Council but on a part-time basis. They both knew that their wealth was now of a magnitude that they could make decisions independent of money considerations.

Over the next few weeks, their every moment together was consumed by talk about the wedding and of moving to Greenwich. It revitalized their relationship. Was Joe sure he wanted to commute? How would that work with his schedule? Was he convinced he wanted to live in the same town with her family?

Yes, I am definitely up for it, he thought. Guys told him you could actually get much more uninterrupted reading done on the train than anywhere else, including your office, and the requirement of catching a particular train compelled you to leave at a reasonable time.

Commuting might even improve his schedule, and he could always get a car and driver if Metro North turned out to be a drag.

Undeterred, she asked if he was convinced that he wanted to live in the same town as her family.

"As for living in Greenwich, it's a big town with a diverse society," he told her, somewhat avoiding her question. "There are literally hundreds of hedge funds there. The joke is that the speed limit in Greenwich is two and twenty. It's not like we were going to live in a family compound and spend our weekends at the Green Acres Country Club."

"That's true," she said. "We actually know far more people in Greenwich than we do in New York. And it's not just me. You know the football group guys. Hey, you could probably get into Green Acres on your own."

"Maybe. Your father tells me there's a lot of resentment of rich hedge fund guys living big and buying their way into clubs."

"Speaking of living," she asked, "what *are* your thoughts on a house and a home for us?"

"Well," he said, "I've been thinking about it a lot. First of all, I have no interest whatsoever in a skimpy starter home. We have to get a big, wonderful house that we're going to live in forever with plenty of room for children and nannies and dogs. I want a huge bedroom for us with a real master bathroom, and I want land, too."

"Joe, that's crazy. We should start out modestly to see if Greenwich works for us."

"We're going to make it work. I'm sure I don't want to live my life and bring up kids in New York City. The way this year is going, I figure I'm worth at least forty million with a lot more to come. I used to feel insecure about my abilities as an investor, but now I'm convinced I've got it and that our model works. It's time to step up."

"We're going to shock my parents and your football friends."

"That's unfortunate, but in the hedge fund world, big, fancy homes *are* how you flaunt it. If we buy some scruffy thing for three or four million, the other guys will think I haven't made any real money."

"Why do you care what they think?"

"Because it involves my image; my reputation in *my* world. A house is not just a house; it's one of the standards people will use to judge me, and for that matter, you, by. If we go modest they'll conclude

I'm just a dog-shit assistant to Mickey who talks big but doesn't get paid much. Homes are the Big Thing. I don't want to be nuts like Perot, but the guys compete with each other to have bigger, fancier houses with more land and other stuff like squash courts, three-hole golf courses, and wine cellars."

Emily stared at him. "You hedge fund people are truly insane."

"Yeah, you're going to marry a crazed man. I want to go whole hog on this house. You'll love it! I can't wait to see your mother's face the first time she sees it. We're going to call our estate *Whole Hog* . . . just kidding!"

"You're sure you got enough money put away that we can afford this extravaganza and the subsequent lavish and expensive lifestyle?"

"Lavish and expensive? What do you mean?"

"Just what I said. We're going to have to live up to *your* house—sorry, *our* house. There are some aerobic social climbers in Greenwich and I know you and your competitive instincts. Some of these people are climbing ladders so fiercely they've got blisters on their hands and feet."

"I've got enough money! I'm totally confident BA can keep making money. We're really rich. We're not upper-middle-class people anymore."

"What's the difference?" she asked, genuinely curious.

He laughed. "Upper-middle-class people have homes with two-car garages, a cleaning lady who comes in twice a week, and who fantasize about airline upgrades. Rich people have estates with wine cellars, a couple of nannies and a cook, and who wouldn't dream of flying commercial; they have NetJets contracts, or if they're *really* rich, their own planes."

"Have we really got that much money?"

"Not quite yet," Joe said. "But, Emily, I've got forty million in BA. Like I told you once before, under our Articles of Agreement with our investors, the managing partners—who are Mickey and me—have to reinvest eighty percent of our earnings after taxes back into BA, and we and our immediate families are not allowed to own equities for our own account. In effect, all our working money is in BA, but it's okay to take out money to buy a home or even homes plural.

It also makes sense to get a big mortgage on the house so I can keep as much compounding in BA as possible."

She was awestruck. What could she say? He was right. Of course, they could afford to spend $15 or $20 million on a house, even an estate.

"And a house in Greenwich is not spending money. It's an investment for the future," he added. "They're not making any more Greenwiches and they are printing more paper money."

He later had to admit that in making this big decision in the back of his consciousness was Mickey's recent revelation to him that he was going to get divorced—again. It was the third time, and Joe knew it was going to cost him almost $50 million as one Susan Cohen, Mickey's ex, was becoming a new, non-fee paying, limited partner in BA. They hadn't socialized much, but Joe had liked Susan. He also noticed that both Mickey's social life and low-slung belly were getting bigger.

As he had come to know Mickey so intimately, he began to understand that Mickey had changed. With success and wealth, he was simply incapable of functioning without at least several adoring, attentive, dependent women embedded in his personal life. *Embedded* was the right word, because the relationship had to have been, at one time or another, physical. Sleeping with a woman symbolized to Mickey that he possessed her.

Mickey was lecherous but it went far deeper than that. In fact, he was fundamentally more comfortable with women than with men. He also was a person who relished physical contact. He was a hugger and an arm-around-the-shoulders person with guys, and a kisser and toucher with women. Joe had talked to Emily about Mickey's womanizing, and they theorized that it went back to his teenage experiences at boarding school, where he was bullied and disparaged as a chubby, uncoordinated Jewish boy. Joe guessed he hadn't had sex in prep school and college and was making up for it now. All these wounds had been reopened when he had initially failed as a value investor in a growth stock firm run by a bunch of California WASPs.

In the past year, Mickey had begun acquiring material possessions in quick succession. He had bought a new penthouse apartment in New York City, a fabulous house right on the beach in Southhampton that must have cost $10 million, and joined Legacy—a fancy golf club in the Hamptons where the initiation fee was a cool $1 million. These adornments went with the ski chalet in Deer Valley that he already possessed.

Mickey also had purchased a new G-5 for $40 million. "Mick" was engraved on its tail. When he told Joe and Joan about this purchase, Joe asked him, "What's the matter with NetJets?"

"It's not classy. Any schmuck can buy a NetJets contract. The big guys like Julian and Stan have their own planes."

"The upkeep, the pilots must cost you a fortune."

"Two million a year, they tell me."

"Sounds nuts to me."

"Yeah, man, but there is nothing like walking with a couple of women across the hardtop to your *own* plane with your *own* name on the tail. And taking off is almost better than sex."

Joe didn't know what to say. Mickey rambled on.

"I'll tell you something, pal. I'm not putting up much real money for my new toys. Mortgages on the place in the Hamptons and the apartment, and I got a loan from Citicorp for thirty million on the G-5."

"It's leverage and overhead, Mick," Joan chimed in.

"Nobody ever got rich or lived well saving money," Mickey told them.

Mickey's latest girlfriend, Vanessa, was 25, worked at Sotheby's, and had assumed a major role in the art buying for his new apartment. Joe had also noticed that Mickey was beginning to leave the office early more often, and not, he suspected, to go to business meetings.

"Don't worry," Mickey jocularly told him. "No more weddings. These divorces are getting expensive."

When Joe mentioned all this to Emily, she grimaced and said sarcastically, "Who are we to question the credentials of the live-in girlfriends of hot hedge fund stars?"

"At least we're more or less the same age. Besides, we're engaged," Joe responded defensively.

"Thank goodness," Emily said. "Seems like all the rest of you guys want ever-younger women."

The new Cohen apartment in New York was over the moon. Joe and Emily had been there for dinner several times. It was a penthouse duplex on Fifth Avenue at 83rd Street in a fine old building. Mickey had done a complete remodeling, and it featured an expansive 25-foot by 40-foot living room with 15-foot ceilings of hand-hewn wood beams, a Venetian glass chandelier, and a massive, eight-foot high fireplace. With its arched windows and stunning view of the park, the master bedroom had been described by *Vanity Fair* as one of the most romantic in New York. The apartment came with a thousand square feet of balconies and terraces, the views from which were exhilarating. Joe reflected uneasily that redesigning apartments, buying houses, joining fancy golf clubs, and dealing with a divorce were all no-no's on the hubris distraction checklist of the hedge fund consultants.

Besides, even he, Joe, had the sense that Mickey was beginning to get a bit too full of himself, that he was spending a great deal of money, and that all kidding aside, Mickey was putting on a whole heaping lot of overhead and leverage. All those houses and apartments had fixed costs, and Joe knew Mickey was drawing almost a million dollars a month from his capital account in BA. Somewhere inside his inner being Joe sensed that he had to ground himself or he could become like Mickey.

While all this was going on, in the winter and early spring of 2003, stock markets had drifted back down toward the lows of the previous year. With the bear market now three years old and nearly 40 percent below its bull market highs, fear and gloom was everywhere. The bears cited the sluggishness of the global economy, its lack of resilience, the desperately overextended consumer, and moaned that this time there was no pricing power anywhere, and no pent-up demand to revive the beast. They worried about the war in Iraq and what the so-called unintended consequences could be. A war between the West and the Muslim world would be disastrous, and one of the first effects would be a shutoff of oil from the Middle East.

Market strategists and wise men were writing about the perils of deflation and quoting Schumpeter, Hayek, Robbins, and other scholarly treatises on the futility of reflating equity bubbles and liquidation cycles. This time, they said, monetary stimulus would not work. An elderly, famous investor and private equity hero wrote a book titled *Running on Empty*. Wise guys said he was "running on empty." Other bears argued the bubble of the 1990s was so big the bust couldn't possibly be over yet. They wanted more creative destruction, additional pain, mansions shuttered, and more redemptions from mutual funds. After Enron and all the scandals, the loss of trust in CEOs, they said, would take a decade to heal.

The great unwashed public in particular showed no inclination to resume speculating in equities. After three years of negative results and scandals, they were still licking their wounds. Tech and Internet stocks were selling at fractions of their 1999 and 2000 prices, and many shares purchased as hot new issues in the glory days of 1999 and early 2000 were now worthless junk.

Mickey's and Joe's religion was to stay agnostic about the direction of the markets, and to concentrate on stock selection. However, their model and research were saying that there were a lot more cheap longs with gradually improving momentum and fundamentals than overpriced, expensive stocks with weak momentum to short. Stocks in the technology, Internet, and telecom space were still appearing in their screens and research as the best shorts. Their net long crept up from 20 percent to 30 percent, and then 40 percent.

In this atmosphere, everyone—the pension funds, endowments, funds of funds, and wealthy individuals—liked the idea of quantitative, market-neutral hedge funds that had proven that they could make money in a bear market environment. Eager new investors poured into BA and other funds with the same religion. The new clients said they weren't looking for cowboys to shoot the lights out, just good, old-fashioned value investors who could consistently grind out 10 to 12 percent a year.

The spring of 2003 was cold and damp in New York, but it was becoming evident that the war was turning out to be an American triumph and there were flickering signs of life in the economy. By April, equity markets were rallying, and as the year unfolded, both the S&P

500 and the NASDAQ surged. By the end of the year, the former was up 28.7 percent and, unfortunately, the latter by 50.6 percent (see Figure 12.1). Suddenly, some of the bankrupt Internet and telecom junk, that they were short, doubled as other hedge funds scrambled to cover their short positions. With their tech-heavy short portfolio, the short squeeze rally hurt the BA portfolio.

For the first time in years, BA lagged the main U.S. market indexes with a gain for the year 2003 of 22 percent after all fees. This performance was only slightly better than the HFRI fund composite, which gained 20.5 percent. As it turned out, no one complained about BA's performance. They had done their job during the bear market years, and with their fixed fee plus 20 percent of the profits, BA earned over $250 million for Bridgestone and once again Mickey and Joe collected big paychecks.

"It's amazing we're making so much money when we actually underperformed the S&P and were way behind NASDAQ. A lot of long-only managers were up forty to fifty percent last year," Joe reflected.

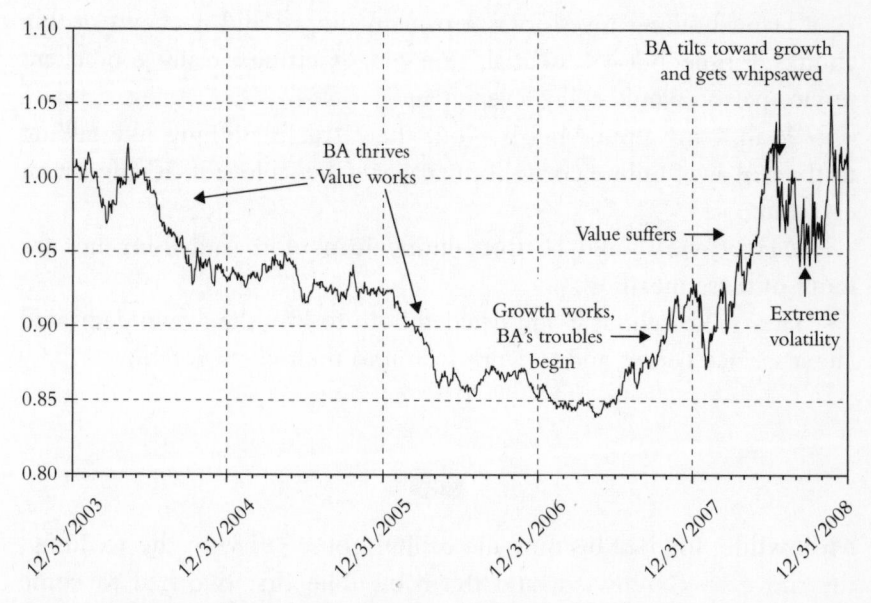

Figure 12.1   The Worm Turns Again: Growth versus Value

"Right now we're in the sweet spot of the best business in the world," Mickey told him, grinning benignly. "Relax. Onward Christian soldiers! Going forth to war! What do you want to do? Cut our fees?"

At year-end they more than tripled Joan's compensation to $9 million, but Joe could tell she was not pleasantly surprised when they told her the number. She obviously had done the arithmetic on their overall profitability. Thinking about it afterward, he reflected that they hadn't been overly generous, as she was now virtually a partner in their business. Mickey was still a little dismissive of her, Joe thought, and he should have stood up for her more. Had he held back because Emily sometimes seemed resentful and jealous of Joan?

They also hired two more analysts, one of whom was to work exclusively for Joan. As the number of investors in their fund grew, they were finding increasing demands on their time from important clients. The Bridgestone client service people were good, but not good enough for the really big, sophisticated investors who wanted to discuss beta, value at risk (VAR), and how the models worked. They began to consider whether they should build their own dedicated staff to include a couple of high-quality client service people to assume some of that burden.

"Hand-holding investors is a pain in the ass and it chews up big chunks of time, but it's essential," Joe said. "Getting a really good client service person would really leverage us."

"Yeah," answered Mickey, "but there still is nothing like talking to the real-live, online portfolio manager. Clients love it. It's almost an ego thing."

"Maybe we should be front-lining Joan more and using her for more of these meetings."

They talked about it and decided both to hire their own dedicated client service person and to work Joan into their client rotation.

Meanwhile, Joe had become increasingly obsessed with the wedding, the move to Greenwich, and the baby. The first two had to come before the baby. This was to be no shotgun marriage, and he was determined that the baby from the beginning would live in his own, secure home, not a rented apartment in New York. Time was of the essence.

With Greenwich on his mind, Joe called Doug Scott, his old friend and mentor from the Grant days. Doug had moved to Hadron as a proprietary macro trader, which was a different religion from what Joe was doing, but they had remained close and talked at least once a week. Several times Joe and Emily had gone out to dinner with Doug and his wife. Now he scheduled a lunch and began by asking Doug how it was going at Hadron.

"Look, prop trading is a highly stressful way to live. It's not a job; it's a life 'cause you take your portfolio home with you, away on vacation with you, to bed with you."

"Yeah, but so do we. Which is why we all make so much money."

"I'm not in your wealth league, pal. In fact, it's like I'm in the minor leagues traveling by bus and playing in cow pastures instead of Yankee Stadium."

"You'll get there."

"But my confidence that I can make money varies from one month to the next. I don't feel at all secure or good about myself as a prop trader. When I was in sales, if I worked harder, made more calls to clients, and traveled, I could be pretty sure I was going to get more business and get bigger paychecks. But as a prop trader, there's no correlation between working hard and making more money."

"I understand. It's rough. See, I feel pretty confident now," Joe told him. "I'm sure our model works in all the different kinds of market environments, and as long as I work it hard we will do well. How about Hadron? Is it okay?"

"All things considered, Hadron is a decent place to do this kind of trading. The other prop traders are all guys in their late thirties— you know the type, former high school jocks with fat necks and low-slung bellies who worked on the trading desks of the big firms. Decent guys—but it's very competitive, every trader for himself; at least there is a little less short-term pressure."

"What do you mean by less short-term pressure?"

"At Grant we were always under that horrible, ridiculous ten percent drawdown sword that completely fucked up your heads. Remember when after two good years I was up thirty percent halfway through my third year and then I lost, like, eight percent? The asshole warlord who ran me, who was really nothing but an accountant, says to me that if I lost another two percent that he'd shut me down. This after I had two great years!" He glared at Joe.

"Yeah, I know the story. So you took all your risk off and sold down to nothing. Two days later the markets turned around, and your former portfolio soared. Of course, since you weren't there anymore you didn't participate."

Doug nodded. "It messes with your head. And to add insult to injury, the young guy who worked as my assistant was so disgusted he quit and hustled a job in the investment management division." He sighed and continued, "The atmosphere is also better at Tamarax. At Grant, the prop traders were surrounded by belching, sweating, farting position traders."

"So how much are you running now?"

"A hundred million."

"And what's your arrangement with Tamarax?"

"I have to pay all my incidental expenses like travel and an assistant if I want one. They deduct those expenses from my profits and then pay me fifteen percent of the total. It's a pretty generous deal by prop trading standards. Most arrangements are at twelve to thirteen percent and sometimes less."

"Do you see much of Tom Tamarack himself? He's supposed to have great market instincts and to be a real winner as a trader."

"Part of each day Tom is on the trading floor with us at his own terminal. He runs a book of about two billion. Once a week, he sits down in a conference room with us sixteen prop traders and his guy who runs us day-to-day and he talks stream-of-consciousness stuff. It's very helpful and stimulating. He also walks the trading floor and kibitzes. He's always looking for ideas, and you'd better not bullshit him on the facts. He's very rigorous. He's into some weird stuff, though."

"Like what?"

"Well, early this month he told us that in late October there could be some spooky volatility. Something about the twenty-seventh day of the seventh lunar cycle. You know the old rock song about *when the moon is in the seventh house and Jupiter aligns with Mars.* Some of the guys sort of laughed, but he pointed out that market panics have consistently occurred in October and he mentioned 1857, 1907, 1929, 1987, and 1997. He has retained an astrologer he consults. Tom says that as a hunter he knows the best time to hunt is when the moon is full, because the animals are stirred up and moving around. Investors are animals too, he said, and they also tend to be more active when the moon is up. Sure enough, late last October there was a mini-panic."

"Amazing! What else does he do to support you?"

"Well, he spent a couple of million dollars building this custom data-base of market history. I can access it and put in a couple of keywords and find the market's historic reactions to every conceivable circumstance and event. History tends to repeat itself."

"Yeah," said Joe, "but I'm skeptical. If successful investing was mostly all about market history, the historians would be running all the money. Each market in its own time does its own thing to fuck up the most traders."

"Well, I find it helpful. Like I said, the atmosphere is pretty good and Tom is around the floor to talk to. Occasionally, he throws a party with live music. Still, it's a tough place. Suddenly he gets moody and pissed and changes the shutdown limits, and out of nowhere a couple of months ago he let six prop traders go. But he gives you fair warning. There's a sign over his office door that says 'I built this business by being a bastard. I run it by being a bastard. I'll always be a bastard, and don't you ever try to change me.'— Charles Revson.' "

They then chatted about living in Greenwich. Doug told Joe that he had bought a house in Greenwich, and that his daughter was now going to the North Street Public School. He had tried—with no success—to get her into Regional Day, the fancy day school that went through ninth grade. He said the private schools were very tough to get into, even in kindergarten, unless you were a legacy or made a big contribution to the endowment. Now, the Greenwich private schools were making a nod to diversity as well. By the time the legacies, endowment, and diversity spaces were filled, he said bitterly, there was hardly any room for ordinary people with no connections, particularly if they were prop traders for a giant hedge fund. The Greenwich establishment viewed hedge funds as *nouveau riche* polluters of the town's pristine atmosphere.

Joe nodded his head in sympathy while wondering if just maybe he might represent the diversity that a place like Greenwich wanted.

Two weeks later, Emily signed up a Greenwich real estate broker. Following Joe's instructions, she told him $10 to $15 million, four-acre zone, new house, large master bedroom suite, four to five additional bedrooms, library, three-car garage, large family room, pool, and so on. The broker said he had a number of houses that met those criteria. Greenwich was experiencing a spec building boom.

Three weeks later, they told their families that they were getting married and that they planned to live in Greenwich. It was hard to read the Daweses' reaction, but Big Joe said little, Dolores was rhapsodic, and his sisters were wildly excited.

They set the wedding date for a month later. Emily made all the arrangements.

It was a beautiful October weekend, and on Saturday morning before the late afternoon wedding, Joe took Big Joe, Josh, and David Dawes to play golf at Lone Tree. The reception was at the Dawes home, where it had all begun. The guests were family, a few close friends of the Daweses, the hard-core members of the football group, Josh, Doug, and three of Emily's college roommates. Mickey, his girlfriend, and Joan were both there, but Joe didn't invite anyone else from BA. Emily was polite but distant with Joan, and her mother looked as though she had indigestion. Otherwise, it was all very jolly. David Dawes was particularly effusive and affectionate with Big Joe, Josh, and Dolores. The Daweses sent a wedding announcement to a broad mailing list the following Monday.

Within a month of the wedding, Emily announced that she was pregnant. But the matter of finding and buying their home was not quite as quick or simple. Emily looked at perhaps 20 houses and narrowed the final selection down to three. Joe looked at each of them twice over the course of a weekend, and he and Emily made their decision on Sunday night. The Greenwich real estate market was hot, and Joe hit the $12 million offer. He got a mortgage for $8 million.

"Man, you don't fool around!" their broker said with genuine awe, thinking that he had should have shown this big, swinging hedge fund guy a larger and even more expensive house. "I wish all my clients were as decisive as you."

"Yeah, well, in my business you have to make buy-and-sell decisions every day, so I guess I'm used to it," Joe replied. He reflected afterward that he must have sounded like a pompous asshole.

They really didn't have to do anything to the brand-new house they had bought, and within days Emily had hired a decorator. Joe gave her a budget of $2 million and emphasized that speed was of the essence. It had become almost an obsession with him that their baby would come back from the hospital to their own home. At the office, Mickey and Joan were amused by the change that had come over him. It was the new domesticated Greenwich Joe. Who would have ever thought it?

Chapter 13

The Years of Milk and Honey

For investors, 2003, 2004, 2005, and 2006 were a time of mild bull markets. For hedge funds—in terms of performance—they were good but hardly vintage years. But it was a delicious moment for gorging with asset growth. Admittedly, in the bull market of 2003 to 2006, hedge funds as a group were not beating the indexes and the traditional long-only managers, but, as their sales people kept reminding everyone, they actually had *made* money in the disastrous bear market of 2000 to 2002 when long-only managers lost at least 40 percent, and in many cases, much more. This statistic was incredibly important! The effect of not having down years on compounding returns was startling. Besides, periods of loss were both embarrassing and unnerving. And long-only managers and long-only investment management firms were no longer where that elusive but fashionable *it* was at. Investment committees around the world became eager to build a new major asset class in their portfolios called Alternative Investments, which was just a fancy name for hedge funds.

Table 13.1   Bridgestone Alpha Total Net Returns*

	2003	2004	2005	2006
Bridgestone Alpha Net Return*	+22.1%	+10.1%	+8.8%	+12.2%
S&P 500 Total Return	+28.7	+10.9	+4.9	+15.8
NASDAQ Index Total Return	+50.6	+9.1	+2.1	+10.3
HFRI Equity Hedge Fund Index	+20.5	+7.7	+10.9	+11.7
HFRI Fund Weighted Composite Index	+19.6	+9.0	+9.3	+12.9
HFRI Fund of Funds Composite Index	+11.6	+6.9	+7.5	+10.4

*After 2 percent fixed fee and manager compensation of 20 percent of profits.

Table 13.1 tells the happy story. The S&P 500 and the Dow Jones Industrial Average worked laboriously back toward the 2000 peaks, but even after a huge rally, the NASDAQ was still 50 percent below its bubble top by the end of 2006. Note that BA lagged the S&P 500 in three out of the four years but did better than the NASDAQ every year except 2003. The more speculative NASDAQ Index, after having fallen almost 80 percent, soared past the S&P 500 in 2003, but then lagged as the broad level of stocks worked higher over the next three years. BA only marginally beat the hedge fund index in three out of the four years, but its clients were still happy, verging on euphoric, because it achieved these results with low volatility, an average net long of 39 percent, and a low level of risk. In other words, the fund generated significant alpha—stock specific performance, which was what the consultants and the funds of funds yearned for.

Dramatic changes were now evolving in the investment perceptions and prejudices of pension funds, endowments, foundations, and wealthy individuals. For the last decade, Yale, Harvard, and Amherst had been big investors in hedge funds, venture capital, and private equity. This unconventional allocation had been spectacularly successful. Despite the much higher management fees they paid, their endowments surpassed the performance of all other large funds by an enormous margin, and David Swensen's *Yale Model* became the rage. Huge pools of money began to gravitate toward hedge funds, and now they were *the* place to be for the *avant garde* investor. Being invested in hedge funds became the bragging, cocktail party chatter of the rich and famous at the watering holes of the upper class. You weren't *with it* as an investor unless you owned some hot hedge funds.

In the mid-2000s, hundreds of new hedge funds were being started by ambitious long-only investment managers, stock salesmen, traders, and various exotic talents ranging from no-good sons-in-law to retired investment bankers. Both the birth rates and the death rates of these new funds were astronomical. A couple of dozen bright *luckies* were becoming *filthy* rich, but many other start-ups were broken, sometimes brutally, on the rack of indifferent performance and inability to raise assets. First-year performance was essential, and the failure rate was high, as new funds either didn't perform or failed to reach critical mass.

As a thousand new hedge funds a year were created, a new industry was developed by prime brokers and capital introduction firms to raise money for these fledglings in return for a share of the management fee. Although there are no official statistics, it is believed that worldwide (in the three years ending in 2006) more than 3,000 new funds opened and 2,000 expired. Hedge Fund Research Inc. says that by the middle of 2008 there were 7,652 hedge funds—and they admit that's a low-ball guess.

The same multiplication was occurring in the fund of funds business. They had become the biggest winner in the entire investment management space with their assets up 10 times from 1999, and with growth in the 2004-to-2006 period of 25 percent annually. In 2000, there were 500 of them. Now there were 2,500. They accounted for almost 40 percent of total hedge fund assets, which was far ahead of the 22 percent share of high-net-worth individuals. The five biggest fund of funds controlled about a third of the business. They charged a fixed fee of around 80 basis points and a performance fee of 10 percent of the profits.

The fund of funds business grew because many investors didn't feel comfortable vetting the plethora of hedge funds or monitoring the development and performance of the funds they were invested in. True, the double fee was a high hurdle to overcome, but as shown in Table 13.1, the funds of funds were doing a decent job. This performance was being achieved in part, however, by using leverage to enhance their numbers. This was leverage on leverage, since the underlying hedge funds used leverage as well, but who cared as long as the band played on?

The big fund of funds were and still are managed by expert professionals who devote their time to studying hedge funds. They use extensive quantitative analysis to isolate the sources of performance and to determine how much risk individual funds are taking on. Portfolios are closely monitored, and they are supposedly not susceptible to hedge fund manager promotional bullshit.

The funds of funds also watch closely for the sociological signs that indicate the evolution of the dread and usually fatal disease of hedge fund hubris. Subtle indications that a manager might be taking his eye off the ball are a falling golf handicap, a divorce, the purchase of vacation homes, multiple foreign nannies, and a rising social and charity profile. Additional signs that a hedge fund manager is getting too full of himself are nonstop pontificating and not listening, which can also trigger the exit button. If they got bad vibes, funds of funds could, and sometimes did, flick $150 million pieces out of a hedge fund for bad table manners.

As time went on, Mickey began setting off such alarms with his extracurricular activities, but that is to come later on.

The hedge fund evaluators were also sensitive to signs of excessive office opulence. A renowned and hot hedge fund that had blown up in 2006 had an office culture and practices that had alerted several fund of fund investors to possible trouble. The managing partner dominated internal meetings and imperiously brooked no dissent. There was a ping-pong table in the trading room, and beer and wine were served after the market closed. The firm was eventually wiped out by a massive short in natural gas that the perceptive funds had sidestepped.

Beginning in 2004, funds of funds became major investors in BA. Mickey and Joe regarded them as a mixed blessing. On the one hand, it was quick, easy money and you were dealing with professionals who didn't ask a lot of dumb questions. On the other hand, funds of funds abhorred performance volatility and so-called drawdowns. [A drawdown is when a fund reports a decline in net asset value for a marking period.] An occasional monthly drawdown will be tolerated, but even a small quarterly drawdown can send up red flags and be the trigger for a quick redemption. A big drawdown is grounds for immediate divorce.

"We're lucky," Mickey said one day as they were chatting. "All this short-term scrutiny can screw up your head big time. You are compelled to respond to market weakness—no matter how irrational—by dramatically reducing your risk. Sometimes as an investor you have to sweat out episodes of stupid sell-offs."

"With our style, it's hard to imagine how we could have a big drawdown," Joe added. "We could underperform for a while, but we keep our net long so modest, even a big market decline wouldn't smash us."

Mickey went on, "The drawdown pressure is really bad stuff. Hedge funds that try to time the market and move their net long around become nothing but momentum-driven prop traders whipsawed and terrorized by the fear of a big drawdown. At the first sign of a softening market, they scramble for the sidelines and then get whipsawed if it doesn't happen."

Joe stared out the tall window of his office into the incredibly brilliant and empty sky from which the morning light poured out over the park. "And even worse," he said softly, "business considerations will begin to dominate good investment decision making. We will be compelled by business preservation to respond to market swings. It's a conflict of interest."

"And a potential recipe for disaster! Well, we've got to at least be polite and meet with these fund of funds guys when they come in and maybe tell them why we may not want their money."

Joe grimaced. "But when you come right down to it, we do want their money. We could get a quarter of a billion from a big fund. It would take a lot less client servicing than getting the same amount from a hundred different investors each wanting their moist little hand held. The smile and a shoeshine gang desperately want us to do it."

The conventional wisdom now had become that hedge funds—because of their incentive compensation fee structure—attracted the best and the brightest investment talent. Admittedly, the fees paid to hedge funds were far higher, but they were worth it. Sure, there were a few good investors left in the big, traditional investment management firms, but in general a long-only investment style was the refuge of unambitious dullards who left work early and didn't take their portfolios home and sleep with them.

Furthermore, since hedge funds could sell short and use leverage to buy more assets, they had the flexibility to exploit an increasingly complex investment world in which the opportunities ranged from emerging market stocks to commodities and even to private issues of public securities, otherwise known as PIPEs. The problem was that some of the best hedge funds were closed to new investors because their managers were convinced they couldn't perform as well with more money. They feared bigness and they were right to. This was very frustrating to the giant pools of money such as state and local pensions and the sovereign wealth funds of countries like Singapore, Korea, and Abu Dhabi.

But there was another powerful force at work as well. These mammoth institutions had actuarial requirements in the high single digits and abhorred volatility. Fixed income, in other words, bond investments, didn't work because their yields weren't high enough to meet the actuarial demands. Also, the plan sponsors didn't like the volatility of the long-only equity managers or of aggressive hedge funds. They wanted investment programs that consistently delivered results in the 8 to 11 percent range. Of course, if the returns averaged out to be even higher, all the better.

Thus, the new class of alpha hedge funds that didn't take much market risk—and therefore had low volatility—and that relied on superior stock selection were very appealing. These funds, their clients believed, were run by smart, sophisticated analysts backed by powerful quant models. They were rationally searching for alpha and were far less risky than trading and macro hedge funds that were making big bets and were driven by beta. The latter class was bound to have more volatility, and the macro superstars had all suffered big loss years at one time or another.

As more alpha funds were created to meet the rising demand for this new style, competition for stocks to put in the funds increased. The investment equations the funds developed had different tweaks, but since they were all basically value driven, the names tended to be generally similar. The BA team found themselves bumping into analysts from other alpha funds at company meetings, and often buying the same longs and selling the same shorts.

There was also bound to be increasing competition for performance as the start-up funds needed to attract attention and raise money. Since

2004 to mid-2007 was a period of low volatility and relative calm in the equity markets, managers began to use more leverage to get better returns. They assumed volatility would stay low, and so they would not be assuming inordinate risk by doing this. In fact, they calculated they could promise their investors modest risk as measured by VAR ratios despite increased leverage.

For example, suppose an unleveraged $100 million portfolio with a 30 percent net long position (that is, long 65 percent cheap stocks, short 35 percent expensive) could earn an annual return of 4 percent with very low annual volatility. Normally, you would leverage it with another $200 million and could then theoretically earn, after interest expenses, 10 percent with a low probability of losing more than 2.5 percent in any one month. Why not borrow still another $200 million and get the return up to 17 to 18 percent and promise you wouldn't lose more than 4 percent? It seemed like a reasonable thing to do, and it increased your returns significantly.

The new breed, however, also had to be big enough to accept large accounts, as the giant institutional pools of money wanted to put out big pieces of at least a couple of hundred million each. It would otherwise be irrelevant to their total fund's performance. BA originally had not been designed to meet this need, but now, by good fortune, it appeared perfectly structured to meet this criterion. Gobs of money poured in, BA continued to grind out the performance, and Mickey and Joe got richer and richer. By the end of 2006, Joe's capital account in BA was over $150 million.

Joe and Emily meanwhile had settled in Greenwich. They loved their big, new house out on Round Hill Road on a little over four acres. Emily's decorator did the whole interior—from wallpaper and contemporary art on the walls to furniture and the giant Viking refrigerator. She even bought some Thai and Cambodian statues for the front hall. It was a wonderful, sprawling yet elegant, mansion. Although way too big for the two of them now, just right for an eventual family of five with a live-in nanny and housekeeper. By 2007, Joe and Emily were well on the way to a full complement. Their first baby, born in the summer of 2004, was a boy, Timothy, and his brother, Ian, came in 2006.

Joe was a doting and loving father, and holding the babies and smelling their sweet, talcum-powdered baby scent and feeling them slump sleepily and so trustingly against his chest was an overwhelming and entrancing sensation like nothing he had ever known. But once or twice, when he was looking into a little face, he thought about that baby of his that Pat had been carrying so long ago and who had been extinguished. There was definitely pain in the remembrance.

"You like being the big daddy, don't you?" Emily said to him one night four weeks after Ian came home. It was really a statement, not a question.

"Yeah," he said. "I never dreamed how much I would like it."

"You like screaming babies in the middle of the night with colic and dirty diapers."

"It's part of the price—but I can't wait until they're old enough to reason and catch a football."

She laughed. "I should have guessed. But Joe, my dear, I'm thrilled the way you've altered your work schedule and even more thrilled the way our life together has grown so much closer again. Even Mother thinks you're a good father and husband."

"That's progress," he replied. "That's real progress."

And he had materially changed his schedule and work habits. Each morning he was driven to work by the housekeeper's husband in his own Mercedes sedan equipped with a customized seat, reading lamp, phone, and a Bloomberg screen. They left every morning promptly at 6:30 to beat the traffic, and he arrived at the office between 7:15 and 7:30. In the afternoon, except under the most pressing circumstances, his assistant knew better than to book meetings that started later than 4:30, and most evenings he made the 5:30 train from Grand Central. The traffic in the evening made driving back to Greenwich a laborious and unpredictable struggle, and he found the peace and quiet of the train relaxing, assuming he could get a decent seat. He had substantially reduced the number of dinners in New York he attended. He wanted to get home in time to see the babies.

At first their social life in Greenwich was somewhat limited, but not for long. He was The Kid, a rapidly rising young star of the hedge fund world; a stud; a guy with an intriguing background. A big-time college football resume; and a four handicap made Joe Hill someone people had heard about and wanted to meet. Throw in a fancy, aristocratic Greenwich girl who had gone to Princeton for a wife, and you had an attractive and interesting young couple who whetted even the whitest-shoe country club appetites.

Well before his move to Greenwich, the seasoned Mickey had advised him that as a new boy in town it would be smart if he made some eye-popping contributions to local charities such as the Garden Club, the local symphony, the Greenwich library, and the Bruce Museum. Joe complied. In fact, advised by his accountant, he even set up his own foundation.

"Don't call your foundation by some mellifluous name," Mickey warned him when Joe told him about it. "Make sure Joe Hill Esquire is on the label so there's no confusion about who the donor is."

A few weeks later, when writing a check for $75,000 to the Bruce Museum, an institution he had never even been to and that mostly housed Greenwich relics, Joe couldn't help wondering if there weren't more worthy causes. A day later, still feeling guilty, he sent a check of similar magnitude to the Big Neck Teachers' Association. Soon he and Emily began receiving invitations to charity balls both in Greenwich and on the New York charity ball circuit.

"Do some of them!" Mickey told him. "They're a total pain in the ass. The formal, money-raising programs at these events are mind-numbing torture, but you *will* meet a lot of people. The object of the exercise is to convince the town's *haute bourgeoisie* that you are not a greedy, blood-sucking hedge fund monster who will ravage the culture of their precious schools and clubs. Undoubtedly, at these events, you will find a number of other hedge fund guys who are also trying to get respectable, and you can babble stocks with them so the socializing is not a complete waste of time. The fact that you have Emily is worth at least several million in contributions to Greenwich Hospital, Brunswick, and Regional Day."

Mickey was right. The Hills quickly discovered they weren't the only ambitious hedge fund couple with upholstered sensibilities trying

to make it in Greenwich. The woods north of town were littered with elaborately obscene estates owned by hedge fund guys where hubris and house vanity knew no bounds. Having your own squash court and indoor swimming pool was bush league stuff. The really big guys like Steve Brown, founder of FAC, had added ostentatious flourishes of affluence like an ice rink with its own Zamboni and an indoor basketball court. Downtown, FAC had leased the top floors of 600 Greenwich Avenue and had installed a soundproofed music room complete with a drum kit and mixing board, three jumbo flat-screen TVs, a custom food court and kitchen, and, of course, a gym and showers. Steve, his own bigger-than-life self, sat in a corner office with views across Long Island Sound at a $50,000 desk that was a single slab of caramel-colored walnut with bronze legs.

Having Emily's parents, deeply embedded in Greenwich, nearby was also a help. The Saturday football game was gradually succumbing to age, but Joe still kept up with some of the old gang. The Daweses took Joe and Emily to dinner at Green Acres from time to time, and David invited Joe to play with him in a Green Acres Member Guest game at which they did well but not too well. Everyone was very friendly. Joe regularly played golf at Lone Tree, and he was continually being invited to member guest tournaments and to brokers' outings. In fact, Goldman Sachs flew him to Augusta in one of their big corporate jets with six other hedge fund heavies for the weekend to play the hallowed Augusta National course.

Joe loved all of this—the golf, the attention, and the interaction with other investors that inevitably occurred on these outings and trips. It wasn't a waste of time by any means, although there was a fair amount of sandbagging that went on. Sandbagging was when a guy glorified his own positions to lure you into them hoping you would buy them to run up the price. Technically, the sandbagging part came only when the sandbagger sold his position into your buying.

Back in Greenwich, he had more mundane thoughts. "Shouldn't we join Green Acres?" Joe asked Emily. "I want the boys to learn at a young age how to play all those country club sports like golf, tennis, and squash. Besides, I like the place. I'm getting to appreciate exclusivity. Aren't you some kind of an automatic legacy?"

"I suppose I probably am," Emily told him. "But it won't be automatic by any means, and if you're going to be the first black member and our children are going to be the first dark-skinned kids, I want them to ask us. Not confront them with it. There's a big waiting list of handsome couples who are other members' best friends and there's bound to be some jealousy."

"I don't sense any resentment," Joe said. "I'd really like to get it done."

"Of course you don't sense any resentment. You're a big-time investment dude and you can hit a golf ball three hundred yards. No one's going to advertise their discomfort to you directly. Nevertheless, it may be an issue. Some member's candidate doesn't get in because they take you. It's bound to piss someone off. Let me be the strategist on this one."

That was the end of that conversation.

Then there was the nursery school issue. Joe was determined his son Timothy was going to go to the best and the fanciest school, which was clearly the revered and blue-blood Greenwich Regional Day School. Emily, on the other hand, was partial to the Montessori School. Joe insisted. His sons were not going to grow up at some artsy-crafty, *avant garde* school crayoning with a bunch of precocious oddballs. In the end he prevailed, and they applied and filled out the forms for the next year's nursery school class at Regional Day.

Greenwich is just as tough as New York City when it comes to getting into the elite schools—even at the nursery school level. At Regional Day, there were four nursery school sections, each with 13 children. The school was very partial to legacies and 30 of the places were already spoken for. Thus, there were 22 spots left, and the Hills were informed there were already 60 applications from beautiful, wealthy, and allegedly blissfully happy families. All applicant parents were invited to an open house on a January evening for a briefing on the school by the headmaster and the senior nursery school teacher.

Joe again consulted with the wise Mickey as to what, if anything, he should do. Mickey gazed out the window at the bleak snowiness of Central Park.

"Okay," he said finally. "I got it. You play the race card here. A school like Regional Day is very sensitive to being too lily-white and perfect. On the other hand, they probably have been taking black kids from Stamford and I'll bet it hasn't worked well. My son went to a fancy elementary school that had some black kids. The third day he got into an ostensibly friendly shoving match with a cute little black kid and the kid kicked him in the balls so hard he barfed. These suburban schools need to take minorities but they want black kids who are homogeneous, if that's the word."

"So you have to be a black kid from the right side of the tracks who won't kick other kids in the balls. How do I send that signal?" Joe asked.

"After the headmaster's presentation, he'll ask for questions. You stand up first and fast. He sees you're of color. You throw up a respectful, well-spoken, softball pitch."

"Yeah, like what? Shout yo momma, dude!"

Mickey laughed and thought again. "Say something like *My name is Joe Hill. Your school is already very impressive, but by the end of your accomplished tenure as headmaster, what further advances and changes would you like to accomplish in both the curriculum and the physical plant?* The *your accomplished tenure* stuff is a bit much, but I promise you the headmaster guy will love it because it gives him a chance to wax poetic. Furthermore, he will register that you're an articulate diversity and remember your name. As long as Timothy doesn't fuck up his interview you'll be in."

"What interview? How can they interview a child?"

"Easy. They put five child candidates in a room with a bunch of blocks and toys while two teachers observe—through windows—what happens, how they behave, how they interact. No mothers allowed. Very subjective. Train Timothy to covertly pinch a couple of the other children, hopefully to provoke an aggressive counter response. Timothy steps away, and the ref throws the unnecessary roughness flag. You know, like the NFL."

"You're kidding," Joe said.

"A little," Mickey told him. "Then there's the marshmallow test. The psychologists at Yale have discovered the best predictor of future success with young children is to put five in a room. The proctor gives each one a marshmallow and tells the children. 'You can eat this marshmallow if you want to, but I'll be back in ten minutes and if you haven't eaten it I will give you two more you can take home with you.' Yale found that children who could postpone gratification at an early age had astoundingly higher social and academic potential."

"Okay," Joe told him. "We'll work on that one, too."

Joe did as Mickey advised at the open house. The headmaster positively glowed in responding to Joe's fat pitch, and afterward, at the reception, he came up to him and asked Joe how long he had lived in Greenwich and what business he was in.

"I run a hedge fund," Joe told him.

"Ah," murmured the headmaster, while visions of a big gift to the endowment danced in his head. They chatted amiably. Later he thought he detected a few dirty looks from some of the other parents, one of whom, a hedge fund guy he knew, gave him a "nice play, Shakespeare" dig with a nasty grin.

Two weeks later, Emily was asked to bring Timothy to Regional Day for the observation session. Joe hadn't trained him for dirty tricks as Mickey had suggested, but he told him not to eat any candies or marshmallows. On the fateful morning, the anxious mothers cooled their Jimmy Choo heels in an anteroom and made polite conversation. After an hour and 15 minutes, the children and the teachers emerged. One little girl had obviously been crying, and one of the boys had pooped in his pants. Timothy, however, seemed serene and unscathed, and three weeks later they were informed that he had been admitted to next year's class. Emily learned later that neither the crier nor the pooper had made the cut.

Chapter 14

The High Probability of the Improbable

I t was the first week of January 2007. More money had come in, and Mickey and Joe's fund was over $8 billion.

"My God," said Mickey, "this number is mind-blowing. All we have to do is just keep grinding it out and we've got a gold mine here. What are you going to do next, big guy, when your net worth hits a billion?"

Joe shrugged. "It's hard to believe. As to what I'm going to do, I'm going to start spending some money. I feel really good about our formula."

"As long as we stick to our model and our risk disciplines, we're going to be fine. We have to keep our net long modest so we're not vulnerable to a market decline and concentrate on being totally focused on creating alpha."

"Suppose value really goes out of style the way it did in the late Nineties? That could screw us for a while."

"Yeah, but our other screens—like price momentum, positive change in the fundamentals, balance sheet strength—will counterbalance. We might not do as well in a growth stock environment, but we should still be okay."

Joe grinned at him. "And in the end, value will win out. That's what you told me, and it's our credo. That's what the hallowed Ben Graham preached. But why did Buffett make that 'beware of geeks bearing formulas' crack?"

"Listen," Mickey said. "Don't get nervous. Buffett likes to deliver cute one-liners. Even if we underperformed both the market and the hedge fund benchmark for a year or even two, we've bought ourselves time with our long stretch of good performance."

"Yeah," said Joe. "Theoretically, with our modest net long, at the very worst we could have a minor down in a year when the market itself was off a lot. But I agree it's hard to conceive of how we could have a big loss. Above all, we can't do anything crazy. We gotta control our egos and not give out any bad hubris vibes."

They sat silently for a while, and then Mickey spoke. "Look, I want to enjoy my money. I figure I'm in my *baroque* period."

"Say again?"

"Baroque is a style. Baroque is living with an overwhelming spirit of opulence, drama, and sensuality. Life is a magnificent feast. Baroque is gorging, exuberantly collecting glorious women, houses, art, even wine."

I don't get it, Joe thought. *What is he talking about?*

"You know," said Mickey, "I am becoming recognized as a big hitter. I got a call today from Larry Fletcher about an art deal involving a lot of money and a couple of pictures."

"Who's Larry Fletcher? Never heard of the guy."

"Fletcher, my child, is the most famous art dealer in the world, or at least America. He owns the big money hedge fund crowd. Larry travels in his own Hawker Eight Hundred and has a helicopter to take him to it. He goes to the estate sales and private auctions, buys good stuff for his inventory, and then sells it at a huge markup to gauche suckers like me. But the guy has superb eye, and his kind of really good art only goes up. It's prudent wealth diversification from paper to tangibles—real things."

"Well, I'm not in that league yet," Joe replied.

"Well, I am!" said Mickey. "I met Fletcher at a cocktail party, and he's a really savvy, smart guy. We hit it off. He's going to put some money in our fund. He's asked me if I would bankroll him on a unique deal that—if it comes off—will be the biggest single-owner sale in art history. He'll give me half of the profits."

"How does that work?" Joe asked.

"There's a collection of six magnificent pieces that a Red Army general took from the Berlin Museum at the end of World War II, and that his heirs want to sell very privately and very quietly. The pictures are the real thing. Rembrandts, a Michelangelo, a large cubist Picasso, and an iconic mechanical nude by Fernand Leger. Unique stuff. Larry thinks he can buy them for fifty million and sell 'em almost immediately in this market for seventy-five to eighty. I put up forty-five, he throws in five, and I get half of the profits."

"I thought you told me Larry was so rich and successful?" Joe asked.

"Successful and rich he is, but he doesn't have fifty million in cash in his back pocket. Besides, he likes me. Wants to do some business with me."

"You'd better be careful. What do you know about serious art?"

"Vanessa knows a lot. It's a layup. Besides, I want to be on the board of the Metropolitan Museum. Classy group! Vanessa very much wants to hang out with them. They'd put me on if I gave 'em an Old Master. It would be a sweet deal. I make fifteen million, give the museum a picture valued at fifteen million, and end up with a big tax deduction and a board seat, all for the forty-five-million-dollar bridge loan."

"Who buys art at those prices?"

"Who do you think? Hedge fund superstars whose second wives are on the make, investment bank CEOs with company money, museums with fat endowments, and now there are art funds. Larry says there are at least a hundred *gros acheteurs* in the world and that we will have *la grande vente* in Paris and then another in New York. How do you like my *artsy* French?"

"Phony impressive, Mick, but as I said, I'm not in that league."

"Just wait, you will be. At first, when guys get very rich, they compete on the grandeur of their houses, then on the pedigree of their kid's governesses, and then finally on their art collections. You're one of the most competitive guys I've ever known. Next thing I know, you'll be buying a Degas."

They were talking freely, openly now, as they had so often in the past. *We are truly investment and business soul mates*, Joe thought. He knew that the smile and a shoeshine gang worried that Mickey was being spoiled by success, and there was the same nagging concern in the back of his mind, too. So he said quietly, "Mick, on that subject, I think you're hitting it pretty hard on the lifestyle stuff. I saw your picture with Vanessa in that society magazine, and *Vanity Fair* had a piece about the villa you just bought on Lake Como and how you refurbished it. That's heavy-duty stuff. Particularly the publicity about how rich you are. The consultants' and fund of funds' hubris red flags must be starting to go up."

"Yeah, I know," said Mickey nonchalantly. "That *Vanity Fair* piece also mentioned how I'm a big donor to the Make-A-Wish Foundation and gave a million bucks to the Kent School for a soccer stadium."

"Right, and they said you gave it to Kent to help your daughter make the team."

"Admittedly, that was a consideration. After all, what's money for?"

"So why not lie low for a while?"

"Because I'm still pissed off at all those fucking growth stock guys who, during all those years when value and I were in the wilderness, made it clear that they thought I was just a loser. Now they're struggling and hurting, and I want to rub what we've done in their arrogant WASP faces."

"Wow," said Joe. "You took it personally."

"Yeah, you bet I did! It was personal and maybe part of it was that I was a pudgy Jewish guy. So fuck them."

Joe decided it was best to drop the subject.

The markets worked higher in January and February of 2007 but then suddenly had a sharp drop in late February and early March, with the S&P 500 down 7 percent. The BA team was disconcerted as their portfolio lagged the early gain and then declined more than the averages.

"It feels like a gathering storm," Joan murmured uneasily one morning.

"Three months don't prove anything," Mickey said. "Relax. It's an opportunity to put money to work." They took in another $500 million on April 1, two-thirds of it from funds of funds, and immediately invested it.

But their performance didn't get better; it got worse. That spring, prices rallied, and by early July, the S&P 500 was up almost 10 percent and the smaller and mid-cap indexes had climbed even more. The markets were becoming more speculative and volatile, and BA was suffering. Macro hedge funds, emerging market funds, and the more aggressive stock investors were reporting gains of around 20 percent for the year, but by July BA was up only 2 percent. Their shorts were going up as fast as their longs, and only their net long position was enabling them to show a positive return.

Alpha funds as a class were struggling, but it was disconcerting that a few, while not prospering, were doing better than they were. Their competition wasn't keeping up with the market averages either, but several of the bigger ones were up a disconcerting 7 to 8 percent. What was happening? What had gone wrong? They were an alpha fund with no alpha. There was just a hint of unhappiness in the questions their clients were asking. As far as the clients were concerned, six months of the vaunted BA value strategy lagging big-time was an aberration. A year, however, would be the cause for an "agonizing reappraisal."

The problem was that Mickey, Joe, and Joan were somewhat mystified as well. One glorious early July morning, they sat in Mickey's office and tried to figure it out. Mickey was very confident.

"I'm sure it's just a lean period when our models have temporarily lost traction. It's inconceivable that expensive, speculative stocks beat the cheap stocks of companies that have strong balance sheets, good free cash flow margins, and improving fundamentals. It's like the tech bubble period. It's irrational. It can't last."

"That's only part of our problem," Joe interjected. "Our competitors are much more leveraged than we are. The returns for value in general are way down, but the other guys have leveraged up from four times equity to seven, eight, even ten times, and so with the same basic unleveraged returns, they are killing us."

"That's crazy bullshit," Joan interjected. "They're going to blow out their VAR number and get into deep shit."

"That's not what they say," Joe interjected, "The DBS fund of funds people were in here yesterday, and they told me that other quant funds are maintaining that markets are less risky, less volatile, and that they can keep their VARs at the limits they committed to even with the higher leverage. In fact, Delta Strategies, which does the same thing we do, is leveraged at ten times, and there's one maniac that's at seventeen. Delta has promised DBS they will cut back the moment they begin to lose money."

"Then we have to jack our leverage up, too!" Mickey said, almost angrily. "We can't just sit here and get our ass kicked."

"But the markets are getting more, not less, volatile. We could take a really big hit if the bad stocks keep beating the good ones," Joe told him.

"It's much more fundamental than that, babycakes," Joan said calmly. "It's environmental and it's not going to go away. Our space, our beloved, fertile, blooming with alpha, pasture, which we once had mostly to ourselves, has become overcrowded and overgrazed." The two men stared at her, startled and uncomprehending.

"It's the so-called 'tragedy of the commons' that social philosophers from Aristotle to Hardin have written about," Joan explained. "Let's say there's a rich pasture open to all. A herdsman grazing his animals on the land will prosper, and soon he will have an incentive to add another animal to his herd, and then another and another. But every other rational herdsman sharing the commons will see the benefits and do likewise. That creates the *tragedy*. Each herdsman captures the benefits from an extra animal, but eventually the cost of overgrazing is borne by all and the pasture becomes barren."

"Yeah," said Mickey. "I see what you mean. Before, it was only us and Goldman Sachs and AQR living off the value commons, but now there's ten to fifteen new herdsmen each with a herd of cows munching the same grass. And guess what! The commons is beginning to lose its grass, and suddenly everybody's animals are getting skinnier rather than fatter."

"God forbid that we have a dry summer or a drought," interjected Joan. "Then there will be a disaster . . . no, a catastrophe!"

"A disaster may even be inevitable," Mickey added, looking thoughtful and concerned. "Goldman Sachs, AQR, all the hedge fund multistrategy giants are *lebensraum*-obsessed firms obsessively seeking rich new farmland. Predators who remind me of Hitler looking at Poland, Czechoslovakia, and the Ukraine in 1939. It's paranoia-inducing stuff."

"So what are we going to do about it?" Joe asked. He always felt a little inadequate when Joan and Mickey reverted to these complex philosophical theories that he had never heard of. Hell, he didn't even know what *lebensraum* was.

Then he answered his own question. "We're going to work harder and refine the inputs to our models. We have more profound algorithms than they do, more analytical resources, and we're smarter."

"You still don't get it," Joan told him. "We aren't smarter. There are a couple hundred quants with genius IQs and PhDs in trigonometry out there searching for anomalies and more profound algorithms. There's too much traffic. No one can maintain an edge for long."

She paused. "You macho guys won't like my answer. It's that we have to stop taking new money and give some money back. Then we find a new, smaller pasture—maybe like small-cap emerging markets that's still alpha fertile—where the other firms aren't, and we start a new business."

They looked at her with dismay. "What's come over you, girl?" asked Mickey scornfully. "We can't run billions in small-cap emerging markets. It's too illiquid."

Joan grimaced, and then said evenly but distinctly: "First, I'm a woman, not a girl. I don't call you boy when you disagree with me." In the silence that followed they all looked at each other, and for a moment their masks slipped. "What's come over me is the truth," she said. "The old truth that's still true. There's no asset class too much money won't spoil. And ours is becoming well and thoroughly spoiled."

"Sorry, honey," Mickey said sardonically. Then he went on. "Well, gang, I'm not ready for shrinking assets. I say we leverage up to seven times and raise our net long to forty percent and then count on our superior investment skills and analytics to make it work. Frankly, folks, I got too much ego here and too much overhead there," and he gestured toward the New York skyline, "to cut back. Business organizations that don't grow, die."

"You realize we blow out our VAR limits if we do that . . . *honey?*"
Joan asked.

Remember, VAR stands for value at risk. In the fine print of BA's
offering memorandum (which was basically their contract with their
investors), they affirmed that they would not run a VAR of more than
five except on a very short-term basis. A VAR of five means that based
on back-testing (using recent market volatility), there is a 95 percent
probability the portfolio will not lose more than 5 percent in a month.
Obviously, a VAR of 10 doubles the size of the potential monthly loss.
Conversely, a VAR of 10 means you could earn twice as much if you
got it right.

"Of course, I realize it," Mickey replied.

"But it's mighty scary," Joan commented matter-of-factly. "We've
committed in our legal client contracts that we won't let our VAR get
above five, and with the markets so volatile, that's where we are right
now. If we violate that number, the lawyers say the clients could sue
the firm and the three of us, directly, for the losses. For everything
we've *got*, incidentally."

"Yeah and I just *got* it," Joe murmured. "Just got it and like it and
don't want to give it back."

"Going to a VAR of eight or nine shouldn't be a big deal. I'll bet
those other guys are higher than that," Mickey said loudly.

"It's a big deal when you committed to not going higher than
five," Joan told him.

"Shit," Mickey replied, his face reddening. "Ignore the mealy-
mouthed lawyers! We have to go for it. Damn the torpedoes. Full steam
ahead!"

"That's crazy, Mickey," Joan said. "With the amount of money
you've got invested in BA, you can live happily ever after on your own
capital. What you should care about is long-term performance rather
than asset size."

Mickey looked at her. "Listen *woman*, you don't know nothing about
my ego or my overhead." Joe noted that Mickey had become prone to
sports talk as in using *good* as an adverb (he is *doing good*) and *nothing* instead
of *anything*. Now Mickey stood up and punched Joe lightly on the arm.

"Like Margaret Thatcher said to George Bush when Iran attacked
Kuwait and he was wavering: 'This is no time to go wobbly, George.'"

They argued it back and forth for another 20 minutes. Then Joe suggested they compromise: increase their leverage to six times from four and their net long to 40 percent, but monitor their VAR and performance twice a day to make sure they weren't crashing.

As they broke up, Joe said, "Maybe we should talk to Spokane and Ravine about all this. After all, they've got a lot at stake too—they also could get sued if we screw up. Ravine is a first-class quant brain."

"Good luck with Ravine!" Joan replied.

"What do you mean, good luck?"

"He's been otherwise distracted the last week or so," she answered, somewhat mysteriously.

"Tell us. No secrets with your investment soul mates."

"Have you noticed that new blond analyst with the wondrous body they hired three months ago?"

"Yeah."

"Well, she seduced him during prime-time working hours in that dim, secluded office of his with all the charts and computers. She's got a big mouth and thinks she's the ultimate *femme fatale*. I heard the gossip in the women's locker room at the gym."

"Go on! I thought Ravine was a man of Yahweh, a monk of finance and above the call of the flesh."

"Apparently not. . . . And it hasn't been just a one-afternoon stand."

"That horny rascal! Carnal activities in the office," said Mickey almost admiringly. "I never would have thought it, but I guess I should have. His wife is an old dog."

By mid-July, markets had soared to new recovery highs with the S&P 500 touching 1550 and close to its 2000 peak. The European and emerging markets were also surging. Then suddenly, out of the blue, in the last week of July, markets around the world plunged as worries about the state of the U.S. housing market and mortgage finance surfaced. There was talk of big losses in subprime mortgages and credit.

The S&P fell in two weeks from a shade over 1550 to 1410. These developments caught Mickey, Joe, and Joan by surprise. They knew virtually nothing about the subprime mortgage market and had only recently heard of so-called liar loans.

The market dip found BA with its leverage, net long, and VAR elevated. As markets cratered, they quickly but reluctantly reduced their leverage and net long to 20 percent, but not quickly enough to avoid a big hit. Suddenly, they were down 12 percent for the year. The inconceivable was happening. Their longs were going down and their shorts were going up. It didn't matter that their net long was now at very low levels, and that the stocks they owned were good, solid, and cheap, and that they were short the high-priced-dream junk.

Now all the other quant funds were being compelled to reduce their leverage and the size of their portfolios because they also were running losses and violating their risk limits. Volatility had skyrocketed. Reducing leverage while maintaining portfolio balance meant selling a percentage of all their long positions and buying back the same percentage of all their shorts. Delta Strategies, the quant fund that had promised DBS a form of portfolio insurance, began to run huge losses and had to liquidate almost its entire bloated portfolio.

"We are all pissing on our own parades," screamed Mickey on the morning of August 5 as the sun poured into their meeting room with a white incandescence. "In my worst nightmares I never could have imagined this happening."

"Yeah," said Joan. "Well, it is. To put it more elegantly, I'd say we're being tortured by a demon of our own design."

"I talked to Cliff Asness of AQR," replied Mickey, still speaking loudly. "He's a value, model-driven quant like us and a very smart guy. He said, 'There is a new risk factor in our world, and it is us.' Remember Ravine said the same thing."

Joe was not intrigued. "It's interesting that you two have got cute phrases to describe our problem, but what I want to know is what we are going to do about it. We're getting killed. Maybe we should close all our positions and go to cash until the dust settles."

"We're going to stick to our disciplines," Mickey asserted confidently. "This panic action is an aberration. Truth and justice will prevail."

"I sure hope you're right," Joe said. "I have to believe you're right. Otherwise, we're toast."

The quant value world was gripped by an old-time, throw-'em-out-the-window panic as giant funds had to buy back their shorts, which drove up their prices, and sell their longs, which forced their prices down. These actions in turn caused a vicious circle of cascading losses for other quant funds.

Bloomberg ran a story of huge possible losses at Goldman Sachs, AQR, and BA, and Mickey, Joe, and Joan were swamped with client calls. It was hard to know what to say. They crafted what they hoped was a reassuring statement:

> *Our models are not esoteric constructs but in our view just thoughtful, intuitive, systematic approaches to choosing stocks and constructing portfolios. What we call the* value spread *difference between the cheapest and most expensive quintiles, which is where we go fishing, is close to record wides. What has happened is an aberration sprung from a panic of inexperienced, speculative investors, and it has created an exceptional opportunity that we intend to exploit.*

In the *Wall Street Journal*, a famous academic quant pontificated that "accidents happen." He continued, "The cause of failure of a complex system is complexity itself. The Iron Law of Failure suggests most things fail eventually, and complex systems fail when seemingly trivial and independent occurrences result through a snowball effect in disaster."

"What the fuck does that mean?" Mickey snarled when he read it.

Mickey seemed increasingly cantankerous, Joe thought. He didn't know exactly what it meant either, but he could feel his irritation with Mickey growing. "It means we, mostly you, talked too much about our ever-loving model, too many people copied us, and we got in each other's way and a disaster was created."

"Complexity compounded becomes fragile and very dangerous," Joan murmured.

The three of them were suffering, each in their own way. It was all so shocking and so terribly inconceivable. In retrospect, thinking about it months later, they came to recognize that it was, so to speak, a classic example of the high probability of the improbable happening.

Joe and Joan were also distraught and depressed by their constant squabbling with Mickey. They all had believed so completely in their *immaculate conception* of a model and its invulnerability that they were crushed and humiliated by its utter collapse. Joe could barely bring himself to talk to other investment friends, and yet he knew he should to maintain his perspective.

For him it was back to the bad old days when he was waking up in the middle of the night in a clammy, cold sweat, desperate about BA's survival. Now he was not just agonizing over the portfolio, but beginning to be plagued by black doubts about whether BA itself, the financial system, and his new wealth would survive this crisis. And in the back of his mind, growing like an insidious cancer, was his fear that they would be sued for their losses from the VAR violation.

He also couldn't help but agonize over how much personal overhead he had assumed. Sure he was rich, but he was still desperately worried. He found that losing sleep and going to work tired deepened his depression. When he got to work, his face from the strain of sleeplessness looked sculptured and hard. One look at him and Joan could tell whether he had slept well. Finally, he went to the family doctor and got a prescription for Ambien. The little pink pills helped a lot, but in the mornings he felt slightly groggy. Joan, with less to lose and less overhead, was holding up better, but she felt sorry for Joe.

On the other hand, Emily was not particularly sympathetic. Her point of view was that they had all the money they would ever need so why didn't BA just go to cash and ride it out?

"What do Mickey and your work-wife think?" she asked him, curling her lip.

Joe ignored the work-wife crack. "They want to tough it out," he replied. "I think Mickey's losing it; maybe *has* lost it. He looks degenerate. I wouldn't be totally surprised if he's smoking pot with that new butterfly of his."

She abruptly changed the subject. She had read an article by George Soros that had deeply affected her. In it, Soros argued that throughout the history of the world—even back before the time of Christ—societies went through long cycles of wealth creation that were followed by crushing cycles of wealth destruction. The cycles of wealth creation lasted about two generations, 60 years, and they were inevitably followed by a 30-year period of wealth destruction. Soros pointed out that the greatest span of wealth creation in all of human history had occurred after the end of World War II. It began in 1947 and, true to form, it lasted for exactly 60 years. Now, this year, was the beginning of the generation of wealth destruction period.

"Do you think Soros has this right?" she inquired.

"Could be," he answered, speaking slowly. "Possible, I'm afraid. The evidence is pretty convincing."

"Well," she said. "I've thought about it a lot. Why does the wealth destruction inevitably follow? First, because the first generation that makes all the money becomes satiated, complacent, and old. Second, because their children and grandchildren grow up spoiled and lacking motivation, they lack the compulsion, the urgency, to work hard. Third, as inequality between the rich and everyone else in the society grows exponentially, the masses become envious and there's a vicious backlash that results in redistribution through higher tax rates, which kills the whole society's initiative. What do you think?"

"Look," he responded carefully. "We could well be entering a cycle of wealth destruction."

"The scary thing," she told him, "is that this time the excesses are concentrated in the investment business—your business. The compensation differential between investment people, hedge fund guys and people in the real economy, are totally insane."

"Yeah," he said reflectively. "We could be in the eye of the storm. It's scary, and the other scary thing is that I don't understand what's happening to the stock markets. Our models don't work anymore and I don't understand why."

"If you don't understand it, why fight it and torture yourself—and us?" she asked. "Why not walk away from BA? Sell everything. Take a vacation. Clear your head. Run your own money. Why are we living like this?" She was impatient with his depression. She wanted more of his attention for herself and her boys. She pleaded, "We should be worrying about preserving our wealth and bringing up our children instead of competing in this manic game you're involved with."

"But I love the game," he told her. "I love winning. I want to prove we can come back."

"You're crazy," she said, almost sadly. "You may be risking our wealth for your ego and your beloved game. It's nuts!" She stood up angrily. "Joe, you've changed! You aren't like you used to be. What's happening to us?"

Her eyes were flashing and Joe could see now she was becoming really angry. "You haven't read a novel or even history for a couple of years now! It's your beloved office, stocks, and golf. You've gone crazy. What's the matter with you?"

He just stared at her and shook his head.

"I'm going to bed," she said and stalked off upstairs.

He sat there after she had gone. He understood her anger and felt badly about not being able to concentrate when he was with the children, but he simply couldn't get his mind off the carnage back in New York and the hurt at the firm. As for reading novels, it was the last thing on his mind. All that mattered was that they get it right!

The following Saturday they had a party for Timothy's third birthday. They had attended several ostentatious children's birthday parties that were more competitive social events than children's birthday parties, and Joe—for some reason he couldn't quite understand—was determined to do Timothy's party on a comparable scale. They were not going to be outdone. They were just as rich, if not richer, than the other parents in Timothy's class.

Emily was somewhat scornful, but Joe insisted that they hire a party planner and a caterer. The children and their parents were invited by an engraved Crane's invitation for mid-afternoon, and there was valet parking, a giant clown on stilts at the front door, gifts for each child, special playhouses, three swings, an elaborate jungle gym, and a live animal show on the lawn. Afterward, food was served for the children, and the parents were offered fine wines and an elaborate assortment of catered canapés.

It had been a brutal performance week for BA, and Joe was distraught and distracted. He spent most of the party standing off to one side talking with Perot and Cliff Ryan, who ran another big quant fund, rather than participating in the games with the children and mingling with the adults. Afterward, Emily was furious.

"For the sake of your precious ego," she yelled, "you insisted on this over-the-top birthday party, and I invite my friends and their children, and then you hide out and talk shop for two hours. It's rude and crude!"

Joe apologized profusely and sincerely. He started to explain to Emily how he could barely face people, how depressed he felt, and that commiserating with someone who had similar pain was such a palliative experience, but she abruptly cut him off.

"It's ridiculous. Greenwich is hedge fund land, and people here are not stupid. They know what's going on in the market, and by standing in a corner and not participating in your own son's party you advertise you have problems. It's dumb! You made a fool of yourself."

The conversation made Joe feel even worse.

"And, by the way," Emily added, "that Perot woman is a jerk. They want to get into the Greenwich Racquet Club. I know some of the women over there. Apparently the Perots have parties of one kind or another almost every weekend, and their house is lit up like a Vegas casino with noise and music. Their guests honk their horns in tribute as they're leaving. It's a quiet, grand-old, back-country neighborhood, and everyone is outraged."

"Tough luck," muttered Joe. "The Perots are just sociable people."

"Maybe so," Emily told him, "but she's really *gauche*. You could do your friend a big favor by telling him to shut down his parties and his wife."

"What's she done?" he asked. "I like the Perots. What you see is what you get."

"Well they're not going to *get* into the Greenwich Racquet Club. She got a list of the people on the Greenwich Racquet Club membership committee, and then had her *personal assistant* no less call them, identify herself as Mrs. Perot's assistant, and invite them for dinner naming three alternative dates. Joining the Greenwich Racquet Club is almost like joining a family. It's not wildly expensive like the new golf clubs, but the waiting list is very long and the approval process is very selective—and very secret."

She shook her head disdainfully. "The wives are an important part of the admissions process. Greenwich Racquet Club wives don't have personal assistants because they're not rich enough to, and even if they did, they wouldn't be so insensitive as to use them to make personal social calls. They think she's blatantly flaunting it, and they're going to blackball her arrogant ass."

As for Mickey, he responded differently to the crisis. He was out every night at dinner parties or splashy charity balls. When he got to work the next morning, often two hours after Joe and Joan, his face looked puffy. His eyes, always restless, now seemed almost frenetic. He continued to live big and spend huge. His socializing and womanizing became even more rabid. It was as if he felt compelled to show the world that he was untouched by the crisis, that everything was fine, and that the rumors about BA's performance problems were untrue.

Perhaps the fast crowd and the socialites Mickey hung out with fell for it, Joe thought, but gossip about their performance and Mickey's behavior was rampant. The hedge fund world is an incubator of animosity with highly competitive, driven, jealous people who want to win at all costs, and if that requires spreading FUD (fear, uncertainty, and doubt) about a rival, so be it. Now their competitors were whispering to the big investors and the consultants that Mickey Cohen was acting like he had a screw loose and that maybe his model had a whole bunch of screws loose.

As for Joan, she was quiet and went home alone at night and licked her investment wounds in solitude. In a way, she was the most troubled of the three because she believed they were enmeshed in an investment version of the tragedy of the commons, and that Joe and Mickey would never understand until it was too late that their investment model was permanently broken.

She also worried about Joe. He cared so much about success. Mickey's problems were his ego, his reputation, and his overhead, but to her they were of less concern than Joe's. And, she had to admit to herself, she was in love with him anyway. Half in love with his toughness, where he'd come from and his journey, and half in love with those broad shoulders, the lean body, and that dark, intense face.

After one final spasm that brought down the whole market, abruptly on the morning of August 12, 2007 when markets opened in New York, the mini-panic ended and prices stabilized. But huge losses had been booked and immense damage had been done to the previously bullet-proof image of value alpha investing in general and BA in particular. BA was now down 17 percent for the year. The fact that two of their biggest competitors were off in the twenties, and that Goldman Sachs' $7.5 billion Global Alpha Fund was down 27 percent and that its Global Equity Opportunities Fund (which was leveraged 6.5 times) had lost an amazing 30 percent in the second week of August alone, was scant consolation. Model-driven value investing was failing—big time.

Goldman now moved aggressively to staunch the bleeding. The firm announced a $3 billion transfusion into Global Equity, of which $2 billion was the firm's money and the other billion came from a select group of big, supposedly astute investors such as Hank Greenberg, C.V. Starr, and Perry Capital. The new money got a great deal. So great in fact that it smelled of panic. No management fees and a 10 percent hurdle rate before paying a performance fee of 10 percent of the profits.

BA's contract with investors provided that redemptions could be made at the end of each calendar quarter with 30 days' written notice. Performance was reported to all investors on the 15th and at the end of each month. BA reported on August 3 that it was down 8 percent for the year to date and then on August 16 that it had lost another 9 percent in the first 15 days of the month. That was the real shocker, even though the Goldman fund had lost even more. How could long/short, supposedly low-volatility value funds lose huge chunks of money in 15 days? It had been a bloodbath! BA, their beloved creation, their Precious Thing, their *Cosa Nostra*, was badly wounded, maimed, and perhaps even in mortal peril.

The timing of the slaughter meant the BA's investors—if they wanted what was left of their money back—had to get a redemption notice in by August 31 or wait another three months until the end of the year. The financial storm had hit so suddenly, savagely, and unexpectedly that their investors barely had time to recognize the damage, much less understand why it was happening. Nevertheless, five of BA's big investors asked for partial redemptions ("just to be safe," as one told Joe) of about 20 percent of their stake, totaling $320 million. Since the portfolio was still leveraged six times, raising the money to meet these withdrawals required BA to close almost $2 billion of positions by selling its longs and covering its shorts. Of course, these trades further depressed BA's performance.

At the same time, the other big value quant funds were experiencing similar redemptions and liquidating their positions across the board. The cheap stocks with strong balance sheets and improving fundamentals that they all owned were going down, and at the same time the prices of the loss-making, hopeless, hapless crap that they were short were soaring. It was all incredibly crazy, frustrating, and very painful.

After the steep, but short, midsummer decline, the major markets took off in late summer with a final surge that turned out to be their last gasp. Although it was not BA's turf, the emerging markets in particular soared, and the spectacular returns collected by the hedge funds that were involved increased the performance pressure on everyone else. Most of the major U.S. and international indexes set new recovery highs in October, although the NASDAQ was still far below its peak from way back in 2000. Then in early November 2007 stock prices abruptly fell again, and drifted sideways during December.

During the fourth quarter, quant funds continued to struggle while most other people were making money. At the beginning of the year, an unleveraged, fully hedged fund using a sophisticated, pure value strategy was earning 2 to 4 percent. Since volatility in 2005 and 2006 had been relatively low, most funds were leveraging their equity five to seven times and running a moderate net long, say 20 percent, which yielded returns after borrowing costs of 10 to 15 percent. For the more adventurous firms, leveraging up 10 times with a 30 to 40 percent net long under the right circumstances could produce returns of 20 percent or more.

The problem now was that value wasn't working and in fact was producing a negative annual return of −2 to −3 percent unleveraged, but at seven or eight times leverage with a substantial net long, the losses were running 20 to 30 percent or more. The rush to deleverage only made things worse as funds scrambled to sell their longs and buy back their shorts. A research analyst at Lehman estimated that from the end of June to the end of September, the amount of money invested in quant programs declined from $210 billion to $154 billion.

One fund run by D.E. Shaw—which was said to have immense leverage (17 times)—lost 18 percent in August and then made 11 percent in October. That kind of volatility, however, terrified many of its investors and there was a flood of redemptions.

"This whole deleveraging, volatility, and redemption process is creating a vicious circle that is in danger of becoming a death spiral," Joan said to Joe one morning in November. Mickey was not in that day, and again they both noted but didn't comment on his repeated late arrivals and absences.

"I know," Joe replied. "I remember you talked about an environmental change one time a couple of weeks ago. Well, it's happening. There's no inherent bias in the market anymore for our value model to work. In fact, the bias is toward growth stocks with momentum characteristics."

"Yeah," said Joan. "I hear some guys are switching to a value-neutral model and buying expensive, crappy companies if they're defensive growth and supposedly high-growth stocks at big multiples of earnings."

"You know Mickey will never go for that," Joe said. "He will be a hard-core, formula-driven, value guy to the end."

"Well," said Joan. "There's a season for value and a season for growth. A time for quality and a time for junk."

"Our models have been too inflexible. I'm beginning to understand that now."

"The trouble is that value beats growth in the long run and most of the time," Joan told him, "but not *all* the time. We know there can be dry spells that last for a couple of years or even longer. Looks to me that we're in one of those now. Remember that from 1996 until 2000 growth beat value huge. Let's get our analysts working on it. We've got to adapt."

"It won't be easy to change Mickey's mind, and if we do, we would have to tell our clients. They think they've bought into quant value, not quant opportunistic."

"They'll be okay with our switch, providing it works," Joan told him.

All through the second half of November 2007 the redemption notices poured in. Each day operations sent them an e-mail summary of the daily toll. They would sit there in the late afternoon dreading to open the e-mail but being unable to resist learning which of their clients whom they had nurtured and cherished were renouncing them that day. By the November 30 redemption deadline, they had received notices of withdrawals of $2 billion at year-end, which, combined with the September 30 redemptions of $320 million, were a crushing body blow. To meet these redemptions they had to do more selling of their longs and more covering of their shorts on top of the deleveraging they were already doing. This combination plus a difficult market resulted in horrendous fourth-quarter performance.

The three of them sat down to talk about it. "It's been a storm of biblical proportions," Joan summarized, her face high and composed. "We got caught with our leverage up in a growth-oriented market and at the same time all the other value quants were frantically deleveraging."

"Great bunch of loyal clients we got," said Mickey bitterly.

"Hey, remember what you told me years ago—at two and twenty we should have known that there's no loyalty. Why should there be? If you want loyalty, charge forty basis points and get a dog," said Joe, shaking his head. "It's hedge fund life—its own ugly self."

"Aren't you the fucking wise philosopher," said Mickey sourly.

For the year 2007, BA finished down 31 percent. Tack on the fixed fee of 2 percent, and the net loss for the full year for an investor was 33 percent. At year-end, their assets had fallen because of the double whammy of redemptions and losses from over $8 billion to about $3.6 billion.

It had been a horrendous year for quants. Goldman Sachs Asset Management's Global Alpha lost 38 percent, and Global Equity Opportunities was off over 30 percent. AQR's Absolute Return Fund and Highbridge Capital Management's Statistical Opportunities Fund had declines in the mid-teens. Some smaller quant funds with poor results and heavy redemptions closed down because as businesses they were running at substantial losses.

To compound their agony, a few quant funds that had switched from value to growth and that had sucessfully market timed did much better. The Black Mesa Fund was up 13 percent, the AQR Global Risk Premium Fund gained 10 percent, and the D.E. Shaw Fund 7 percent. Unfortunately for them, the non-quant rest of the hedge fund space had posted a pretty good year despite a fourth-quarter fade. The weighted HFRI Hedge Fund composite gained 9.9 percent and many emerging markets and Asian funds were up 20 to 30 percent.

It was proving to be a strange year for markets in general. The S&P 500 was up 5.5 percent but on the New York Stock Exchange almost twice as many stocks fell as advanced. Something was rotten in Denmark and there was an uneasy feeling in the air.

The hard, unpleasant truth that Mickey, Joe, and Joan still had not come to grips with was that the great value run was over. The fantastic value bull market that had begun as they started in 2000 and during which their model had worked so well with only minor interruptions had reversed again in 2007. Now the market, perhaps sensing that the global economy was faltering, had reverted back to growth, and value and BA were suffering. It was no more complicated than that.

Their deal with Spokane and Ravine was that they—Joe, Mickey, Joan, the analysts, and client service group—got 70 percent of the carry and 25 percent of the fixed fee. The firm, Bridgestone, took 75 percent of the fixed fee for providing the infrastructure, back office, operations, trading, and marketing. At the time they had struck the arrangement, it seemed to Mickey and Joe that it was a great deal.

In this disastrous year, however, it was another story. They had never envisioned a big down year with huge redemptions. Since there were no gains, 20 percent of nothing was nothing. The 2 percent fixed fee on their average assets for the year was $110 million, and their 25 percent of that was just over $27 million. They were now carrying and were responsible for paying a research director, six analysts, three research assistants, and four secretaries. The firm paid for their three dedicated traders, but the salaries plus bonuses for their staff had been budgeted at $28 million, which assumed a 10 percent increase in the bonuses. Plus there was Joan.

The hedge fund incentive fee is 20 percent of *net* profits. If a fund loses money in a year, it must earn back its losses before it gets paid again. For BA it was a simple but daunting calculation. The fund would have to be up 50 percent before they would earn any incentive fee. This was the curse of the high water mark system.

With all this in mind, Mickey and Joe sat down and talked about money one early January afternoon. The discussion was as grim as the bleak January sky outside their windows, with a cold rain falling. They both were depressed and gloomy. So far 2008 was off to a dismal start.

"We have to pay our people up from last year despite our lousy year," Joe said.

"Why?" said Mickey. "They should suffer like us."

"Because the hedge fund business in general had a decent year and almost everybody else is paying well. Our guys did their jobs as analysts and as quants. We're the ones who ran the portfolio into the ground. We have to pay 'em on budget because they'll leave if we don't and the turnover will look very bad with our clients. Furthermore, they know we're way below our high water mark so they'll be amenable to listening to offers from other funds that don't have the same problem."

"Shit," said Mickey. "I suppose you want to pay Joan more, too."

"Yeah, I do. We screwed her last year. In retrospect, we've been greedy. The big clients know she's a major player here. If she took a walk, it would be another huge black mark against us."

"We were dumb to get into this situation. We should never have given her the power to hold us up like this."

"Come on, Mickey, that's ridiculous! She's not holding us up. We have to pay her fifteen million dollars."

"That means, *Mr. Hill*, that with the analysts and her you're talking about us having to pay sixteen million dollars, each of us eight million, out of our own personal highly beloved capital accounts. And I'm bleeding money—a million dollars a month. Man, this is tough shit!"

"Yeah, it is. But we had the roller coaster ride up and now we're going to give some back to keep our thing, our beloved BA, afloat. If we don't, we could lose our business completely. And we've got to work like madmen this year to make some good numbers or we're toast."

"Unfortunately, you're right," said Mickey ruefully. "It's pay the people and perform the portfolio or perish. We blew all our accumulated goodwill last year. And until we earn back our losses, we get no incentive fee."

"Good! Thanks Mick, it's the right thing to do."

"Yeah, but I'm the one with all the overhead."

Joe felt he had to say something. "You can always cut back, live more gently."

"Easy for you to say, dude. Women don't like to get cut back. You know I got two ex-wives now and a girlfriend. I never knew how fast a month went by until I started paying alimony."

"I understand. But the golden times are gone—probably for good. It's going to be hard to ever get back to the size we were. Our credibility with our clients is shot. Nobody ever conceived we could lose 30 percent."

"I never did either," Mickey said softly. "I never did."

Chapter 15

2008: *Annus Horribilis*

Those whom the Gods would destroy, they first make proud.
—Ancient Greek Proverb

A s the new year began, most investors and soothsayers were optimistic, although there was a mournful chorus of Cassandras warning of impending doom from the mortgage market. January was a tough month and ended with a sickening decline and the S&P 500 down 6 percent. The business news was uniformly grim, and the high- frequency data on the U.S. economy indicated that a mild recession loomed. Employers were beginning to cut back on hiring, and house prices were continuing to drift lower.

In late January 2008, Joe went to an investment dinner put on by Lehman Brothers in the wonderful, old, vaulted wine cellar in the basement of the 21 Club. In a way, Joe dreaded going, but it was like a gathering of the tribe and he knew he should attend just to take the temperatures of the hedge fund war party. But to attend events like this you must be in the mood to put on and keep wearing your game face, because although everyone ostensibly is friendly and jovial, the guests at dinners like this are among the most intensely competitive people in the world. There was always an edge to the interaction. Hedge fund investing is a blood sport. It would not be a friendly, relaxing evening with old, tried-and-true comrades in arms. Everyone knew BA's troubles and would be observing him to see if underneath there were even deeper wounds.

There were 12 slick, glib, opinionated, aggressive hedge funds guys at the dinner. The salesman from Lehman Brothers did a good job of drawing the group into general discussion. Joe had always felt a little inarticulate on these occasions as some of the other guys were so outspoken and seemed so confident. At these dinners there was always bound to be a lot of gilding (as in gilding the lily), some lying, and once in a while some sandbagging so you never knew quite what to believe. (*Gilding* is when you dress up your stock story by exaggerating the fundamentals.)

That evening there was unusual tension in the room, and the dinner got rowdy as the evening wore on and the wine flowed. Joe had never felt easy about prettying up merchandise he was about to sell, and, when his turn came and he presented a stock, he was not amused when Peter Brandise, who was always a wise guy, interjected, "You ought to be ashamed of yourself, Hill, for trying to put lipstick on that pig."

"It's not a pig and there's no lipstick," he snarled at Brandise. "The stock is five times earnings and two-thirds of book value with plenty of free cash flow."

"You don't get it," Brandise replied, grinning evilly. "We've transitioned into a growth stock market. Growth is going to continue to kick value's ass."

"That was last year's story," Joe replied. "Value is historically cheap versus growth."

"Wrong!" said Brandise loudly. "Wrong! Volatility is increasing and when the VIX index is climbing, growth always beats value. You better adjust your models or you and Cohen and Bridgestone are going to be choking on growth stock fumes . . . again."

The investors around the table were staring at him, half-embarrassed, half-amused. "Fuck you," Joe replied, and lapsed into silence as another guy went on and on about emerging markets.

"He was up thirty-eight percent last year," the man sitting next to Joe whispered to him. "Thirty-eight percent!"

Listening to the others bragging about their 2007 performance made Joe feel both dumb and defensive. He was still reeling from the beating BA had taken. Sitting there, he was angry and even more determined to somehow put up some good numbers for the new year.

The next morning Joe reported to Mickey and Joan that the theme in the candle-lit wine cellar was that the January market weakness was an aberration. Over the last few months, equities had already suffered a bear market–like decline, were very cheap relative to bonds and inflation, and sentiment was extremely bearish. The environment was nothing like 2000 when valuations were to the moon and craziness reigned. The feared liquidity crisis seemed to have abated, and the banks had managed a successful round of recapitalizations. Furthermore, after its big rate cut, the Fed was no longer behind the so-called *curve*.

The consensus seemed to be that real growth in the U.S. was likely to be around 1 or 2 percent for the year, and corporate profits should be up 10 percent. Overlaying this view on a benign inflation and interest rate outlook suggested at least a 10 percent gain for the S&P 500. The conclusion was, as one guy had put it, that it was a time to "suck it up and load up."

That morning they agreed to tweak their models to adjust for the new market environment, which favored stocks that were growth- and momentum-driven. By mid-February, the BA portfolio had more of a growth orientation than at any time in their history, and their performance improved. Almost 30 percent of their long positions were cheap technology stocks. Then suddenly the market plunged again, and all tech stocks, expensive or cheap, got crushed indiscriminately as talk of a recession increased and long-only, fundamental managers began to rotate out of volatile, cyclical-growth shares like tech into value.

Once again, BA's performance was abysmal. They had been whipsawed and had given up on value at exactly the wrong time. BA ended up the first quarter down 8 percent, and a new flood of redemptions began. Joe could sense that their clients, even the long-standing ones who had booked big gains, had totally lost confidence in them and their model. Now twinges of outright fear mingled with his depression.

In fact, he, Joe Hill—the ever-confident quarterback, the impenetrable defensive back, the golfer who always came through with the long drive or the winning putt—was losing his confidence. He was sleeping badly again and his consumption of Ambien was up to two five-milligram pills a night. He found himself dreading not just investment occasions but also social events at which he knew his demeanor would be scrutinized for signs of stress that could be gossiped about. A year, or 18 months ago, when he and Emily went to a dinner party, he had been buoyed by the knowledge that he was recognized as The Kid, a very successful guy, a "big hitter." Now the gossip around was that BA had lousy performance and was enduring massive redemptions. He knew there was some gloating—"How the mighty have fallen!" Now the not-so-subtle implication was that he, Joe Hill, was a flash in the pan, a loser. Even golf at his beloved Lone Tree Club was an ordeal, but at least his playmates were suffering too, and they could lick their wounds together.

As spring came and it got light earlier and earlier, he found himself waking well before Emily and the boys were even up and going to the office at 5:30. The family didn't like it, and Emily told him he was a "sour, old grouch to live with." Those were her exact words. Even his libido had diminished.

Angry calls from their big clients didn't help his mood. Schapiro, of the Florida golf game and the giant fund of funds White Rock, had withdrawn half of his money at the end of 2007. Now he called asking why they were still doing so badly. Joe tried to explain how they were adjusting their model. Schapiro would have none of it.

"We didn't hire you to retroactively adjust your asshole model to what just happened. You told us you that your value-driven strategy would always work, rain or shine, to create some alpha. The amount might vary but you promised you'd never be down big."

"We never promised anything except that we'd work like dogs."

"Well I'm sick and tired of your excuses and tweaking models bullshit. We're getting big redemptions ourselves. I'm gone at the next opening, and don't try to pull any gates on me or I'll sue you."

Furlman of Texas Teachers was more soft-spoken but the words he mentioned were "betrayal of fiduciary responsibility."

"My staff asks how you could be losing this much money if you'd adhered to your VAR guidelines. Joe, I like you guys, but we're going to have to look at this and consider whether legal action is appropriate."

Joe felt his heart sink. This is what he had always feared. This was his worst nightmare. Furlman went on, "I'm sorry Joe, but the trustees are frantic. It's become a major political issue in the state. This is the teachers' pensions we're talking about. The state may have to raise taxes to replenish the fund. I've had to forfeit my bonus."

When he later told Joan about the conversation, he almost broke down. "You know, what makes me feel worst is that we have lost the money, the pensions of ordinary people who worked for years to save it and were counting on it for their retirement and for their grandchildren and all that kind of stuff. It's a terrible thing. It's almost a crime against humanity."

Joan reached out and touched his arm. "You're right," she said. "*It* is a terrible thing, but it's not a crime against humanity. You didn't steal it. You did your best. You just got *it* wrong."

"Wrong and arrogant," he said sadly. "Wrong and stubbornly arrogant."

Consolations for Joe that long hot summer were his land and being with his boys. He felt mysteriously drawn to working the land and found himself playing less golf on the weekends and instead spending his free time building a long and elaborate dry stone wall down at the tree line of his property. It was hard, strenuous work. The stones had to be dug out of the ground, moved by wheelbarrow, lifted, and then wrestled into place. At the end of a couple of hours of work his hands were roughened and his arms, legs, and shoulders felt deeply used. A dry stone wall is a work of masonry art in which each piece has to be snugly fitted into place. *It was not just manual labor*, he told himself, *this wall was the work of an artisan*. He found the exercise and the satisfaction of seeing the wall grow, sturdy and real, profoundly therapeutic. He might be losing the battle for investment survival but he could win the struggle against the rocks.

Equally important, when he was working, the two boys were always with him with their own small wheelbarrows with which they brought him stones to add to the wall. Timothy chattered incessantly, and both boys were immensely proud of the wall that they felt they were helping to build. In this common enterprise with them, Joe found the stress of the day melting away. As the summer progressed, he would come home from the office and the three of them would go outside in the early evening and work on the wall until dinner was called. He loved it!

But the pain and hurt of the unfolding debacle was always there. One steamy, bright yellow afternoon in late September he had lunch with Dawes on the porch at Lone Tree. The two of them had grown even more intimate over the years, and Joe poured out his woes. His father-in law listened sympathetically and counseled him, saying, "This too will pass." Then Dawes changed the subject and enthusiastically told him that he thought he could organize a push for membership at Green Acres with Alan Reid proposing him.

"I've talked to Sam Comly, who's the chairman of the membership committee, and he's very encouraging. It's a wonderful club, Joe, and the boys will use it a lot for sports as they get older. They can go to camp there, and learn squash, tennis, and golf. And there's great family events, unlike this place, which is just a men's golf club."

"That's exciting news because we would love to be members, but this may not be the best time," Joe told him. "You know how my firm is struggling."

"Hell, everyone's struggling," Dawes told him.

"Not like us."

Dawes ignored him. "Alan is going to get the ball rolling. Usually, it would take a while, but with what's going on this could be an opportune time to apply. This financial crisis is beginning to really hit Greenwich and even Green Acres. The board expects a number of requests for leaves of absence and even some resignations."

"You're joking. It's that bad?"

"It's that bad or even worse. Families are taking their children out of private schools and even canceling piano and fencing lessons."

"Okay, I guess we should try for Green Acres," Joe replied. "I think I can still afford a country club." They chatted on idly, drinking ice tea.

"It's death and destruction," Dawes said. "All the banks and investment banks, including Grant, are doing massive layoffs. They're called RIFs, stands for reduction in force, and they're brutal. Management is not allowed to warn the victims. An employee, man or woman, comes to work one morning, thinks he's doing fine, but is asked to come to the Human Resources office. There, in a scripted interview, he's told he is being *fired!*"

Dawes paused and shook his head. "Then he's informed that he will get one month of salary for every year he has been at the firm, and that he is not allowed to go back to his office. His personal possessions will be sent to him. He must turn in his ID card, and right then and there, a security guard escorts him out the door on to the street. No recourse, no goodbyes, nothing."

Joe was shocked. "This is Mother Grant? I thought this *great* firm was paternalistic and looked after its own?"

"This *great* firm, like every other *great* firm, is desperately fighting for its very life. Legally, these procedures have to be religiously followed. These separations are not *for cause*, in other words, for poor performance, the expense of which must be charged to operating earnings. They are layoffs, true reductions in force, and as such can be treated for accounting purposes as a nonrecurring, nonoperating expense that is below the net income line expense. In other words, they don't reduce net income as long as the dismissal process has followed this very cold-blooded procedure. Managing directors who have been with the firm for twenty years and who thought they were family are being dismissed in this humiliating manner."

"It must be having a terrible effect on morale."

"It's contaminating; ruining the culture of the firm, but even worse, it's destroying lives. The younger people who are being laid off can go on unemployment and hopefully get jobs in the real economy when it gets healthier. The forty- and fifty-year-olds that are getting RIFed will in all probability never work again. There are no jobs—none—available in the securities business. What decent-paying job in the real economy is a guy qualified for who has been an investment banker, an analyst, or a stock salesman for twenty years?"

"Well, presumably they've been well paid for years and have some serious savings to live on."

"I'm afraid not. The run-of-the-mill managing directors at these firms were getting comp packages like two, three million dollars, but they were sixty percent cash and forty percent in restricted stock. Taxes, kids' private school tuitions, over-the-top vacations, and an extravagant lifestyle ate up the cash. Furthermore, most bought bigger homes and places in the Hamptons and Aspen. Some even used their restricted stock as collateral to borrow from banks to get more cash for personal spending. After huge mortgage payments, taxes, and expenses, these people were saving nothing and blithely counted on their stock in their firms as their retirement fund. They assumed financial stocks could only go up because they always had." Dawes shook his head in a gesture almost of despair.

"You know the total destruction of financial stocks! Lehman went to zero, Bear Stearns almost went to zero, and the others are all down seventy to ninety percent. Our stock has gone from ninety to fourteen. It hit seven one day. The big houses those guys bought are now worth less than their mortgages."

"So what happens next?"

"People are in shock and denial. They can't believe they're not going to find another job. They're grudgingly cutting back. At Green Acres, locker rentals are getting canceled and guys are carrying their own bags instead of paying a caddy, but eventually they're going to have to materially reduce their lifestyles and maybe get out of town."

"Yeah, Emily told me the new bargain hair coloring in Greenwich is *bear market brown*. Some cheery soul confided to her that the Greenwich house price index so far is down only fifteen percent, but did she know that between nineteen twenty-nine and nineteen thirty-three, Greenwich real estate prices fell ninety-three percent?

"A year ago, those guys were masters of the universe. Now, they have no jobs, no money, and no self-respect. The press, and even the President for that matter, prefixes every reference to an investment banker with *greedy*."

Dawes paused and they both looked reflectively out over the rolling green fairways of the golf course baking in the white glare of the summer sun. An automatic sprinkler went on, and they could see a foursome with two caddies laboring up toward the eighteenth green. The whole scene looked so normal, so much like every other summer, yet it wasn't; there was decay and rot. They both had heard about the resignations from Lone Tree, and how in reality you couldn't resign until someone wanted to join who would buy your debentures. A year ago men were salivating to join the club. Now there were no buyers, only sellers.

"The sad, the tragic thing," Dawes said, "is that the guys that are ending up high and dry are decent, smart people. They went to good colleges and to first-rate business schools and were effective investment bankers or analysts or sales managers. They weren't stumblebums. They had relationships that produced business for their firms. They thought—and their parents and their wives and their children thought—they were winners, but they were in the wrong place at the wrong time. Their businesses were built on exotic financings, structured products, and securitized loans, and the clients they had relationships with have gotten laid off, too. This bust has made their skills and Rolodexes worthless."

Joe didn't know what to say. He could sense that Dawes was hurting. "What's happening with your guys in the investment management division?"

"It's getting tough. I can protect them only so long. I've had to RIF two of the five analysts you worked with, and you know what, those guys won't get another job in the business for a long time. Nobody's hiring. But they're young; eventually, they'll find something out there in the real economy. The investment management business has been the most overpaid profession in the history of the world, so they won't ever get the money we did. But they'll survive."

"Yeah," said Joe. "For that matter, hedge funds are letting analysts go, too."

"But that's just the beginning," Dawes went on. "What's the value of an investor who for the last five years hasn't beaten his benchmark? Seventy percent of all active managers underperform the index they're judged against. Who's going to buy their funds or give them money to run when they can buy an index fund and pay ten basis points? In the old days, our retail sales force sweet-talked those funds down the public's throats, but no more. Remember that tech fund we did back in your Grant days?

"Sure."

"It's down eighty percent. The portfolio manager got so many harassing phone calls, he had to change his phone numbers. The hate mail was even worse. The guy had to go to a shrink."

"So what happens to these failed portfolio managers and analysts? Do they get fired?"

"Yeah, I'm afraid so. They've been with us a long time, but, like I said, they don't add any value and they get paid a lot of money. But it's not just us; it's the entire financial industry. Never in the history of commerce have so many been paid so much for so little."

"It's a secular bear market that will make fools out of all of us," Joe said reflectively. "A killer bear market like none of us has ever seen."

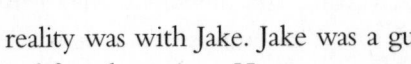

Joe's next encounter with the new reality was with Jake. Jake was a guy in his late forties who had been around for a long time. He was respected as a very smart, free-thinking, analytically intensive investor who made mammoth bets. In early 2008, he was on top of the world running a billion-and-a-half-dollar hedge fund out of a Philadelphia suburb. Jake was intellectually, and in fact socially, very arrogant, but with good reason because his record in recent years had been fabulous. He scornfully disdained Wall Street analysts and salesmen, and instead read trade magazines, talked with businessmen, and used other unconventional sources.

Back in the fall of 2003, Jake's fund was small, maybe $200 million, and sitting down there in Bryn Mawr he became convinced there was going to be an industrial and infrastructure boom and that commodity prices were going to go through the roof. He loaded up on long dormant, half-dead copper, aluminum, iron ore, and steel stocks and to a lesser extent just plain old dirty, rusty manufacturing companies. "Smokestack America," he called it. Joe had run into him at meetings and was impressed with his incredible intensity and conviction and with how concentrated his portfolio was.

In the following years Jake, as the expression goes, shot the lights out. He was dead-solid, perfectly right. Commodities soared, and his Smokestack America names went up even faster. For a case study, take a look at Figure 15.1, which shows the performance of Cleveland Cliffs (CLF), an iron ore and coal miner. In the fall of 2003 it sold at $3 a share, the same price more or less it had sold at for 20 years. Then as the price of iron ore rose, the stock began to climb. Jake started buying in the summer of 2005 when the price of CLF was 18. As the mania for resources and particularly iron ore grew, the price of the stock kept going up. Jake continued buying CLF and similar stocks such as U.S. Steel, the Brazilian miner, Vale do Rio Doce, and the Australian giant BHP, all of which had languished, been asleep for years. Rip Van Winkle stocks, he called them.

By 2006 and 2007 it was a full-fledged mania, and Jake's fund began putting up monstrous numbers. Fifty, 60 percent, some years. By 2007, his fame (and his self-confidence) was spreading, and the money was pouring in. Jake belonged to a fancy country club in Bryn Mawr. It was a family club, but it had a sophisticated membership and

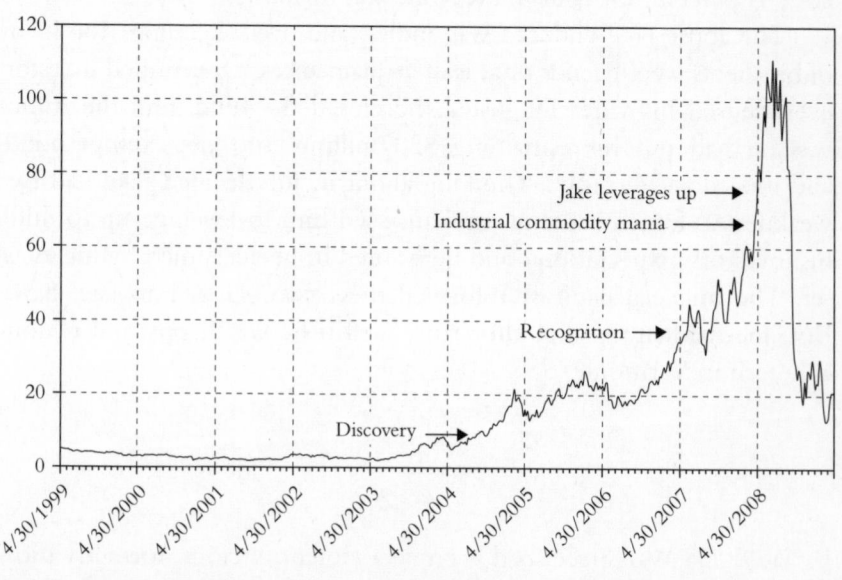

Figure 15.1   The Rise and Fall of Cleveland Cliffs

CNBC was on all day in the Fitness Center. As the word got around that he was a hedge fund genius, suddenly his fellow members and their wives were clamoring to get into his fund. They put him on the all-powerful Admissions Committee, and the trustees of his college asked him to join the board and to be chairman of the endowment's investment committee. This was heady stuff and hubris reared its ugly head. Jake became even more outspoken at investment dinners, and often verged on the obnoxious. He wouldn't listen to anyone who argued that the resource stocks were in a ridiculous bubble.

By the spring of 2008, his fund was up to $4 billion. A third of the members of his country club were now in the fund, and when he took his gap-toothed boys to their tennis lessons, starry-eyed members were coming up, visions of sugar plums dancing in their heads, asking what stocks he liked and how the fund was doing. Jake, a very smart guy, then did a very stupid thing. He leveraged up. As you can see from looking at Figure 15.1, CLF and the resource stocks peaked in mid-summer 2008. On August 29, 2008, CLF was at 101; a month later, it traded at 29! Two months later, it was at 17. Over the same time, U.S. Steel plunged from 184 to 23. With leverage, it was death and destruction. Joe heard that for the year the net asset value of Jake's fund was down a cool 82 percent. Of course, everyone was furious.

The abuse Jake endured was endless and overwhelming. Too many of his clients were friends or at least acquaintances. Disgruntled investors even abused his wife. Disgusted, he closed the fund, and the rumor was he had put his remaining $20 million into tax-exempt bonds and moved to Vermont. Thinking about it, Joe decided Jake had two weaknesses. His investment arrogance led him to leverage up to fulfill his investors' expectations, and he wanted to be acclaimed by his social set. The financial panic transformed these two errors into fatal flaws. But, Joe meditated, were they truly fatal if he was happy and reasonably rich in Vermont?

By late 2008 Wall Street had become a violent, vicious, formerly prosperous and presumptuous city, like bombed-out Dresden in 1945.

When night came, the fear, pain, and loneliness was equal for its citizens, whether they huddled in Park Avenue duplexes or lived in big brick mansions with long driveways in Greenwich. Day after day, markets were plummeting, and then suddenly out of nowhere would come a powerful rally that would have all the technical characteristics of an important reversal. Interday swings of 5 percent were not uncommon, and there were even a few days when they reached 10 percent. With everyone jittery and staring at their screens all day long, the hyperactive, momentum-oriented professional trading money would be sucked in to the rally, usually buying the S&P futures, an exchange-traded fund, or some other volatile index. Almost always, these traders entered a stop-loss order 2 to 5 percent below their purchase price to limit their losses.

Three days later, and sometimes even the next day, the market would fall apart again, and the traders would be stopped out with another loss. After a number of these 5 percent hits, even the most arrogant and self-confident hot money players began to get the message that the old rules had been repealed. This was a gigantic bear market storm like nothing they had ever experienced, and that by buying they were going against the tide and were sure to swept out to sea and drown.

Groups of short sellers, often hedge funds, were bear raiding stocks, particularly the investment banks, by selling deep, short-dated, out-of-the-money puts, selling short the stocks without first borrowing the shares (so-called naked short selling), and then buying and bidding up the volatile and thinly traded credit default swaps. Until 2006, shares could not be sold short without an uptick, but with that rule no longer in effect, the short sellers didn't have to wait while their broker arranged to borrow the stock. They could just pile on and drive the price of the stock down with their selling.

This lethal, triple sucker punch called into question the ability of these investment banks to finance themselves because the higher the price of the credit default swaps went, the more expensive it was for them to finance their leveraged balance sheets. Bear Stearns, Lehman Brothers, and then Merrill Lynch were bear raided in this manner. When Lehman failed, there were 32 million shares of stock that had been sold short that could not be delivered.

Citicorp, Morgan Stanley, and Goldman Sachs were targeted by the short sellers as the next victims. Grant was almost certainly on the list. As recently as December 26, 2006, Citigroup's share price had been at a new high of 56. That year it earned $4.22 a share and paid a dividend of $1.96. Its stockholders were reassured by the knowledge that its executive committee chairman was the revered former secretary of the treasury Robert Rubin, and that a great mutual fund manager from Baltimore maintained Citicorp, the premier financial franchise and brand in the world. The brilliant Bob Rubin who had saved the world in the Asian debt crisis wouldn't let Citicorp do anything really stupid, would he?

As Figure 15.2 shows, a mere 28 months later the share price had cascaded to a low of 1.50. On the way down, in November of 2007 with Citicorp's stock price in the mid-30s, the Abu Dhabi Investment Authority made a $7.5 billion equity investment in Citicorp, momentarily propping up the price of the stock. A year later that stake was virtually worthless, so it wasn't just the widows and orphans who owned the stock for its rich dividend, the value managers who thought it was so cheap it was safe, or the growth stock investors who were convinced it was a priceless global brand who were wiped out. No

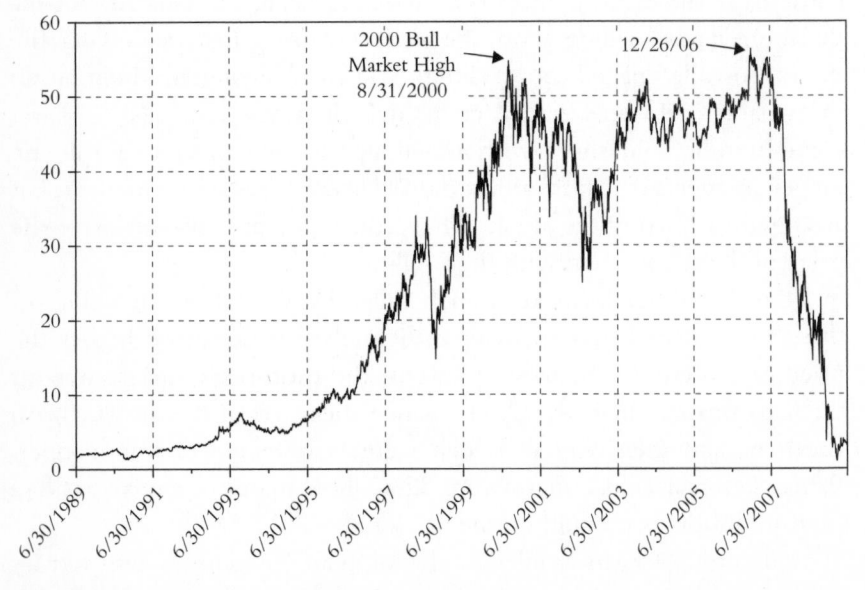

Figure 15.2 The Rise and Fall of a Titan—Citicorp

one had ever imagined there could be such a waterfall decline in such a supposedly great institution.

As the organized and concerted bear raids drove down his stock price, the courageous chairman of Morgan Stanley, John Mack, and other people who understood what was happening, complained vociferously to the SEC about these tactics. The hedge fund short sellers, enraged, punished Morgan Stanley by pulling their prime brokerage accounts from the firm. Prime brokerage had been Morgan Stanley's most profitable and fastest-growing business, so this exodus really hurt and—as rumors swirled—exacerbated the weakness in the stock price.

Also, other hedge funds, worried that Morgan Stanley might fail, transferred their prime brokerage accounts as well, and, fearful of bankruptcy, some long-only institutional investors, mutual funds, and investment banking clients suspended doing business with the firm. With this onslaught sucking its lifeblood, Morgan Stanley teetered perilously close to going down despite having reduced its leverage and cleaned up its balance sheet. In the press and on CNBC, hedge fund managers piously defended their supposedly inalienable right to sell stocks short without an uptick and without having borrowed the shares. It was a time out of the early 1900s of bear raids, rumors, and panics. A verse about short people was circulated by a market letter writer that went like this:

> They got little hands
> And little eyes
> And they walk around
> Tellin' great big lies . . .
> Well, I don't want no short people . . .
> 'Round here.

Eventually the Securities and Exchange Commission imposed a temporary ban on short selling by financial institutions, but the damage had been done. Confidence in the great investment banks had been undermined, and their employees had been demoralized by financial terrorism. Senior managers and employees were quaking in their Gucci loafers.

Now the panic was in full flood. The S&P 500 fell 9 percent in September, 17 percent in October, and another 7 percent in November.

By November 30, it had fallen 38 percent for the year with the steepest angle of decline in history. Only the Great Crash itself was comparable. Nevertheless, the S&P's percentage drop was less than that of almost every other major bourse in the world. The so-called BRIC (Brazil, Russia, India, and China)—the anointed, superstar emerging markets— were off a shattering 70 to 80 percent. The prices of all assets, not just stocks but houses, commercial real estate, private equity, timber-land, junk bonds, you name it, were collapsing. This was true wealth destruction on a scale and at a speed that was beyond any modern soul's comprehension. The world was in shock.

Meanwhile, BA was still afloat but leaking badly and threatening to broach in the most severe financial and economic storm since the 1930s. Tempers were short and the fabric of relationships was fraying. Mickey had never been a second-guesser, but one morning after a late night he turned mean and nasty as he berated Joe and Joan for their ill-timed foray into growth. He was as passionate as ever that value was the only true religion, and that they must stick to their core beliefs. Sure, there might be short periods when growth outperformed, but the historical record was clear that value was best by far. When Joe reminded him that he seemed to be forgetting that during value's last years in the wilderness he had suffered intensely for what seemed an eternity, he stormed out of the room. They looked at each other.

"He's wound as tight as a violin," Joe murmured.

"Not the state of mind from which to make good decisions," Joan added, "The punishment of this bear market is getting to us all."

"It's like in a football game when you're getting beat up and blown out. Some guys react badly and start pointing fingers," Joe said. "Trouble is, you don't forget it. Like they say, character will out."

"This bear is stripping us bare, revealing all our weaknesses."

Meanwhile, volatility was soaring, and their performance was continuing to suffer. After a discussion that verged on a shouting match, they tilted toward a more growth-oriented portfolio, and then abruptly the next month was of strong value. They had been whip-sawed again.

"We can't do anything right," Joe grimly said to Joan.

"We're out of step and continually being wrong-footed. It's not good that Mickey is so adamant. He's screwing up our heads."

"Yeah, adamant yet disengaged." They both had noticed that Mickey was out of the office even more frequently and, in addition, was spending considerable in-office time on the affairs of his high-profile charitable activities. One or two glasses of wine at lunch were also becoming habitual.

"Raising a lot of money for the Metropolitan Opera isn't going to help our numbers or stem our redemptions," Joan said bitterly.

"I know," Joe said. "And I'm worried some of our savvy, long-time clients are noticing. If we were doing well, it would be okay—not doing great but just well. But instead, we're doing badly. Now it's a clear warning sign, and at worst it makes them wonder if without Mickey involved you and I can't cut it."

Joan said nothing. She just stared out the window at the park and the chilly, impersonal blueness of the sky against which was visible the tips of black boughs with tattered rags of leaves attached to them.

After a few minutes, she murmured, "You know what one fund of funds guy said to me? He said, *Did you three geeks ever think that it's your models that are simple, not the world? Maybe that's why they're not working.* And just maybe that's why Buffett says, *Beware of geeks bearing models.*"

Joe just shook his head. He felt a growing sense of despair. It was as though he were imprisoned in a glass cage. Those great, tall, steel and stone skyscrapers ringing the park in serried ranks that to Joe once had seemed temples of wealth and stability were now like authoritarian sentries, almost images of their judgmental clients, observing them in their mortal agony. The luxurious, opulent fittings in the Bridgestone offices somehow made things worse. It all seemed phony and ephemeral as though it might melt away at any moment. He wondered what was real. Playing with his boys, building stone walls with them, talking into their fresh little faces had become a reality and a release from the markets. But Joan was still talking to him.

"And he's drinking martinis before dinner and swigging those expensive Burgundy wines of his and getting fatter and fatter. Yesterday, he admitted to me he'd made a fool of himself at a party the previous night. *Don't know what got into me*, he said."

"Not good!" he responded as he was brought back to reality, "What did you say?"

"I didn't say anything," she replied, "but what I thought was: I know darn well what got into you. Two martinis and a bottle of Burgundy." Joe laughed in spite of himself.

"What scares me," she went on, "is that I'm sure there's even more dangerous stuff than martinis at these parties. I hear pot and even snorting is going on."

"You think Mickey could be doing coke?" Joe asked incredulously.

"I don't know. He's hurtin' big time and there's a lot of people in this town who are hurtin' too. Everyone is trying to dull the pain."

"Jesus!" Joe murmured. "This really is a killer bear market. It's not just wealth destruction but people destruction, too."

As they were talking, Ravine strolled by. He paused and came in. In contrast to them, he seemed relaxed and at peace. Maybe his affair had done him good, Joe thought.

"So what do you guys think?" Ravine asked.

They told him of their anxieties about their model and the chaos that was enveloping them.

"The velocity of events is terrifying because we have never experienced anything like it," Ravine reflected. "What frightens me is that history teaches that highly complex, adaptive systems—like empires, the global economy, and the financial markets—can function in a productive equilibrium for long periods of time; but inevitably, suddenly, because of some relatively minor shock, collapse and crash with inconceivable rapidity. Think of Rome, the Ming Dynasty, the Ottoman Empire, the Bourbon Monarchy. The chaos of World War I that changed the world began with the assassination of an obscure archduke, even the sudden dissolution of the British Empire after World War II, and the fall of the Soviet Union. In retrospect, the collapse of each was totally unexpected, sudden, and triggered by what seemed at the time a rather insignificant event that fatally tilted the system. Complex systems are both durable and then become terribly fragile."

He paused and gazed at them. "The world, our complex system as we have known it, is being crashed, perhaps fatally, by the stupidity of a few million people who overreached with subprime mortgages and the ingenious mendacity of a few hundred bankers. Human intelligence itself is a complex system. And guess what? Your precious model is a complex system trying to decipher another complex system, the financial markets. Both are crashing simultaneously."

Joe and Joan just stared at him. They knew what he had just said was profound, but it was too deep and too frightening for them.

"Insha'Allah!" Ravine turned and walked out of their office.

Now the tsunami-like momentum of the global financial and economic collapse was devastating markets. Random volatility soared to previously unimaginable highs and growth stocks fell less than value names. This distortion was torturing value-based models and their performance. Across the world, markets in stocks, commodities, oil, and futures were swinging 5 to 10 percent a day, and the daily changes in individual stocks were even more violent. With the frantic deleveraging, price action was totally irrational as funds scrambled to buy back their shorts and sell their longs.

Thinking about all this, Joe realized that the real problem was that their carefully crafted value-seeking model was totally broken, busted, shattered. As he bitterly said to Joan, "Our precious *cosa nostra* that we thought was so special is basically no different from the twenty other value-seeking models out there. As a result, we all own and are short the same stocks, so when the shit hits the fan, we are all screwed. There's no concentration factor in our equation, and it's killing us. In fact, the terrifying truth is that we may already be dead!"

"Yeah!" Joan told him. "Yeah! Remember what I told you and Mickey a year ago? F. Scott Fitzgerald once wrote that the test of a first-rate intelligence is the ability to hold two deeply opposed ideas in the mind at the same time and still retain the ability to function. We don't have that ability; we hold only one idea, and in managing money in an environment like this, it's a terrible disability. The unexpected is the killer."

He looked at her trying to understand. Sometimes she was too deep for him.

"We didn't see this credit crisis coming," he said. "I was reading the boys an ocean book last night and it told how the dolphin, always vigilant, the most intelligent of fish, sleeps with one eye open while still swimming. We were swimming with both eyes closed."

Panic and fear were everywhere, and with them came the overwhelming desire of owners of wealth for their money. Treasury bills now actually had a negative yield. People weren't concerned about the return *on* their money but rather the return *of* their money. Many hedge funds were imposing restrictions on withdrawals—raising what was called *gates*. A gate stated that an investor could not get his money back when he requested it as originally agreed on. Instead, a form of investment *force majeure* was being imposed, and investors' supposedly liquid capital would not be returned until the hedge fund felt like it or could find it. The trapped investors understandably were furious.

Various lame excuses, such as illiquidity and the large number of withdrawals, were proffered by the gating hedge funds. The ugly realization that some highly reputable funds such as Citadel and Tudor were imposing gates was extremely unnerving to investors. It called into question whether you could get your money out of a hedge fund, any hedge fund, when you wanted to. One fund of funds told Joe that when he told a famous hedge fund manager that he wanted his money back, the guy rudely replied. "Listen fella, you got it all wrong. It's not your money; it's our money. You're like a stockholder in us. You gave it to us. We'll give your investment in us back to you when we think it's the right time for all of us and that's not now. Take a walk."

Then in early December 2008, the Madoff scandal exploded. The investment world was shocked and mortified that reputable funds of funds, venerable and supposedly wise Swiss banks, and sophisticated investors could get sucked into such a massive Ponzi scheme. Confidence evaporated and the liquidity panic that was already under way became a deluge.

The funds, such as BA, that did not have a provision for gates or did not choose to erect them received the full force of the enormous surge in redemptions. In the month of November, for redemption on December 1, BA received notices for $950 million, bringing withdrawals for the full year to $1.5 billion. Since they couldn't imbalance their long and short portfolios, they had to sell a major portion of each long position and buy back a proportionate amount of each short to raise the cash, further crushing their performance. BA had begun the year with $3.6 billion, down from $8 billion on January 1, 2007. Now they were at less than a billion! The brutal truth was that after two straight big down years, their clients had totally lost faith in them, and were absolutely terrified by the financial panic. Under those circumstances, why would they stick around and pay a 2 percent fixed management fee?

Two of BA's remaining fund of funds clients had leveraged their portfolios and as a result were suffering staggering declines in their own net asset values. They also were getting heavy redemptions, particularly from their individual investors, some of whom had been talked by their banks into borrowing money using their BA investment as collateral to enhance performance. The theory had been that with a long-short fund such as BA this was perfectly safe leverage, as until the last two years BA's returns had been consistent and almost bond-like. Now the banks were calling the loans, and the individuals had no choice but to redeem. Essentially, the underlying hedge fund was leveraged, the fund of funds was leveraged, and the individual investors in the fund of funds were leveraged. Leverage on leverage on leverage.

The bear market had devastated investors of all financial religions, but its pattern of schizophrenic returns had been particularly damaging for long-short hedge funds that trafficked in pure alpha and were supposed to be immune from bear market volatility. For the full, horrendous year of 2008, BA's net asset value, including the 2 percent fixed fee, was down 31.5 percent. The S&P 500 was off 37 percent, a broader index of worldwide stocks in dollars was down 44 percent, and the MSCI Emerging Markets Index sunk 53 percent (see Figure 15.3). Many hedge funds lost 50 percent or more, but a few fixed income macro funds actually made money and Treasury bonds had a total return of 20 percent.

The destruction of BA's assets from losses and redemptions had been so fast and so unexpected that they had not reduced their cost structure anywhere nearly enough. They belatedly let go three of their analysts and all the research assistants, and Joan's compensation for the year was cut by two-thirds. Nevertheless, their operating loss for the

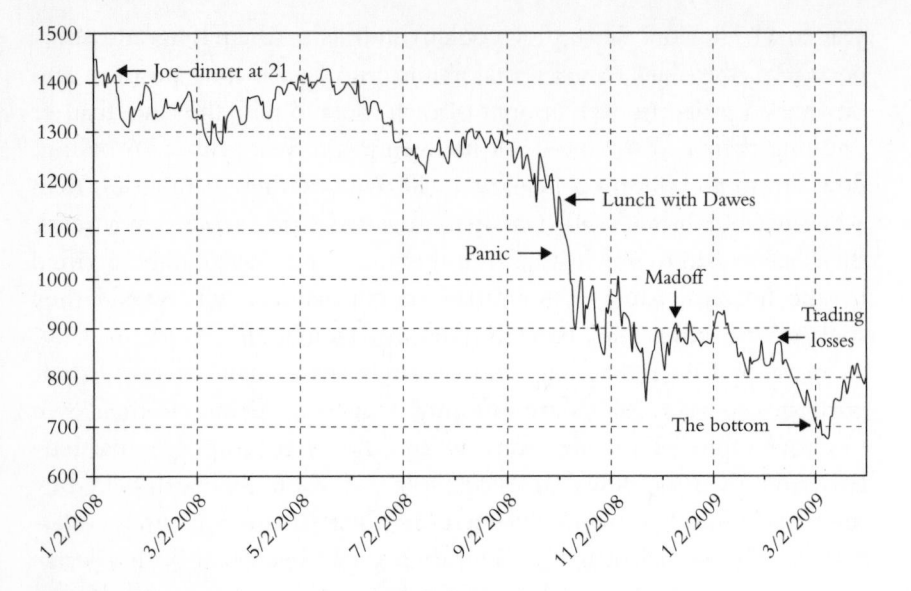

Figure 15.3 *Annus Horribilis*; Anatomy of a Bear

year was $10 million, meaning that Mickey and Joe each had to come up with $5 million. At their peak two years earlier, Joe had $170 million in the fund. After paying taxes on 2006 earnings in 2007, two years of losses, and the withdrawals he had made to cover his domestic expenses, he was down to $15 million before writing a check for the $5 million.

As for Mickey, he was, as he put it "really hurting." At the very beginning, he had invested $20 million, all of his inherited money, in BA, and at one time, despite his extravagant lifestyle, he had almost $375 million in the fund. But the divorces, taxes, losses, apartments, beach houses, airplane, artwork, and major living expenses had him down to $20 million by the end of 2008. He owed Citibank $30 million for the plane and had $17 million of mortgages outstanding. Finally, he had year-end pledges that he had made in the flush times to five different charities for a total of $7 million. They were tax deductions then; now they were an embarrassment.

The Old Master deal with Fletcher had been the ultimate killer. He had gone into the art partnership with Fletcher in late 2007, and they had ended up buying the five Old Masters for $57 million of which Mickey had put up $50 million. After the lousy year BA had experienced in 2007, he knew it would look bad if he made a major withdrawal from the fund. So instead, he borrowed $35 million from Citi and withdrew only $15 million from BA.

The art deal had closed in Paris, and Mickey, Fletcher, and Vanessa were jubilant after the signing. The Russian seller had been holding out for $70 million, and they had been prepared to go as high as $65 million. To get the pictures for $57 million seemed like a bargain. That evening they had celebrated at Taillevent with a couple of $600-bottles of 15-year-old Bordeaux.

The actual display and selling of the pictures was not a minor or inexpensive undertaking. In New York, Fletcher had rented a fine, old townhouse on 63rd Street, and in Paris a grand salon off the Rue de Babylone from Saint Laurent. In the New York townhouse, the gallery was at the end of an oval lacquered hallway, and the pictures, elegantly lit, hung above an array of furniture by designers from the Art Deco period as well as small seventeenth-century statues of muscular Greek gods, rampant animals, and other *objets d'art*. The overall effect as the *Economist* described it was "one of glamour, intelligence, and luxury." A prominent art historian with impeccable credentials had written essays on each work for the glossy catalogue.

The problem was that the *art moment* had evaporated in the heat of the financial conflagration. In late September, 2008, immediately after the failure of Lehman Brothers, the high-priced art market (like the price of all precious collectibles) had utterly, totally, and completely collapsed. It was as though row after row of different asset dominoes sympathetically and simultaneously cascaded.

The chairman of Lehman, Dick Fuld, had been a serious and discerning art collector, but by October his collection was for sale and there were no bids for anything. As for Fletcher, serious art lovers were flocking to his gallery and sipping his dry Chablis while murmuring and gazing raptly at the masterpieces, but there were no buyers anywhere near his proposed purchase prices.

"I'm, like, running an art museum, choking on inventory," Fletcher complained to Mickey. "The market's frozen. We have bids for two of the pictures that would bring us $10 million but nothing for the other five. We're well and truly artistically screwed!"

Mickey was frantic. The idea of a gift to the Metropolitan in return for a board seat was totally unappealing now that he had no income for the year to write the gift off against. Besides, Vanessa was sullen and not much fun anymore.

"Can't we get Sotheby's or Christie's to auction 'em?" he demanded of Fletcher. "My girlfriend used to work there."

"Not a chance," Fletcher told him. "They both had big losses at their fall auctions and are loaded with inventory. Besides, they charge ridiculous commissions."

"You told me it was going to be easy to sell these. What's happened to all the buyers? Why aren't the museums with the big endowments like the Getty interested?"

"Because they're leaking money like everybody else. They've relied on formula payouts from their endowments to support their operating budgets. The endowment values are going to be off thirty percent or more this year, so their payouts are way down, and to add insult to injury their funds are loaded up with private equity and real estate opportunity funds. Both asset classes are at the bottom of the sea, and the funds are making capital calls. The foundations are savaging budgets, staff, and spending."

"Hey listen, Larry, whatever. We have to sell those two. I need the money."

"Well, I don't," Fletcher told him coldly. "Your leverage is not my problem. Relax, fella. It's a highly cyclical business. I thought you knew that. The market for art will come back, but right now we can't get even close to what they're worth."

"Who's going to pay fifteen million bucks for a picture in the midst of a fucking financial panic and a depression?"

"There are at least a hundred so-called *gros acheteurs* still left in the world, and maybe I'm being presumptuous, but in the longer run they will be unable to resist the combination of quality, provenance, and fame. Take a couple of the pictures to your apartment, hang them, and enjoy them. The only rub is that the insurance on them is expensive."

"Yeah, great!" grumbled Mickey. "Just what I need—more overhead."

Meanwhile the muted whispers in the halls at Bridgestone were about how badly most of the firm's funds were doing. One macro fixed income fund was up 15 percent for the year, but BA and all the other big funds were down anywhere from the mid-20s to the high 30s. Assets under management were evaporating, and the firm unquestionably would have a substantial loss for the year. With its main engines barely turning over, the once great ship, the U.S.S. Bridgestone, was wallowing in the eye of the storm.

Spokane stopped by their office and came in and closed the door. He was as fashionably dressed as ever and looked as though he didn't have a care in the world. Without preamble he said to them, "Boys and girl, we're floundering. It's the perfect storm and we're taking in water too fast for the pumps."

"What does that mean?" Mickey asked him.

Spokane rose and glided athletically toward the door. "It means that Bridgestone is *H.M.S. Titanic*, and it gives formal notice that it's every man for himself. Women and children last."

That evening, Joe recounted the message to Emily. She responded casually, "Okay! Easy come, easy go."

"It's not okay," he told her. "We've got to practice austerity. I don't know what's going to happen with BA or at the firm. I may not have a job."

"It can't be true," Emily reassured him. "And even if it is, you've still got a lot of money."

He shook his head. All his capital had been in BA.

"Not anymore. I'll be lucky to get out of Bridgestone with ten million. And I feel terrible about the losses for your mother, Josh, and my parents. They came in too late, after the good years. It's a disaster."

The redemption notification from Emily's mother had been particularly personal and painful. One Sunday, after dinner with the children at the Daweses' home, that formidable character took Joe aside in the library and without preamble said, "I'm withdrawing my money from your fund as soon as possible. Your performance is abysmal."

"You're right," Joe replied. "I'm extremely sorry."

"Being sorry is useless, Joe. I've lost several million dollars. You persuaded me to invest by telling me that I couldn't lose any money."

"I never asked you to invest in our fund, and I certainly never told you that you couldn't lose."

"That's not the way I remember it." She stared at her manicured fingernails. "And what's more, I've been paying you fees all this time you've been losing my money. I distinctly remember you telling me I only paid a fee if you made money."

"With all due respect, I never told you that. I believe I said you only paid the incentive fee if you made money."

"Well, that's not what I recall at all. The whole experience has been very disappointing, a disaster!" and she turned and stomped back to the family room where the children were playing.

She was right, Joe thought, it was a disaster, or maybe a *catastrophe* was more like it. The hard, dreadfully indigestible fact that Mickey, Joan, and Joe now had to swallow was that BA's assets under management totaled only about $1 billion, of which $120 million was Bridgestone's and paid no fee and maybe $40 million was Joe's, Mickey's, and Joan's, none of whom paid a fee, either. They calculated that they were so far below their high-water mark in BA that only after their present net asset value had doubled would they again begin earning an incentive fee.

Furthermore, after two big, back-to-back down years, no self-respecting investor would ever put new money into them again. A few of their existing investors might keep money with them because they would understand they had a free ride back up to the high-water mark. They would have to pay the 2 percent fixed fee, however, regardless.

The reality was that if BA were to keep going, they would have to let most of their staff go and run the whole thing, models and all, by themselves. That made no sense either because if they took such drastic action, the rest of the fee-paying money would in all probability evaporate in the next six months. For the upcoming redemption date, they had already received notifications for $120 million in withdrawals. BA was out of business and everyone knew it. Both the hedge fund magazine, *Absolute Return*, and the *Wall Street Journal* had published articles to that effect and speculation was rife that Bridgestone itself was going to close.

A few days later Mickey confided in Joe. "If the world is headed for another great depression, the S&P is going to five or six hundred, and

Bridgestone is going under, then, like the bears say, I'm wiped out. Sunk without even a wine slick to show where I went down. Gone! You know, I'm almost bust right now."

Joe just stared at his partner, his friend. Mickey looked awful. All of his old ebullience had evaporated. No longer were there extravagant gestures and warm, friendly arm squeezes. His face was splotchy and he now kept his hands either in his pockets or under the table. Were they shaking uncontrollably? Joe thought to himself, *Of course, Fletcher had no incentive to sell because he had put up no money.* But what could Joe say? In fact, he suspected Mickey was already wiped out.

Meanwhile, Mickey ranted on. "Overhead! You know how many people I have working for me? Including the pilots—eight full-time. That fucking airplane is eating me out of house and home and there are no buyers or even renters for the damn thing. Citi wants more collateral for the loan. Plus I got two mortgages to service."

"My God," said Joan when Joe told her about Mickey's plight. "He was such a brilliant guy, and then with success and the acclaim and great wealth, it was as though he'd lost his mental moorings, talking about living *baroque.* He became a different person, like he'd gone crazy!"

"The money affected me differently," Joe reflected. "I didn't go crazy but I became investment complacent. I thought we had *the* model, *the* algorithm that would work forever. I didn't realize the brilliance of our model, our complex system, and our performance was only a momentary thing that could reverse and eat us alive."

"Yes," said Joan. "We were all too smug, too self-satisfied. We should have been tinkering with it. Above all, we should have been listening to the market."

"We did tinker with the model," he told her, "but we were always adjusting for the way the market *had* been rather than what it *was* becoming."

"The seriously dangerous thing for us now," Joe went on hesitantly, "is that Mickey's financial distress is messing with his head. He's not thinking straight about anything."

"I think he's depressed and on the verge of some kind of a breakdown," Joan said. "He should see a doctor and get help."

"You're probably right. I'll try to think of a way to tell him. What do you do in a situation like this? Do you confront him or do you do it gently?"

"Gently must be the answer," Joan told him. "Gently. Tenderly. After all, he *is* our Mickey. We came to the party with him."

Mickey, of course, was not the only hedge fund guy suffering from stress, anxiety, and humiliation. They were hearing of other prominent brigands who had come down with what were being called "investment nervous breakdowns" where they simply collapsed in the face of the enormity of the professional and personal disaster that was confronting them. Guys who you used to talk to regularly, would suddenly just drop out of circulation; you would stop hearing from them. Then a few weeks later, you would learn that they were staying home or had gone to Florida or someplace where they could hide out.

In one sad case, a guy whose fund was down a lot and who was getting massive redemptions left the office one afternoon without saying a word to anyone. He went home to his bedroom, drew the blinds so there was total darkness, put in wax earplugs, and pulled the covers up over his head, and just stayed there. When his wife came home he told her he was very tired and wouldn't be getting up for dinner. He wasn't taking any calls—not from clients, not from his partners, not from anyone. For the rest of the week he stayed in bed. Nibbled on toast and soup. Ignored his wife and seemed to have no interest in the children when they came to visit him.

Finally, after five days of this behavior, his wife exploded. She stormed into the bedroom, threw back the draperies and the covers, and almost threw him out of bed. But the guy still did not go back to his office. As a matter of fact, his hedge fund was effectively being liquidated to meet redemptions. It was messy—lawyers, auditors, all that nasty stuff. Later, Joe heard their home was on the market, and they were planning to move back to Ohio where the wife's family had an insurance brokerage business.

In an instance that hit closer to home, Doug Scott, Joe's old prop trader friend, called, and they had a long talk.

"I've been laid off by Hadron," Doug told him.

"I'm so sorry."

"Tom is cutting way back on prop trading. He had maybe thirty prop traders and he's going to nine or ten. We all have lost big money and some guys are down fifty to sixty percent."

"I thought you guys used stops?" Joe asked.

"Stops are no protection when the market is having ten percent intraday swings," Doug replied. "We all were using leverage, and it's been a total disaster. The amazing thing is that Tom himself is up, like, fifteen percent on the year. The guy is a fabulous trader! It's like magic. I don't understand how he does it. He's a born gambler. If five guys were betting on which fat raindrop would make it down the window pane first he would win every time. It's feel; intuition."

"So what are you going to do?"

"I'm packing it in," he told Joe. "I just can't take it anymore. I've been whipsawed over and over again, and I'm just so discouraged. I have to get away from it."

"Take some time off," Joe advised him. "You've got a family. These tough times aren't going to last forever."

"I'm disoriented. Jeannie tells me I'm like a zombie with her and the kids. She's threatening to go home to her mother in Michigan."

"You can't let that happen. Haven't you got some money from those good years?"

"No. Can you believe it's gone, gone with the wind? But it is. I was trading for myself as well; leveraged up big so I've lost almost everything. You know two years ago when I was doing great, I bought a house in Rye. Not a big deal. Two million bucks, but I took out a mortgage for a million eight 'cause I wanted to keep my capital for trading. The payments are eating me up, so I put it on the market. The broker says I'd be lucky to get a million four. Hell, I can't even repay the mortgage."

Joe nodded sympathetically. He suspected he was under water on his mortgage too. Greenwich real estate was plummeting.

Joe didn't know what else to say. Doug had been such a strong, confident, attractive guy; it was doubly shocking to hear his despair. Why would he have leveraged up? Joe knew the answer, of course. He had been doing well with his trading, and success was like drugs or alcohol. You came to believe it could never end, that you were bulletproof. If you were truly invulnerable, kissed by the gods, why not leverage up and double or triple your profits? Make hay while the sun shines!

Toward the end of the year, Spokane asked Joe, Mickey and Joan of them to come to his conference room.

For once, Mickey was on time, and when they were assembled in the familiar room, the site of so many epic confrontations, Spokane entered. He was surprisingly gracious but he couldn't resist an occasional snide crack.

"It's been a tough time for us all," he said with no preamble. We've blown up. All our competitors are badmouthing us. Fuck them! Anyway, we're going to close the firm and all the funds, including BA, as of April 30. We'll send out a letter to the clients next week. They'll get their money or what's left of it around the third week of May. We do have two funds that are so illiquid they won't be able to pay out until God only knows when. We're worried about lawsuits.

"You're the first ones to know because you're our most famous, or should I say, our most *infamous*, fund. Ravine and I will take big hits, as we're going to have to eat the last year and half of our lease here and, as you know, there's no demand for space in New York now that the world has fallen apart. We've also got to provide severance pay for the back-office and support staff. The investment staff has already been paid for 2008 so their last salary check will be at the end of next month."

He paused. "It was a great, bumpy ride, a fabulous party while it lasted, but it's over. It's painful. Ravine and I are going to walk away with a lot less money than we had two years ago, but we're not going to starve. I'm moving to Palm Beach. Presumably you three, despite the hits of the last two years, will leave with enough money to keep the wolf from the door. Ravine regrets he couldn't be here, but he had personal stuff to attend to."

"Can we stay in our offices for a few months while we figure out what we're going to do next?" Joe asked. "We'd pay some nominal rent and get a couple of Bloomberg machines."

"I don't see why not," Spokane replied. "Every little bit of income will help us swallow this monster of a lease. You realize we're going to strip the offices, and that there'll be nobody here but a security guard. It won't exactly be a vibrant, cheery atmosphere."

No one said anything. The four of them just sat there. After a while, Mickey got up and walked out of the conference room. Joe and Joan shook hands with Spokane, who still seemed relaxed.

"So what's Mickey's problem?" Spokane asked them when Mickey was gone. "I guess I know," he said, answering his own question. "The story around the watering holes is that he's been wiped out. Hope you guys are at least solvent."

Neither Joe nor Joan said anything.

"We could start a new fund and begin all over again," Joe said to Joan that afternoon as they sat in Joe's office.

"Who's *we?*" she asked.

"You and me and Mick and maybe two of the quants who run our models and a trader."

"No thanks," she said. "Mickey is toxic waste. I don't like sounding cold-blooded, but both the investment world and the art world know he's careened off the tracks. As for our models, they're discredited. We blew it."

"What are you going to do?" he asked her.

"I don't know. We could blame the disaster on Mickey, and a lot of people would probably believe it. It has the added virtue of being at least partly true. Then we could start our own fund with our own money and try to scrape up a little more and go it alone. You got any ideas?"

"No, not really," he said, "and there's no new money out there for start-up hedge funds, particularly ones run by two pilots who just flew a Boeing Business Jet from fifty thousand feet into the ground at supersonic speed."

"Once upon a time you had a really good investment reputation."

Joe looked at her thoughtfully. "But that was long ago and far away. I've been thinking about it a lot. We didn't know it at the time but purely by chance Mickey and I started BA at the absolutely perfect moment for our value strategy. The greatest bull market in growth in history was peaking, and the biggest bear market in value was bottoming.

We aren't and never were investment geniuses; we were just lucky to be in the *exactly* right place at *exactly* the right time with a decent line of bullshit. I have no confidence anymore that I'm a good investor."

"But what else besides investing do we know?"

"Nada! But Joan, you're far less tainted by what's happened here than Mickey and I are so you can maybe get a job at a mutual fund company or somewhere else in the money management business."

"Lousy time to be looking for a job," she replied ruefully. "Besides, I'm convinced the golden age of the investment business is over. It's going to be asset allocation, index funds, and fixed income for the next ten years. But listen, Joe, I'll be okay. I've still got ten million dollars put away so it's not exactly like I'm impoverished."

Joe looked out the window for almost a minute. "We have to reinvent ourselves. The problem is we're getting older and we have a bad rep in the only profession we know. I'm not qualified for anything else."

"You're right. The party's over—over not for a while but for years."

"Yo momma," he told her trying to lighten the mood, "but I'm going to keep coming in here and am going to try to make some money and trade my own account. I sure don't want to sit around Greenwich sucking my thumb with nothing to do all day but play golf and listen to other guys' hard luck stories."

"I'll be around too. Can I ask, how much money you got left?"

"After everything, taxes, paydowns, settlements, maybe fifteen million. Ten million in BA and five million outside. I took that ten out of BA at the end of last year. Figured it was the smart thing to do. Then I lost half of it."

"I did the same," she told him with a wry smile. "Rats deserting the sinking ship."

He looked at her thinking how constructive and open their discussions were. With Emily now there was so much anger about his fall from grace, and, he had to admit, an undertone of distrust because of his relationship with Joan. It was as though the glass through which they saw each other had become not only cracked but blurred and distorted as well.

Chapter 16

The Age of Malevolence

The game of professional investment is intolerably boring and over-exacting to anyone who is entirely exempt from the gambling instinct; whilst he who has it must pay to this propensity the appropriate toll.

—John Maynard Keynes

T wo weeks after his meeting with Spokane, Joe got a call from Perot. "I'm having a dinner at Lone Tree next Wednesday for a group of us bruised brigands. Everybody I've invited is hurting. Fuck, everyone I know is hurting. We all desperately need some therapy, and my idea is we sit around, drink some good wine, and bare our shattered souls. It'll be hard, but I'm convinced it'll be therapeutic. You okay with that?"

Joe liked the idea a lot. "Yeah, I'm definitely all for it."

"Should I invite Mickey?"

"You can try. It would be very good for him, but I doubt he'll come. He's become a proud guy, and right now he's in denial."

"Yeah, I heard he's in bad shape. I saw him the other day, and he had a martini and then two glasses of wine at lunch. You guys okay with each other?" Perot asked.

"Yeah, I think so," Joe told him. "Why do you ask?"

"Because I hear all kinds of wild stories about hedge fund guys who have been partners for years squabbling with each other, even blaming the other guy in public. Guys who have been friends and comrades are now splitting up with vicious recriminations."

"I'm not surprised. It's always easier to be lovey-dovey when you're winning."

"You know Sal Linowitz and Jeff Corzon who run and own Madison? Last week at their annual meeting with investors, Sal—in his review of their positions—made it clear that most of the losers had been put on by Jeff. Understandably, Jeff got pissed and nasty and, with fifty people watching, confronted Sal and called him an arrogant, stubborn asshole. It was really ugly. It'll be the end of their fund. Talk about wealth destruction!"

"I know," Joe told him. "I know. Mickey once said every great financial crisis in the end becomes truly malevolent. Malevolent for the people involved, for the society, for the country. Have you ever heard of anything like what we're going through?"

"Yeah," said Perot, "and it was called the Dark Ages! And it lasted three hundred years! Or maybe a better analogy is to Icarus. Like him, we flew too high, too close to the sun, and now, like him, we are falling, 'hurtling headlong through the affrighted air on unfaithful wings.' His were wax and feathers; ours were just as unfaithful."

Joe was nonplussed.

The dinner was a therapeutic but frightening event. The interest in the details of the Madoff Ponzi scheme was at full flood. At cocktail hour, guys stood around talking about Madoff, how his family must have been involved, and how the high and mighty who should have known better lost big money in his fund. There was a lot of gossip exchanged about redemptions and guys who had crashed and burned. One unfortunate had used Lehman London as his prime broker, and when Lehman failed, the British authorities had frozen his account. Now they were telling him it might be a year and a half before it would be released. Everyone agreed it was the ultimate and final indignity. The dinner was like an Alcoholics Anonymous meeting with the addicts confessing their anxieties and their sins.

They, as hedge fund people, had all been the stardust-kissed children of a Golden Age, of the magnificent bull market that emerged from the ashes of the 1970s. Now the lyric dancing had ceased, and the party was over. The band, the music, had stopped playing a couple of times before—briefly back in 1987, once in the 1990s, and then after 2000, but they all knew this one was different. This time the musicians had been scattered to the proverbial four winds, and their instruments smashed and broken. The bedraggled, brutalized dancers at the dinner sensed it would be years, maybe even decades, before those sweet, beguiling songs that they had thrilled to would be played again.

The world had produced way too many investment bankers, proprietary traders, structured products specialists, and yes, hedge fund managers. Now the bubbles, all the bubbles, had burst, and it was the time of revolution, witch hunts, and creative destruction.

It was all immensely bleak and depressing. Day after day Joe was hearing horror stories. He began to feel that he and everyone around him were doomed. If someone had a relatively minor character flaw, an Achilles heel, but brilliant, life-enhancing body armor everywhere else and a magnificent, crested helmet, the crushing bear market would find and not only expose the weakness, but magnify it, seize on it, and destroy the unfortunate guy.

Hedge funds were going out of business right and left and not just because of poor performance. Funds were closing down simply because their assets had shrunk so much that they couldn't support their overhead. In addition, they were so far below their high-water marks that there was no prospect of earning an incentive fee for a long time. The math was simple—if you're down 30 percent, you have to be up 50 percent before you're going to get paid again.

Joe knew a guy, Sam Spencer, who was a macro hedge fund specialist and member of Lone Tree. Sam was glib and charming, had been to the best schools, and had a slug of inherited money. He was inclined to eat too much and was overweight, but his fatal flaw was not obesity; it was rather his lack of attention to risk management. He'd been careless with leverage and had blown up a macro fund in the Russian debt crisis of 1998. The mistakes had cost him his jobs. You would have thought he would have learned his lesson, but Sam was nothing but resilient, and he repotted himself and resurrected his career. In 2006, he started a macro hedge fund, got $60 million at full fee from a wealthy investor, but with the proviso that he would never have a drawdown of more than 20 percent. If he did, the investor warned him repeatedly, and in fact had put it in writing, that he was automatically going to pull the entire commitment.

Sam's fund got off to a good start. As it grew to $130 million, Sam added overhead and analysts. By October, the fund was up 10 percent. Then, incredibly, there was the regime change of all regime changes as markets began to sicken. Like a lot of people, Sam didn't believe it and he didn't hedge his bets at all or pay attention to his risk management. He allowed his analysts to make investment decisions, and there was no central control of the portfolio. It was happy-go-lucky, momentum-oriented, bull market portfolio management.

By the end of January 2008, before he knew it, Sam's NAV had fallen 22 percent from its peak. By now, his rich benefactor was frightened, angry, and probably felt betrayed. He was looking for a way out and the drawdown provision provided it. He exercised his prerogative and pulled his money. The other investors saw the big withdrawal, and scrambled like rats to leave the sinking ship. By mid-summer 2008, Sam's fund was down to $10 million in assets, and two months later, he closed it down. He was out of business.

Sam had always been a little crazy in regard to lifestyle extravaganza, and he had blithely loaded on a lot of personal overhead. Besides a nice but socially ambitious and expensive wife, he had three children in private schools, including one at Deerfield. In addition, he had just acquired a sprawling mansion, huge decorator bills, and had a couple of rooms full of antique furniture on order. Plus, during the boom, he had signed up to be chairman of two charitable balls and to be the head of the finance committee at his son's day school, all of which meant big contributions.

However, the real leverage was the apartment he had bought virtually sight unseen at the Fields Hotel. In the full flush of the times, in early 2007, Sam had paid $15 million for a supposedly glorious two-bedroom, living room, dining room, library apartment on the seventeenth floor of the magnificent old hotel at the corner of Central Park West. Since the building was under total reconstruction, buyers made their purchases based on the plans and a three-dimensional video representation.

Sam had purchased the apartment based on the theory that an apartment in this glorious landmark would be a trophy property and a great investment. There were only 182 condominiums in the building, and the location, the views, the ambiance were unmatchable. Russians, Arabs, other hedge fund guys would be all over them once they could actually see the space, he reasoned.

Now construction was complete, and the magnificent old building was as beautiful as ever from the outside, an empty disappointment in the inside, and was even worse financially. Of course, the building's sales agent wouldn't reveal how many condos had actually been sold, but the rumor was only half. When he finally saw his apartment, Sam was appalled. The roof overhang restricted his view, and there was a wonderfully scenic, giant steel pillar right smack in the middle of the living room. Admittedly, on the blueprints there was a circle on that spot, but Sam hadn't paid attention and no one had told him it signified a pillar. The décor in the public spaces was glitzy tawdry, the fixtures in the apartments were fancy-tacky, and the workmanship was mediocre at best.

Sam was furious but he had no recourse. He was supposed to be a big boy. He told the property sales agent he wanted out. She ignored his bilious outburst and told him what he already knew—the New York real estate market was a disaster. "I think I can get you six," she murmured.

He was apoplectic, but then his accountant had an idea. He should give three equal interests in the ownership of the apartment to each of his three charitable obligations.

"Look," the accountant said, "so after a decent interval they get together and sell it for six million. Let's say they get two million each, but you file for a charitable deduction based on your cost of fifteen million. It's a little risky. People do it all the time but not usually in this size. At worst, if you're unlucky and the IRS audits you and really digs into the transaction, they might disallow it and you might be liable for back taxes on the difference between fifteen and six."

"Done!" Sam told him. "I'll be off the hook with those charities forever."

Joe had heard only snatches of all this directly from Sam. It was locker room chatter, but he was pretty sure it was true. He ran into Sam at Lone Tree, and they chatted sitting in the oak-paneled bar amidst the usual hum of golf talk. Sam had always been heavy, bordering on fat, but now he was positively obese.

"My back is killing me," he told Joe. "I've gained a lot of weight and I sprained it getting out of my car. They got me on muscle relaxants and heavy pain killers. Now some asshole client is trying to sue me. That's the last thing I need."

Joe said he was sorry. He could see Sam was keeping a stiff, albeit quivering, upper lip. He was retiring, he said, and was going to "trade his own account." Joe wondered, *Retiring at age 50? Trading his own account when it was maybe four or five million dollars? With tuitions to pay for kids in private schools? Sounds like the kiss of death!*

Two weeks later Joe heard that Sam had resigned from Lone Tree, that his house was on the market, and that he had pulled his kids out of the private schools. The problem with his home in Darien was that he had paid $6 million for the house, the mortgage was $6 million, and the only bid he had was for $4.5 million. The math didn't work.

Another victim was the great Perot himself. His fund hadn't done all that badly, but it was down 25 percent in 2008 after a mediocre year in 2007. The indexes were off far more, but his investors had gone from being surly to downright mutinous. He received massive redemption notices in both the third and fourth quarter, and by early 2009 his fund had shrunk from $2.5 billion to $800 million. Perot was a stock picker and an information freak, not a trader, and he had built up an expensive research staff of 10 analysts.

Eight hundred million dollars of assets with a fixed fee of 1.5 percent amounted to $12 million in revenues. With back-office staff, space, legal, compliance, the 10 analysts, and three other partners, the firm had 40 mouths to feed and was running an operating deficit of $2 million. Furthermore, his analysts had done the high-water mark arithmetic, and as soldiers of fortune, were light in their loafers and looking for a new home that wasn't under water.

Joe told him to hang in there. "Fuck your precious analysts. They're just glorified, overpaid reporters. If you can survive this tsunami and put up some good performance numbers, you'll live to fight another day."

But Perot was still close enough to his past, the damage to his net worth was crushing enough, and his overhead big enough that he was panicked.

"That stupid Greenwich mansion I've built is obese and obscene. What was I thinking? The pool house alone costs $14,000 a year to heat so I turned off the furnace and the pipes froze and shattered. I've got too many automobiles, maids, butlers, personal assistants, and toys. Nancy's pissed, but they're going!"

He went on to tell Joe he had suspended the Southampton beach house building program, canceled his order for a Citation Ten (forfeiting his down payment), and just plain welshed on his charitable commitments. One school, for which he signed a commitment letter, was angry and threatening to sue. Joe advised him not to overreact and not to burn too many bridges, but Perot would have none of it.

"I'm hunkering down. It's every man for himself." Joe couldn't help but agree. It was a time to concentrate on just surviving. But fate had one final punch for Perot. One day, he took his two boys to a musical in New York City. As they walked up Broadway, a kid bumped hard into Perot while another kid from behind shoved him, grabbed his left arm, ripped his gold Rolex watch off, and took off. Perot—with his kids staring wide-eyed—lunged after his assailant, taking four giant running strides, and then suddenly screamed in pain and fell to the sidewalk grasping his left leg. He had severed his hamstring.

Then there was the saddest case of all: Randolph (Lord Randolph was his affectionate *nom de plume* because of his patrician demeanor) from London, whom Joe had first met five years before at an investors' golf outing at the National in Southampton. The man had incandescent personal charm. Joe could remember how beguiled he was by the aristocratic accent, the impeccable manners, and his quaint British expressions. They had been paired together in a golf game. Joe had played exceptionally well that day, and they had won their flight. At the end of the round, Lord Randolph had embraced him, "Oh well done, sir! Well done! And I was so enriched by your super investment insights. I do want to keep in touch, sport, and from time to time have a word with you!"

Joe was flattered. This sophisticated, fancy European nobleman wanted to *have a word with him!*

At the time Lord Randolph was in his early forties, darkly handsome with striking brown eyes that seemed designed to flash interest and charm. He was the ultimate bespoke man with impeccable boulevardier taste—meticulous, made-to-order tailoring, suspenders, and bright Hermès ties. He belonged to the best private clubs, smoked fine cigars, and hunted birds in the fall in Scotland. From the beginning, Joe sensed his ambition and believed in his trajectory.

Lord Randolph's father was French, allegedly from an old family and had served with distinction in the Foreign Legion. The father first married an Italian countess some years his senior, and when she died, wed her daughter from a previous marriage. He was a broker who knew everybody in Zurich, London, and Paris, and eventually ran the Zurich office of Lehman Brothers.

At his father's knee, Randolph had learned that the keys to financial success were cultivating the very rich and *savoir faire*. Wealthy people were more inclined to trust advisers with exquisite manners. The old man sent his son to Le Rosey, a fancy Swiss boarding school, not renowned for the rigor of its academic program but rather for its sobriquet of "the school of kings" because its alumni include the Shah of Iran, Prince Rainier III, and the Aga Khan. As a measure of its seriousness, Le Rosey moves its campus to Gstaad during the ski season.

The young Randolph, however, was not just a callow social climber. He was ambitious and no fool. Hedge funds were where the money was and, after a stint at the private bank Pictet and Cie, he started his very own fund in 1995. He was a superb collector of information (sometimes *inside* information), knew the right people, and was also an alert, momentum- and trend-following trader. As a result, his fund prospered and he became rich. He grew his hair long and wore beaded necklaces and gold bracelets. His clothes were impeccable, and artfully concealed his growing waistline.

For years, Randolph virtually lived with Gertrude Gallingo, the Swedish supermodel. They never married. "No squaws for me, sport," Randolph told Joe once. Everyone was addressed as "sport." "Can't remember names for the life of me," Randolph confided once. "Just call everyone sport and it works like a charm. No stammering over names; no hurt feelings."

In 2003, at Liza Minnelli's star-studded fiftieth birthday party for her husband, Randolph met the beautiful heiress, Felicity Pioline, and that was the end of Gertrude, whose charms had waned with the years. Gertrude kept the children and Randolph paid monthly child support, and played the devoted father on the occasional weekend.

Lord Randolph had always been a grandiose spender, and he and Felicity frolicked through the London–New York high life for the next couple of years. He acquired a ski chalet in Zermatt and a 7,000 square-foot condominium in St. Tropez with an incredible ocean view. He used these luxurious leisure digs for his women (he kept score) and also to entertain prospective clients. As time went on, he talked less about stocks and more about golf, the clubs he belonged to, and the yacht he was having built in Norway.

In 2004 and 2005, he had made big investment scores in Russia, and to advertise his cosmopolitan investment skills, he played the Russian theme hard in the St. Tropez condo. The walls were covered with fine copies of paintings from the Hermitage, and one room displayed a collection of Fabergé eggs and boxes. Another held, in glass cases, copies of priceless, intimate letters from the Romanov family, which Randolph hinted several oligarchs were desperate to buy back from him. There were also two Romanov bedrooms complete with the elaborate, ornate bedsteads allegedly used by Czar Nicholas. The master bedroom was one level above the beach and featured a broad terrace adorned with two Rodin sculptures.

Lord Randolph's Achilles heel was that he had always been capricious—verging on perfidious—about valuing his portfolio positions for client reporting. His fund was domiciled in the Antilles where the local administrators tended to turn the proverbial blind eye on accounting niceties. What that meant was that he could value his more illiquid holdings virtually any way he wanted to. When he was having a good run of performance, Randolph would price some positions below the market, and if he was in a slump he marked them up in order to mitigate the bad news. Only in exotic places like the Antilles can you get away with this kind of performance manipulation.

When Joe had asked him about his administrator, Randolph airily waved the question away, "The chap does what I tell him to, sport. He has no choice. He works out of an office that looks like an outdoor toilet."

It was not as though Lord Randolph hadn't had a warning about the dangers of fabricated valuations when the shit hit the fan. In the Asian crisis in the late 1990s, he had been hung upside down from the yardarm with some very illiquid, highly speculative junk and had spun the stuff off into a side pocket private equity fund. A *side pocket* is when, without any warning, the depressed, illiquid shares of companies that have become a boulder around your neck are put into a new, separate fund; in your *side pocket*, so to speak. Then you inform your clients that you've created a new fund for "these incredibly high potency, underappreciated, private equity investments that eventually will be huge winners." In the meantime you charge them the usual management fee, and gently inform them they can't withdraw their money from this new fund until further notice. Invariably, and rightfully, side-pocketing both worries and pisses off investors big-time.

Nevertheless, he had managed to sweet-talk and squirm his way through that crisis with only minor damage and had rebuilt the lucrative hedge fund business that had made him wealthy. He and Felicity were seen everywhere—charity balls, Wimbledon, conferences at the Hôtel du Cap. In the fullness of the moment he talked of buying a house on Gin Lane in the Hamptons. Always on the make, he was a shameless name dropper, maintaining he hung out with the very rich and famous, including the King of Spain, whom he alleged was invested in his fund.

However, the killer bear market proved to be another story. Fast, quick on the trigger, as momentum-oriented as Lord Randolph was, the year had just been one whipsaw after another. He trafficked in the story merchandise that all the other hot guys were in, and he got trampled in the rush for liquidity. Toward the end of the year, he was down over 55 percent and the redemption notices were pouring in. He also owned even more illiquid stuff than usual, including a mammoth position in Gazprom and a huge holding of a small Thai bank that was supposed to have been acquired by Bangkok Bank at a giant premium. Unfortunately, at the last minute, the deal had aborted. Now, he knew that in the present panic environment, he could sell these positions only at catastrophic discounts, which would knock down his net asset value another 15 percentage points.

Around that time, Randolph suddenly appeared in New York, and Joe met him for lunch at San Pietros. Joe had not seen him since January, and he was curious and worried. He had heard that Randolph's fund was down big and was experiencing massive redemptions. Even worse was the talk that Randolph had misled, even cheated, his investors. Joe was shocked, but not totally surprised. In the back of his mind was the memory that Randolph almost always *forgot* to pay golf bets he had lost.

When Joe saw him, he was surprised at his appearance. Randolph's previously tanned and handsome face was drawn and haggard, his shoulders slumped, and the old-time, effusive *bonhomie* was gone. He seemed to have developed some kind of twitch in his right eye.

"It's you, Sir Joseph, hale and hearty with all your feathers," Randolph greeted him, but with only a shade of his former effusiveness. "I'm afraid mine are a bit bedraggled and tattered these days."

"Hey, I don't have hardly any feathers left," Joe told him. "Are you okay?"

"No, I'm not okay, sport," Randolph told him. "Nothing's okay. My health is poor, and I've had a horrible year. I have constant twitches and dizzy spells and killer cases of insomnia and diarrhea. I was literally in bed for five days straight! The portfolio is loaded with illiquid stuff, and I'm faced with big redemptions. Plus Felicity has left me."

Joe murmured condolences. He wasn't surprised about Felicity. She seemed spoiled and pretentious, and she had a foul tongue. Joe had never warmed up to her; he just couldn't get accustomed to an aristocratic woman with a cultured, upper-class British accent who spouted four-letter words.

"We'd been drifting apart for a while," Randolph told him, "but she got really pissed about the money. She now tells everyone she'd been warning me a bust was coming, and that I didn't respect her judgment. Some truth to the accusation." He shook his head.

"She put most of her inheritance, which incidentally was never as big as advertised, in my fund, which I confess has done badly. I foolishly, but generously, gave the young *national champions* I hired segments of the fund to manage, and they've had total wipeouts. No judgment. Bought crazy private stuff and sold short blue chips. Now she wants to sue me for palimony payments."

Why weren't you supervising them? Joe wondered, but instead asked, "Why can't you meet the redemptions by selling the liquid stuff?"

"Because I'm the biggest investor in the fund. I've always eaten my own gourmet cooking. What's left of my fortune," he grimaced, "is in this cancer-ridden, crippled fund of mine. If I honor the redemptions, sport, I'd be left owning over half the fund and with most of it in overvalued, totally illiquid shit."

His past sins were catching up with him, Joe thought. *The man for all his breeding and manners was essentially a cheat and out of business! Done! Like we soon may be. And he has an immense amount of overhead.*

"So what are you going to do?" Joe asked him.

"I'm trying to sell all the liquid stuff and I've suspended redemptions indefinitely. I have no intention of raising the gate until after I've got my money out. I put all the crap in a side pocket, and since I've got to have some income, I'm going to keep charging the clients the two percent fixed fee on the side pocket. Of course they're furious and want to sue. Fortunately, lawsuits don't work in the Antilles. Like I told you, my administrator will value stuff at whatever I tell him to. But I'm going to have no clients left. I'm done."

He shook his head and the apparently uncontrollable twitch was back.

"What about the guys who worked for you?" Joe asked, almost dreading the answer.

"I let all my chaps go. I couldn't afford to even pay them for the last couple of months, much less any severance. Just closed the fund and changed the lock on the office door. They're bitter. Can't say I blame them, but they should have known it was a dodgy go. They've hired a lawyer and have attached my bank accounts and the house in London. Won't they be surprised when they find it's under water on the mortgage."

"But you're okay financially, aren't you? You yourself?"

"Barely. I've got some money in Switzerland but it's going fast. I'm trying to cut back but it's not easy. I counted up the other day. I have four houses and seven full-time housekeepers! You can't just walk away from the upkeep of a house. And I belong to a ridiculous number of clubs. They're money suckers! I resigned from Old Oaks outside of London, but what I didn't realize is that you have to keep paying the dues, which are twenty-four thousand pounds a year, until someone buys your debentures. There's fifteen chaps ahead of me in the queue and no buyers."

He sighed and stared at Joe for a long moment, and Joe could feel the weight of his eyes on him. "And you know what, sport? It turns out I have a tumor on my colon that is cancerous. I've come to New York Hospital for the procedure."

"Jesus!" said Joe. "The gods really are frowning on you."

"They're not frowning, they're glaring. They despise me! Remember after Gertrude and I split, but before Felicity moved in with me, I had a fling with that countess woman in Paris. Well, when we broke up she told me she was pregnant and wanted to have the baby. I tried to persuade her to have an abortion, but she was determined to have the baby."

He looked at Joe mournfully and sighed. "That was five years ago, sport. She was rich then and the subject of money never came up. Her first husband had been forced to give her a great stack of his options on Société Générale. But that was then, and SG stock is down eighty-five percent since. Now I got a five-year-old son I've never seen, running around Paris. She sends me pictures. Cute little bugger. Looks exactly like me at that age. Three weeks ago I get a letter from her solicitors demanding monthly child support and a settlement for past years. It's not insignificant money. I'm already paying Gertrude monthly palimony. Yesterday's supermodel is now old and ugly and can't earn a shilling."

"Hey, Randolph," Joe interrupted, trying to cheer him up. "It's a bear market. Everybody's hurting." But inwardly he was appalled that Randolph didn't seem more concerned about his son, his own flesh and blood, whom he didn't even know.

"Not hurting like me." His eyes were cold and abstract. "You know what, sport? I'm going to get my colon fixed, and then I think I'm just going to bug out. Take some money and disappear—maybe for good. No more greedy ex-girlfriends, no more pissed-off clients who want to have a word with me, no more lawyer chaps, no more fucking irrational stock market."

"What does that mean? Where are you going to go?"

"Don't ask. Better you don't know, sport. I'm just going to go. One night soon I'm going to run down the streets in the shadows under the murky lights and keep on running out to where it's dark and there's nobody who knows me or wants anything from me and where everybody, everybody, will leave me alone."

Joe was deeply concerned. "We're all stressed, but you're heavily stressed. Maybe you should see a psychiatrist and get some help."

"Fuck that! As Sam Goldwyn once said, 'Any chap who goes to a psychiatrist ought to have his head examined!' My problem is not my head. It's my domestic overhead. It's my office overhead. It's my net worth." His surly reaction made Joe feel better. They embraced warmly, but Joe wondered when, if ever, he would see him again.

Of course, it wasn't just the high and mighty hedge fund managers who were hurting. Ordinary people—analysts, assistants, vice presidents, secretaries, and back-office clerks—were suffering too as the big and small Wall Street firms were doing massive layoffs. The desperately dispossessed were standing in lines for hours for five-minute interviews at job fairs in New York, Chicago, and London. Equally demeaning so-called Pink Slip Parties promoted by blogs with the tag line "If you've got misery, we got company" were drawing huge crowds who aimlessly milled around hoping to connect with recruiters and ending up mingling only with other lost souls and crying in each other's wine.

There was carnage everywhere.

Now, after dinner when the children were in bed, he and Emily would sit in the library, he scanning his BlackBerry and she reading one of her endless think-tank books. To make conversation, he would start to relate to her one of the human tragedies that were happening out there. He wanted to tell her, wanted to share the pain he was suffering. At first, he assumed she would be interested because she had met Randolph, Sam, and the Perots and, of course, she had known Mickey for years. But she would have none of it.

"I don't want to hear your salacious gossip," she told him, almost angrily.

"Emily, it's hardly salacious. It's tragic."

"You're right," she said. "It's the pathetic whining of a bunch of peevish losers who finally are getting their just desserts."

He just shook his head as she ranted on. "I never liked that Felicity or those flashy women of Mickey's. He went off on a world-class ego trip, and now he's getting what he deserves. And as for Nancy Perot—I just saw her a couple of days ago. She's another spoiled brat. All she could talk about was how the fancy stores on Greenwich Avenue had closed down, and that her husband had fired the butler and one of their two maids. The *poor things* are down to a cook and a maid. Am I supposed to feel sorry for them? It's their own fault, what with that gigantic house and all their phony pretension. I hope he's wiped out and she has to start doing the dishes and cleaning toilets again."

"You're tough," he replied mildly. "Think of what people are saying about us. All the good burghers of Greenwich must be licking their WASPish chops."

"Of course they are, and that's exactly why I don't want to add fuel to the fire. They're thrilled we're getting our comeuppance. Order is being restored to their world."

He winced. "Sure, they're probably gloating, but they must also be licking their wounds as well as their chops. Their net worth has been cut in half—providing they weren't leveraged," he remarked wryly. "They're going to have to sell their homes in Florida. If they were leveraged, had mortgages or whatever, they could be down seventy to eighty percent. A lot of people are."

"And their mistake," she told him, still angry, "was that they were gullible and fell for the magic bullshit the likes of Madoff, Sam, and your buddy Randolph dispensed. Gullibility is a far lesser sin than greed, pride, and fraud."

"I guess that applies to me, too."

"No Joe, you were just naïve. We're just lucky the attention and the tongues of Greenwich are focused on the Madoff scam and the poor souls who have lost their jobs. But who knows, I'm just the half-wit they keep locked in the attic."

Joe knew that she had lost any illusions she might have had that he was a gifted investor. For several years, she had maintained their intellectual communion was deteriorating, and that he was too obsessive about the markets and his portfolio. Her view was that if he was successful and really good at this insane, crazy profession that he was in, these habits were tolerable, but only barely so. But in her eyes, now it had turned out that he had worshipped at the altars of a false religion, a god that had failed.

Unfortunately, he also recognized that it wasn't just the business stuff that was bugging her. She had become much more critical of him in other ways as well. She picked at him for everything, from his clothes, which she thought were too "hedge fund casual" as she put it, to his squeezing the toothpaste out of the tube from the middle instead of the bottom. The dress thing was symbolic of the change in their relationship. Back at the beginning, she was intrigued and cherished that he was different, tougher, than the callow boys she knew from Greenwich and Princeton. That had all changed; perhaps it was their two boys, but now she wanted him to be more conventional, to join the club, so to speak.

She had become disenchanted with him. In a world where every-one was disillusioned with everything, his fall from grace tore at him. Once she had been an imaginative and athletic lover, but now their love life was sporadic and perfunctory. He suddenly felt as if she and the world had cut him open and torn out slowly and imperceptibly something incredibly precious, like his soul, his love mechanism, and discarded it as worthless.

Now that Emily was so critical, she reminded Joe of her mother. Was it his imagination or was she beginning as she got older to look like her mother, too? Sometimes he wasn't even sure if he loved her anymore.

Thinking about it, he knew that in many ways he had become more compatible with Joan than with Emily. In the past, Emily had been his soul mate, but that had been at another, very different time in his life. He had been an inexperienced novice back then. It seemed as though so much had changed since they first met, and somehow, almost without knowing it, they had drifted apart. Investing, BA, the hedge fund world, golf, even Joan had intervened. As a result, his connection with Emily—their precious soul link that had dispersed his adolescent loneliness—had deteriorated over the years. These days they seemed to have so much less to talk about.

On the other hand, Joan was his new soul mate, and he sensed, no, he *knew*, that she loved him and would welcome a more intimate physical relationship. He wanted it, too. He looked forward to seeing her every business day, and when they were separated on weekends there was often a dull ache, an emptiness. He couldn't imagine not being able to talk to her about the markets, the world, the future. They had so much to share. Her mind was so clear and concise, and they had the same reaction to so many things.

Yet his relationship with Joan was another point of contention with Emily. Emily had never been happy about the amount of time he spent with Joan, and now that, as she put it, "they were bunking together in a deserted office" it had become a real irritant. Only a week ago she had snapped at him, "I'm not in love with the two of you in communion all day long." Joe bit his lip and said nothing.

In spite of these arguments, Joe knew that he and Emily still had their boys to keep them together, sustain them. He was doing more and more things with the boys. The stone wall was finished, but now they begged him to play catch with them. They were growing up; they were becoming real people, and he cherished and loved them.

He couldn't conceive of being separated from them. Could he and Emily sustain their relationship just from their interaction with the boys and then finally repair it? He had to try, didn't he? But the thought of life without Joan tore at his being.

Afterward, ruminating on the chaos of his life and of so many around him, Joe concluded it was all part of the malevolence of the great bear market. None of these circuit breakers would have been activated if the world had hung together. This credit crisis, this financial apocalypse was becoming a life-threatening crisis. He thought of all the guys he knew who once had been successful, revered hedge fund managers or investment bankers. They had been on top of the world, confident, affluent, nay, rich, but now they were shrunken, shaking shadows of their former selves, their personal lives shattered—lonely, broken men trying not to cry. The gossip in the press was all about hedge funds that had been broken by redemptions and internal squabbling and of investment bankers and traders who were being summarily laid off. The media gloated that these golden children of the magic years had lost a major portion of their wealth and could no longer support the extravagant lifestyle that they had become addicted to. Shouldn't they have had the internal reserves of strength and family love that now should be supporting and sustaining them? Instead, there were divorces and separations from children. Had the foundations of their lives been so shallow and so fragile all along?

It was the leverage and the hubris that was fatal, Joe concluded. The leverage, born of greed, terribly magnified their financial losses, and the arrogance that compelled them to flaunt extravagant lifestyles. The combination bankrupted them financially and emotionally. It brought tensions to the surface and ripped apart the fabric of lives. It also exacerbated relationships if, in addition, they had, like he did, a wife in Greenwich and an investment soul mate at the office. A great longing for simplicity swept over him.

Chapter 17

The End of the Affair

*If men could learn from history, what lessons it might teach us! But
passion and party blind our eyes; and the light which experience gives
is a lantern on the stern which shines only on the waves behind us.*

—Samuel Coleridge

A t the end of 2008, BA was faced with a final deluge of
redemptions that cleaned out almost all of their remaining
capital, and had basically liquidated the fund. All of their positions were closed, and the cash was invested in Treasury bills that were
yielding nothing. Bridgestone had dismissed what was left of its staff
with a one-time payment equivalent to each of their one month's salary
multiplied by years with the firm. It was a pittance. There were no fond
farewells, no hugs. Everyone was scared and pissed.

When it was done and BA was essentially no more, Joe initially
felt as though some kind of massive clot had suddenly dissolved in

his chest, the center of his being. For weeks afterward, he had the impulse to weep, the forgotten sensation of a flowering, a release, coupled with an almost desperate sense of loss and danger. It felt as if one of his limbs had been amputated. Over the holiday break, working outside in the pale winter sun building a log fort with the boys, the pain gradually subsided. Christmas in a demoralized, unhappy Greenwich was dreary, and the parties he and Emily went to seemed forced and contrived.

The first business days of the new year found Joan and Joe hanging out by themselves in their old offices at Bridgestone. It was an eerie time. Even the great throbbing metropolis of New York seemed despondent and depressed, its animal spirits and vigor diminished. The traffic had noticeably thinned, and the ambient roar of the city was at least several decibels less. Far fewer black cars idled outside the midtown office buildings, and the Fifth Avenue stores seemed strangely deserted. Restaurants were empty. Joe had discharged his driver, and now commuted to work by train.

With the firm closing down and the support staff discharged, the once opulent, vibrant offices of Bridgestone, now empty and stripped of furniture, seemed stained and secret. Other than the lone security guard, no one else came in regularly. The café, of course, was shut, and all the elaborate equipment in the gym had been sold, so they couldn't even work out. The fancy fittings in Spokane's and Ravine's suites had been removed, and every piece of the made-to-order Dunbar chairs, desks, and couches that had been in Joe's and Joan's offices had gone to auction. They had to scrounge a couple of abandoned chairs and tables from the cafeteria to set their Bloomberg terminals up on. It was all rather bleak and dismal.

However, in late December and the first few days of January, markets rallied. Their dark moods suddenly lifted, the sun sparkled off the snow in Central Park, the battlements of the surrounding superstructures shone again. Everyone, including Joe and Joan, both of whom had voted for Obama, were enchanted with the new president's charisma, his physical elegance, and his articulate language.

The conventional wisdom was that following the president's inauguration in late January there would be the usual 100 days of honeymoon for the new administration. His Dream Team of brilliant advisers would craft a powerful stimulus program and would create some ingenious scheme to relieve the banks of their toxic assets. As they sat there in their bare office looking out over the winter skyline of New York, both Joe and Joan came to believe that these actions would trigger at the very least a playable rally in markets.

Joe had become obsessed with rebuilding his net worth. "I have to get back to thirty million," he told Joan. "Then with your fifteen we'd have enough to at least start a new fund. This time, right now, could be a great opportunity. The markets are incredibly oversold. Hedge funds are way underinvested. Everyone knows all the bad news. I'm gonna take a big shot with the S&P futures at nine hundred."

"You know what you're doing is trading, not investing," Joan warned him with an edge to her voice. "It's not really our *thing*."

"I realize that, but our old *thing*, our model, can't be replicated by just the two of us, and besides, it's failed, broken. I've lost confidence in it. I'm feeling I can make some money."

"Well, I think you're right on the rally. Stocks have had a huge decline and should be due for a bounce. I'm gonna do the same. But in case we're wrong, I'm putting in a stop loss on my trade down five percent at eight fifty-five."

"I will, too. At this point, I definitely can't afford a big loss."

That day they both bought the S&P at around 900. A week later, the price was 935. It wasn't much, but it was something, and they luxuriated in an intoxicating mood swing. There was nothing like making some money again. They added to their positions.

But their elation was short-lived. Contrary to general expectations, the rally petered out after a few days and everything seemed to go wrong. The economy got sicker by the day, Cabinet nominees had to withdraw for stupid, careless transgressions, the stimulus program became politicized by Congress, and when it finally was announced, the Treasury's financial rescue agenda laid a huge, amorphous egg. Because of his uncertain, deer-in-the-headlights demeanor, cynical investors began calling the Secretary of the Treasury "Tiny Tim." The president's honeymoon seemed to be over before it had even begun.

In the second week of January, the S&P 500 plunged again, and three days later their stop-loss orders were activated. They had lost $2 million between them. *Why was it,* Joe agonized, *that the market always seemed to go in the opposite direction from that which he was positioned for?* In the early evening as he walked through the jostling streets toward Grand Central, he felt a deep sense of loathing and hopelessness crushing his mind and his heart.

That night Joe woke after a few hours of restless sleep. As though compelled by some mysterious gravitational pull, he drifted out of their bedroom where Emily was sleeping, and quietly, without turning on any lights, carefully made his way to the library. The blinds were drawn, and the darkness leaped suddenly at him like a live thing and clutched him. In the total blackness he was aware only of a pitching motion, a drumming in his head, the blood pounding, beating at his brain. He stood there transfixed, staring into the blackness — or was he enclosed inside the infinite circumference of his own head gazing inward into the vast chasm of himself where there was only confusion and blackness? His breath was coming in great gasps, and the pounding in his head became more powerful and accelerated until it cascaded into a pervasive, pulsing roar. Slowly, he sank to his knees on the floor.

He had no idea how long he stayed there. The pounding gradually subsided, his eyes regained their focus, and he emerged from the blackness. He found he was drenched in a cold sweat and totally confused. What had happened to him he couldn't comprehend, but he did know that it was as though he had experienced a stroke, a seizure of the soul. He worked his way upstairs and, still unwilling to wake Emily, went to the guest bedroom and lay down on the bed there. There was an eye mask in the drawer of the bed table, and that was where Emily found him in the morning. He awoke with the sunlight streaming into the room and her standing over him.

"What's going on with you?" she asked.

He lay there collecting himself. Somehow he couldn't tell her what had happened. She wouldn't understand. He himself didn't understand it. It was all too strange. In a strangled voice he said, "I woke up in the middle of the night. It was like I had a really terrible nightmare."

"Yes," she replied, looking hard at him. "It is a nightmare. Our world has become a nightmare. Something's got to give!"

"I know," he said quietly. "I know." When she had gone, he lay there for a few minutes, forcing his mind to work over the meaning of this dark agony and the morning visitation.

After the horrendous 2008, January 2009 turned out to be the worst January in stock market history, with the S&P 500 down 8.4 percent. February was even poorer, with a further decline of 10.7 percent. Hopes that the new Obama Administration would produce fresh and dynamic economic programs had not been fulfilled. In late February, Obama proposed a populist social program that seemed to be primarily focused on the redistribution of wealth. Proposed increases in the tax rate on capital gains, dividends, and ordinary income were greeted with anger by conservatives and dismay by moderates who thought it was the wrong time to raise taxes. There was much talk of the world falling into either another Great Depression like the 1930s, or suffering a long period of stagnation and lingering deflation such as Japan had endured from 1990 until 2003. Both were grim scenarios implicit with wrenching bear markets, vast wealth destruction, and the end of modern financial capitalism. At a New York conference Joe attended, over half of the 200 investors present believed the S&P 500 eventually would settle far below present levels of 800 somewhere within 100 points, either up or down, of 500.

By now, many great and famous investors were extremely bearish and scorned anyone who disagreed with them. Even Warren Buffett was derided. In February, as markets around the world collapsed, technicians and strategists warned that it was crucial that the indexes rally and not break through the lows of the previous fall. They maintained that the creation of a "double bottom" formation would be very bullish, and that, conversely, a penetration of the November lows would indicate further falls to between 500 and 600 on the S&P.

One morning in early February, Joe and Joan watched an interview with Buffett on CNBC. The Great Man argued, folksily but forcefully, that stocks were very cheap, sentiment was extremely depressed, and that the market was so oversold that it was a great time to buy. "Buy when terrified," he firmly asserted.

They were impressed. Buffett had been right about the danger of being a geek, and he would be right again. "The November lows are going to hold," Joe proclaimed.

"Well, there's no doubt we're terrified," Joan said.

Once again, they bought index futures with a stop loss 5 percent below their purchase price. As markets churned down toward the old lows and the acid test approached, everyone's anxiety soared. On February 23, the market seemed to hold and to bounce off the November bottom. Emboldened, they again added to their positions.

Then, the very next day, the pathetic little rally aborted, and, to their horror, the S&P plunged through the November 754 low. In early March, the level of fear and despair around the world soared as markets approached their November 2008 lows of 754 on the S&P 500. The last line of defense, the Maginot Line, had been breached. Joe's stomach was churning and his head ached. They both were stopped-out of their positions, and they had sustained yet another deeply depressing loss. Joe was shattered.

Eventually in the second week of March the index bottomed at the devilish number of 666. At that ominous level, with everyone deathly bearish, in cash or short, and doom and gloom the thickest, the market beast, so intent on inflicting pain, satiated, took a deep breath, and a powerful rally began. As time went on, the rally was fed by the first "green shoots" of better, or at least less bad, economic news from around the world. Figure 17.1 shows how difficult it is to trade a bear market from the long side as Joe and Joan were attempting to do, and how easy it is to be whipsawed. Bear in mind that when they began trying to trade it, the S&P 500 was already pretty much straight down 44 percent from its October 2007 high.

By the time the market turned and what was to become the true, great, monster rally began, Joe and Joan were so demoralized and frightened that they missed it. Missed it totally, utterly, and completely. They just sat there paralyzed, quivering, "sucking their thumbs (as Joe put it)," not believing it was for real, afraid to stick even their toes into the water. Their three previous trading forays and the losses they had suffered had so diminished their capital and their courage that they were frozen, unwilling to risk the remainder. More significantly, their confidence in themselves as investors

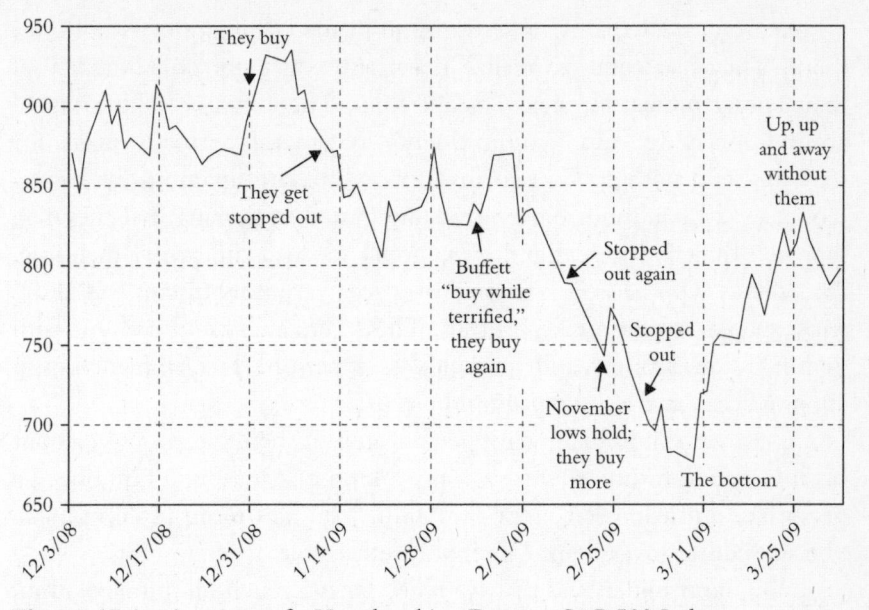

Figure 17.1   Anatomy of a Heartbreaking Bottom: S&P 500 Index

had been burnt away, consumed in a flash like snow falling into fire. They were both deeply depressed, Joe more than Joan. For him, the stock market had been transformed from a powerful racehorse whose moods he knew and that he was capable of mastering into a wild, vicious, totally unpredictable beast that was determined to buck him off, trample, and destroy him.

"We're just losers!" Joe sadly told Joan in April with stocks soaring. "Losers! We went back in on a whim because Buffett sounded good on TV and then get scared out and have no balls left at the bottom. I don't trust my instincts and judgment anymore."

"We got wrong-footed on that first trade at the beginning of the year," she told him, "and then it's so hard to get back the rhythm."

"Missing this rally or new cyclical bull market or whatever is disgraceful," Joe groaned. "Buffett was right. He hung in there. We got stopped out like a couple of amateurs."

"Don't be so hard on yourself. Buffett has all the money in the world and can afford to take the long view. We couldn't. Our backs were to the wall."

A profound lethargy, a sense of suspended animation, swept over them. They had come to realize that there was there no possibility of their raising money for a new hedge fund. There was very little capital around for hedge fund commitments in general, virtually none for start-ups, and nothing for two investors who were infamous for having blown up a huge fund. No one was interested in hearing that they had scrapped their old model and were going to do it differently this time. The clients who had once fawned over Joe were now distant and aloof. Most would not even take his calls. They were angry and had lost faith in him as an investor and implicitly as a person. The ambient gossip about Mickey was also tarnishing them.

They were humbled, whipped, beaten. When Joe thought about his investment future, there was only a kind of paralysis, a numbness, a pervasive, dull pain that crept over him. Joan was more philosophical. She sensed her investment career was retrievable.

"We didn't understand that we relied far too much on our algorithm, had too much analysis that was like everybody else's, and that an obsession with relatives eventually destroys the understanding, the intuitions, of wholes," she philosophized.

"Yeah, yeah, yeah!" Joe snapped. "We are all so wise now that it has happened. Keynes said, 'The power to become habituated to his surroundings is a marked characteristic of mankind.' In other words, our problem was we believed our own bullshit was going to work forever."

Although Joe put on a tough guy act, Joan knew how deeply he was hurting. The next morning as he was sitting at his desk she walked over to him and put her hand on his shoulder. She had written out in her own hand, a snatch of poetry from Longfellow.

> Be still, sad heart! And cease repining;
> Behind the clouds the sun is shining;
> Thy fate is the common fate of all,
> Into each life some rain must fall,
> Some days must be dark and dreary.

He read it and was moved both by the poetry and her hand, which was still on his shoulder. He reached over and squeezed it. "Well, at least it rhymes," he murmured.

"So do we," she said.

"I know," he replied and put the scrap of paper in his pocket. They both realized in that moment they had reached a new level of intimacy. On the train that evening he pulled it out, read it again, and then thinking what Emily's reaction would be if she saw it, tore it into little pieces.

One dark, rainy afternoon Joe got a call from the building's security desk in the lobby. "That fellow Mickey Cohen who used to work here is back. Says he wants to visit you. Can I send him up?"

Of course they assented, and minutes later the security officer called again. He was an older man, Armenian, and perhaps from boredom had always taken an interest in the more prominent tenants whom he insisted on greeting by their first name as they went in and out.

"He's on his way up, Joe. Mickey doesn't look so good these days, pal." *Neither do I*, thought Joe, but he just grunted, repelled by the man's intimacy. He rose and went to meet Mickey in the bare reception.

"Great to see you, old friend," Mickey shouted, throwing an arm around Joe's shoulder and hugging him. For a moment, Joe was thrilled. It's the same old physical, effusive Mickey, he thought. Then he smelled the humid scent of alcohol on his breath.

When they got to their makeshift office, Mickey boisterously hugged Joan as she kissed him on the check. But now they noticed there were dark hollows under his eyes, and that his jowls were puffy; but then he'd always looked a little degenerate.

"So, how you guys doing and what are you doing?" Mickey asked jovially.

"We're trying to figure it out," Joan told him. "Strangely, these days there doesn't seem to be much latent demand for our money management skills."

"Don't I know," replied Mickey. He looked directly at Joe. "How about money? You still filthy rich?"

"Are you kidding? No, I'm squeaky clean poor! I've just managed to lose some more trying to trade this vicious market."

"So what are you two worth now? We've been comrades for so long we gotta have no secrets."

Joe hesitated, "I'm at about seven," he told him glumly. 'I've got a mortgage on the house and the property but I don't think I'm under water. And I've got a lot of overhead what with the interest, living expenses, and the kids' tuitions."

Joan said she still had four million.

Mickey's head slumped. "I was hoping against hope you guys were in much better shape than that. I need a loan bad." He grimaced and seemed to sag. "I'm in big trouble. My leverage is killing me. I've got loans from Citibank and J.P. Morgan of roughly eighty-five million and assets of maybe fifty or sixty million that in the good old days I paid north of one hundred million for. Who knows what I could get for the G-5, the art, the condo, and the houses in the midst of this disaster. Sixty is probably optimistic. Nobody's buying anything. Old Masters and G-5s are both down at least thirty-five percent. The banks are pressing me for a token payment."

Joe felt he had to offer something. "I could loan you a couple of million," he told him, a spasm of fear gripping him at the thought of being a creditor of Mickey's. Like Big Joe once said, "Lend money, lose a friend." But Joe sensed Mickey was already lost.

"I need a loan of ten to fifteen or they're going to foreclose." He buried his face in his hands. "I can't believe I've blown it all. Greed and stupidity and leverage! My greed, my stupidity, my leverage! Once I was worth three hundred fifty million, but the crazy toys I bought and the leverage has killed me. At the end of last year, I took fifteen million out of BA but that's almost all gone. My overhead is eating me alive. The interest on the loans alone is almost five million, and then I got alimony payments to two wives and upkeep on the houses, the plane, and the condo. I'm broke! Busted!"

It was severe, magnificent honesty, and the stupidity and immensity of his predicament stunned them. The Piper was being paid in full. Suddenly Mickey started to weep. Great, rasping sobs. "She's left me. The money's gone. What will become of me?" he kept repeating over and over. Joe was paralyzed with embarrassment, but Joan quickly got up and stood over Mickey. She put her hands on his slumped shoulders and handed him a tissue.

"What can we do to help? We'll do anything we can. It's almost five o'clock. Let's go down the street to The Four Seasons and have a drink."

Abruptly, Mickey stood up and pushed her hands away. He wiped his eyes and headed for the door. "I'm out of here," he gasped as he half staggered, almost ran down the corridor toward the elevators. "I've had too many drinks already for too long! Please don't follow me! It's all over! Everything is gone."

They let him go.

Joe walked to the window and looked out. The sky was an undifferentiated gray. He could not even find on such a lowering day the formless splotch of lighter gray, scarcely luminous, that marked the position of the sun. It somehow seemed fitting and symbolic. Below him, there was the great soft mass of Central Park. Spring was just beginning to touch it, and he could see the individual boughs hung with that uncertain, irregular green that seemed in that fading light almost purple. He had always loved this time of the year. The foliage so fragile and tender yet sweet, and then as the days lengthened the leaves gradually thickening in the gentle sun. He remembered the beauty of standing with Josh in the soft twilight of a Virginia spring gazing up at the highest boughs where the last rays of sun struck a pale gold. There would be no spring this year in his life.

In early May, Joan took a call from a headhunter. He told her that the research director at Alliance, a giant investment management firm, had seen her at meetings over the years and had been impressed. He had heard she was "on the beach," so to speak, and he was looking for someone to be his assistant director, and had asked the headhunter to approach her. The job would be to manage, motivate, and sharpen the analytical skills of the 14 analysts in the firm's research department. Was she interested in talking, he wanted to know. By the end of the month, a series of meetings led to a job offer. The compensation package was modest by past standards, but it sounded pretty good now—a salary of $300,000 and a potential bonus that could get the total package to $400,000.

Joan and Joe talked about it intensely, chewed it over—a little gingerly, as though it were too hot to bite into freely. Their discussions were frank and open; however, they left completely unsaid their feelings for each other and what such a parting of the ways meant. Both were so enervated by the trauma of the last two years and now their recent trading losses that they simply couldn't muster the energy to try to break through the wall of restraint that engulfed them.

"I've got to take it," she finally told him. "It's positively unhealthy for us to sit here like two zombies in this empty office, paralyzed by our past sins and stupidities, staring at our Bloomberg screens, and doing nothing. Soon we'll be completely detached from the investment world and useless."

All Joe could do was nod. "Fortunes of war," he murmured. He wondered if there were any job offers out there for him. He also knew it was now or never for Joan and him. He'd thought deeply so often, struggled so desperately with the dilemma of what he defined as *it* presented; the issue of leaving Emily for Joan, and now *it* was staring him in the face.

Once again, he was overwhelmed with the flux and confusion of his thoughts and his life; he desperately needed some point of reference, no matter how arbitrary, some hypothesis on which he could base his calculations. Fragments of memory like dirty dishes in the sink piled up in his mind. Had he and Emily drifted apart, or had the market *torn* them apart? She was no longer his soul mate; Joan was, but then suddenly like a flash of light, he knew. He just simply couldn't do *it*.

The boys were the decisive factor in his decision. They followed him around when he was home, gazing at him, asking him questions, wanting to sit next to him. Besides, if he and Joan didn't have an investment future together, he wondered what would be their life-link? They had never even spent a weekend together. Were they truly compatible? He wasn't sure, but there was an aura of mystery and potential about her.

She was trying hard not to look wistful. "What are you going to do?" she asked. "Will Grant take you back?"

"Not a chance," he said. "There would be the nepotism issue, and no one would want me as a portfolio manager after what's happened. I couldn't go back to being an analyst. I'm not even forty years old, and yet I'm spoiled, ruined goods."

"So, are you going to stay in Greenwich and the business?"

"I don't know." He shook his head. "But you know what? I want to sleep through nights again. I need time and space when I'm not worrying about whether I've got too much risk on when I'm throwing a ball around with the boys. I want to look at the sky and read three good novels. After you leave, I'm going to shut this office down, turn in my damn Bloomberg and BlackBerry, and just take hunks of time off to soak in and to lick my wounds."

"Joe, are you going to stay in Greenwich?" she asked, not bothering now to conceal her anguish.

"I don't know. I've been talking to Josh. Told him I'm terribly sorry I lost most of the money he invested with us and about my problems. Josh is a wonderful man. He said, 'Why don't you take that beautiful fifty-acre parcel of land that I bought down by the river and build a house on it? You and I can work together on stuff. I haven't got a son to leave my business to, and maybe you could coach football at the high school. The living here is easy and cheap.'

"I told you about how the night he bought that piece of land and the two of us walked out in the twilight with just the sky and the stars, and that land was so green and so beautiful and the earth and the grass smelled sweet and clean. I dreamed then I might live there some day. I've always been drawn to the land, like Mickey and New York are drawn to money and power. Now I have an opportunity, maybe a chance to start over."

She looked at him intently. "You really mean it, don't you?"

"I'm very tempted. I have no future here; just a toxic past. I've got to get out of Greenwich. My home is a decayed, haunted house. I could put what I got left, seven million, into tax-exempt bonds at five percent, get three hundred fifty thousand a year tax-free and live a normal, sane existence without the market and where I can sleep at night and work the land, get my hands dirty, during the day. It's like that Robert Frost poem that Josh quoted to me: 'The land was ours before we were the land's.' I need to make that land mine. It's about the only real thing I've got left. The stock market, Greenwich, this life, it's not mine anymore."

"Work the land? Wouldn't you miss investing? Miss the intellectual challenge, miss the rush, the ecstasy when you're winning, miss the action? The market, *our* game, has been your life for the past fifteen years. Can you just turn it off and walk away forever?"

"My life has turned to shit. *Our* game, the market, *our* model, what we used to call our *cosa nostra*, tortures me now, humiliates me, and I torture the people I love. There's far more pain than joy in our game now. Too many terrible nightmares and doubts haunt me. I gotta get out before it all consumes me."

"You know, of course, that once you're out of the investment business for a couple of years, there's no coming back. You'd be obsolete."

"I know."

"What about Emily? Will she go for Virginia and that life?"

"She might."

"You know I would," she said softly.

"I know," and he leaned and put his lips close to her ear. "I love you. I know you would and I know you'd be my soul mate." He quietly moved away and continued, "But Virginia is not New York, and there's the boys. If I divorced Emily, she would get them, and it wouldn't work for me being separated so much from them. Besides, what would you do in Big Neck? I don't think you'd be happy."

"Maybe I could teach economics at the high school. Home is where the heart is."

Joe groaned. "This is Big Neck, Virginia. Hicksville. You'd be teaching home economics."

"I'd be all right. I want to share the journey with you. Like I said, home is where the heart is."

She turned away from him, and the mid-spring afternoon light falling on her face made the flesh take a golden tinge. He knew that her eyes were green, but in that light he could not make out their color; they appeared so dark, and he saw how her shoulders moved and hunched together a little. He knew she was trying to suppress a sob. But there was nothing to say.

The fog and mist had cleared. The ball of the earth revolved on its appointed course as it had forever, and the two of them sat there staring into the enormous emptiness of the incandescent blue depth of the sky, the awful emptiness tugging at them like an abyss.

Meanwhile, out there, the stock market rally continued without mercy, cruelly, indifferent thumbing its nose at them.

Epilogue

The following week Joan accepted the job she had been offered as assistant research director at Alliance. The position is challenging, and she enjoys working with the young analysts. Alliance has survived the hard times but its asset base is depleted. Her compensation is mostly salary plus a meager bonus.

For the first few months after they separated, Joan and Joe thought and worried about each other obsessively. They kept in touch almost daily by phone. Both knew a meeting would be dangerous and destabilizing. As time passed, they found they had less and less to talk about because their lives were becoming so different, and their calls became less frequent and then gradually perfunctory. She is now going out with an older man, a portfolio manager at Alliance, but there is not the investment intensity or the passion in this relationship that she once felt with Joe. She wonders what will become of her.

Joe left the BA office that day and never went back. The first few months he felt physically tired and he knew he was demoralized. Initially, he was torn between staying in the investment business and joining Josh in Big Neck. The powerful rally in stock markets that began in spring, which he missed, further depressed him.

Moreover, in the months that followed, much to his chagrin, he received no serious job offers. At first he kept himself occupied with his boys, playing golf, going to the gym, and watching *Bloomberg*. As time went on, he found hanging around Greenwich all day enervating and depressing. There were a lot of other guys in the same, sad boat, but that was no consolation. It was like being in the company of invalids, lost souls babbling about golf scores, trying to fill up the time with aimless activities.

Maybe it was his imagination, but it also seemed as though people who still had jobs, or whose hedge funds had survived, disdained him, viewed him as discarded goods. Once he had been the brilliant, sought-after Kid; now nobody asked or cared what he thought about the market or wanted to hire him. How could he have fallen so far so fast? He consoled himself by noting that literally thousands of hedge funds had gone out of business and that he wasn't the only experienced, supposedly talented guy on the beach.

By the fall of 2009, he was bored and deeply depressed, and in December, Emily reluctantly agreed to move to Virginia on a trial basis.

Disgusted with the stock market and worried about another decline to new lows, Joe had put what remained of his money into tax-exempt bonds. When he moved to Big Neck he bought Josh's land that fell gently in a meadow down to the river and eventually built a house on it. These days Joe works some with Josh in his business and coaches football at Big Neck High. He will probably be named the head coach next year. However, he sometimes finds his involvement with the team frustrating because, with Big Neck High's enrollment declining, the team is at a competitive disadvantage to the other bigger high schools in Virginia whose student bodies are growing.

Living in Big Neck proved to be a difficult adjustment for Emily. She was bored and lonely, and her relationship with Joe became increasingly distant. Sensing her unhappiness, her mother reminded her, "This is what happens when you marry beneath you." As the boys got older, the Daweses and Emily insisted with increasing vehemence that they go to the better schools in Greenwich, and Joe had to admit that the environment at Big Neck Junior High was not great.

Emily has now moved back to Greenwich to be closer to her family. Although Joe and Emily stay in touch and spend holidays and part of each vacation with the boys, they are legally separated. She wonders if she did something wrong. Why did the love she and Joe once had evaporate? Was she insensitive to the depth of Joe's investment agonies, or was their relationship and life built on the shifting sand of the investment world and thus fundamentally unsustainable? Emily currently sees a lot of a professor at Columbia whom she met at the Council on Foreign Relations.

Unfortunately, Grant & Company, disillusioned with its investment management business, sold it in early 2010 to a private equity firm that in turn replaced David Dawes with a younger man. He has been unable to find another job and is restless. The decline in the price of Grant's stock destroyed a lot of his personal net worth and has made him more dependent on his wife's wealth.

The art deal, his debt, and the carrying cost of his possessions wiped out Mickey, and he apparently lives year-round in an apartment in the Hamptons . . . without Vanessa. Joe has called him a number of times, but their conversations have been unsatisfactory and neither confides in the other. Lord Randolph has simply disappeared, although Joe heard he was living in Kuala Lumpur with a Chinese woman. Doug has moved his family back to Cleveland, where he bought a gas station. Perot is running a small fund from a so-called hedge fund motel in New York. He is happily, but expensively, divorced from *my Nancy*. Spokane is in Palm Beach, and Ravine moved to Arizona, where he is involved with the Santa Fe Institute. The process of closing down Bridgestone and settling the attendant lawsuits has materially depleted their wealth, but since neither was leveraged, they are hardly impoverished.

But as this book was written in the fall of 2010, and although markets have been listless for almost a year now, The Money Game goes on around the world. Wealthy individuals are dissatisfied with the performance of their hedge funds and fund-of-funds investments, and they have withdrawn massive amounts of capital. They are licking their wounds and have retreated to cash or bonds. Over 3,000 hedge funds have failed or closed down since the bear market began in the fall of 2007, and the funds' partners and employees have lost their jobs and are searching for gainful employment. The business is becoming more concentrated, with the 200 largest funds now controlling 80 percent of all the assets. There is virtually no seed money for hedge fund start-ups.

Bridgestone and BA were certainly not the only large hedge funds to suffer stunning declines in their assets in the aftermath of the Great Financial Panic. Other even bigger multi-asset entities that erected gates in 2008 and that subsequently had poor performance either have closed down or are dying slow deaths. At the end of 2010, many funds are still below their high-water marks and thus are unable to adequately incentivize their most talented employees. There is also beginning to be fee pressure.

The big pension funds, state funds, and sovereign wealth funds, however, are adding to their hedge fund commitments. Their hedge funds lost only 20 percent in 2008 when their active U.S. equity managers were down 40 percent or more, and small-cap and emerging markets portfolios were off 50 to 60 percent. Other asset classes such as commercial real estate, private equity, commodities, and venture capital did just as badly—if you could get valuations—and proved to be totally illiquid.

In 2009 the hedge fund survivors were up around 23 percent; so from August 2007 through 2009, the time of the eye of the storm and its aftermath, hedge funds outperformed most other strategies and asset classes. Quant funds like BA did far worse, however. When BA closed down, it was off 78 percent from its high, and one gloomy afternoon Joe calculated that personally he had lost 96 percent of his peak wealth. The S&P 500 finished 2009 up 26 percent, and he still tortures himself for missing that rally.

Studies show that in the first decade of the 2000s, so-called aggressive hedge funds earned 15 percent a year but with high volatility, and lost money in a third of all months. The low-volatility, more market-neutral, alpha-oriented cohort generated 11.5 percent a year and had losses in only 11 percent of the months. The big institutions know what they want, and it's the latter, low-volatility group. That's where their money is going. After two secular bear markets in 10 years, they and their overseers can no longer tolerate the violence. They have also put a massive amount of capital into fixed income investments ranging from Treasury bonds to emerging market debt.

As for Joe, he plays a lot of golf on the Big Neck public course, sporadically dates a teacher at Big Neck High, and wonders with a touch of desperation what he is going to do with the rest of his life. The truth of the matter is that he is bored. He makes a valiant effort to spend time with his boys, but there is a deep sadness there as he knows they are growing up away from him.

When he reads of the European sovereign debt crisis, considers the threat of a double dip in the economy, and sees the volatility and flash crashes of 2010, he is glad to be out of The Money Game. But there is also an emptiness there. He misses the excitement and action of the years in New York but also vividly remembers the pain. He feels bruised, and he winces when he reads of the benefit reductions being implemented by the big state pension funds whose money he once managed.

Joe Hill today is profoundly bone-weary and lonely. This man, who once celebrated love as a solution to spiritual isolation, is still looking for someone or something to come home to, and he remembers Joan telling him "home and heaven are where the heart is." He once had a heaven with Emily and a home at BA, but success, the tragedy of the commons, hubris, and then the great financial panic destroyed his heaven and home. Or were his excessive reach and grasp the cause of his ruination?

The End

About the Author

Barton Biggs is the cofounder and managing partner of Traxis Partners, a billion dollar macro hedge fund. He spent thirty years as a senior partner at Morgan Stanley, where he formed the firm's top-rated research department, and created and built its investment management division. He was also Morgan Stanley's investment strategist and was on numerous occasions elected by *Institutional Investor* magazine as the number one ranked global strategist. He was on the board of Morgan Stanley for a number of years. His previous books, *Hedgehogging* and *Wealth, War & Wisdom*, are also published by Wiley and are international bestsellers.

Biggs lives in Greenwich, Connecticut and has three children and nine grandchildren. His foundation provides funding and mentoring for college experiences for African-American men and women.

Disclaimer

This book's story and characters are wholly fictitious. None of the people or hedge funds ever existed. However, the descriptions of financial and stock market events are meant to be accurate depictions of markets and of what happened in the periods covered. The figures included are true, and, unless otherwise sourced, are from Bloomberg.